FROM PRISONER TO PRESIDENT – ENDORSEMENTS

"What a captivating story that kept me riveted to the book, from beginning to the end. You just don't imagine that things like this exist in the world, because we have been trained to look at the outside appearances and not see what is going on in the inside. Jeanette has captured the true essence of what it means to be a 'battered wife' and how this could happen. I think all of us always wonder how someone could let this happen to them, or why don't they just leave. Jeanette explains so clearly in this book how this could happen to anyone who has a heart and mind to love. This story is one of hope, love and victory in Christ. I strongly urge anyone who is lost in their circumstances, doubtful of life and wanting to quit, to read this encouraging story of how someone who just wanted to love and to be loved, found that love in the end." – Kyle Flores, International Vice President/Sale and Marketing

"'Wow!' is the first word that came ~ of my mouth after reading this incredible sto~ ~ 1 a ride of young dreams that turn ~ ~nd up in victory. Jeanette recounts ~ 1ave lived or are living through tod ~ ~nade her a bitter woman giving into (~..₃ a story that through the grace of God has seen success and triumph. Her story will make you angry, will raise questions of why; wondering why no one noticed, but will take you to a place of hope and dreams being fulfilled. I am so proud that Jeanette has been willing to tell her story, to face her past, to find healing and to now be in a place to help and encourage others." – Tim Stevenson, Senior Pastor, Horizon Community Church

"Jeanette's story brings hope. She openly shares her life as she grew up in total innocence, married into a life of chaos and destruction, but was completely restored by God's grace." – Angie Martin, BS, NM Technologist

"Unbelievable and encouraging! Jeanette has detailed a real life experience that so many women have endured and can relate to. Even more importantly, Jeanette's boldness to bring her story to light can and will continue to encourage thousands who feel trapped out of guilt or fear. She reminds us that God will never leave us amidst trials and tribulations." – Christopher Hudson, Chief of Operations, Still Light Studios

"Jeanette Towne wished this sad story during her 20s never happened. But it did. And through her transformed life today, Jeanette looks back, and courageously uncovers the 'silent terror' of her torture and abuse, and the emotional paradox of her 'domestic prison,' a similar prison which many others are 'captive in' today. This book is not a voyeuristic tour, but rather a story of reality, and a gift of hope to those who still cry out to God to be rescued, and for their friends and family who will be part of the rescue. And even more, it shows everyone there is a path to building a beautiful new life of hope, strength, giving, trust, and genuine love." – Rod Howard, Co-Founder of Vocari, *Vocation to Calling*, and father of six daughters

"In *From Prisoner to President*, Jeanette Towne captures the survival mentality and pain of those entangled in domestic abuse, allowing the reader to understand the complexity, perversion, and emotional conflict that terrorizes victims of such abuse. While her story recounts the ugliness and sorrow of her labored journey, the raw realities of true redemption shine forth, reminding readers that God does not shy away from the hard and impossible." – Emily White Youree, Former Randall House Acquisitions Editor

"*From Prisoner to President* is the eye-opening and heart-wrenching ten-year true story of an abused wife who chronicles what it's like to be beaten down, emotionally and physically on a 24/7 basis. Jeanette Towne has woven the fabric of a married life spinning out of control and who bares her soul honestly and convincingly. Faced with the sad fact that the husband she only sought to love and cherish does little but beat and break her down, Jeanette comes to grip with a seemingly hopeless situation. She never falters in her goal of being a good wife and mother and in spite of the adversity at hand emerges as the winner and more

importantly a beacon of light to battered women everywhere." –
Joseph Miani, Training Administrator, Major Aerospace Company

"This is a must-read book for every young girl getting ready
to leave the protection of her family." – Alisha Steinheimer JD,
Corporate Vice President

"A very real story of abuse and salvation that will encourage
women in similar circumstances to realize there is hope for a
better tomorrow. This story speaks life to anyone in overwhelming
circumstances showing that prayer and faith can bring inner
strength to escape unspeakable misery." – T.L. Crutchfield, B.S. in
Criminal Justice, Sacramento State University

FROM PRISONER TO PRESIDENT

JEANETTE M. TOWNE

Dec 2010
Sarah —
I pray you
will learn
to trust
God and
always listen
to your
heart
I love
you! ♡
Mom

From Prisoner to President

Published by:

Intermedia Publishing Group, Inc.

P.O. Box 2825

Peoria, Arizona 85382

www.intermediapub.com

ISBN 978-1935529590

This book is dedicated to my late-father, Dominic Miani, and to my husband, Sam Towne. My father was my very first love and the hero of my life and Sam Towne is the only man I have ever met who embodies the values and lives the life my father modeled to me as a girl.

I want to thank my friend Angie who gave me the courage to write this story and to my first readers, especially Leah, who encouraged me to continue and endured countless hours of my incessant editing in quest of the perfect copy.

Last but not least, I want to give honor to God for calling, saving, and never leaving me.

TABLE OF CONTENTS

Chapter 1	The Last Straw	1
Chapter 2	First Meeting	7
Chapter 3	Iris	21
Chapter 4	The Parents	29
Chapter 5	Club Escape	35
Chapter 6	I Do	49
Chapter 7	Corona Del Mar	61
Chapter 8	First Abuse	71
Chapter 9	A New Life	81
Chapter 10	Northern California	87
Chapter 11	The Perfect Little Family	103
Chapter 12	Married?	117
Chapter 13	The First Eviction	133
Chapter 14	The New Job	141
Chapter 15	A Wild Party	147
Chapter 16	A Teaching Opportunity	157
Chapter 17	The 25K Gift	169
Chapter 18	A Box Explodes	175
Chapter 19	Reconciliation	187
Chapter 20	Guns	199
Chapter 21	The Shameful Disease	209
Chapter 22	The Garbage Disposal	219
Chapter 23	The Mustang	229
Chapter 24	Kitty	235
Chapter 25	Casa Clara	241
Chapter 26	The Dream House	253
Chapter 27	Nothing but Trash	261

Chapter 28   Fortune 5   265
Chapter 29   New Roommates   271
Chapter 30   The Confrontation   279
Chapter 31   The Escape   283
Chapter 32   Lake Tahoe   289
Chapter 33   The New Life   293
Chapter 34   Modern Day Miracle   295
Chapter 35   Building an Empire   299
Chapter 36   Leah's Rescue   303
Chapter 37   President   309
Chapter 38   Healing a Heart   311
Final Chapter Epilogue   317
Questions for Discussion   319
About the Author   325
Author's Note   327

CHAPTER 1
THE LAST STRAW

I knew better than to leave out any type of tool. Throughout the years, I had trained myself to be meticulous when it came to using sharp objects around the house such as knives, barbecue utensils, or anything that could become a weapon.

Getting ready for work was a challenge. I had to walk softly and towel-dry my hair; any loud noises in the house could cause him to wake up. After a late night of drinking, drugging, and partying, if I woke him up while getting ready for work, the punishment could be anything from a screaming tirade delivered an inch from my face, to hits, kicks, choking, airborne projectiles, or body slamming—or it could be worse, and he would pull out a knife or a gun to punish my actions.

At this point in my life, the violence was surreal. This was my life. I was a hostage in my own home and fairly certain I'd be dead before the end of the year.

Raised Catholic, I learned that suicide was a mortal sin. Not only did I live in hell on earth, if I killed myself to escape, my sentencing would be eternal damnation to burn in hell. I prayed daily for God to *please let me die in my sleep*, or for God to take *him* through cancer, illness, or some freak accident.

No one had a clue what went on in my house. From the outside, I looked perfect: perfect family, perfect life. People assumed I had it all together—a nice-looking young woman working for a Fortune 500 company; married to a strikingly handsome, funny, intelligent, wonderful husband; and raising a darling and obedient young stepdaughter.

No one would believe I was a prisoner in my own home. No one would believe I was followed, threatened and could be killed on any day. No one would believe my husband had already been involved in murdering several people, and murdering me would come easily. I could not escape.

Why couldn't I just take off, change my name, and start a new life? Maybe that was possible in the early days, the days when things weren't very violent. In those days, I was a young wife, raising a darling two-year-old baby who had been abandoned by a cruel mother. I wanted her. I wanted to be the mommy, the good wife ... the perfect family. Now, I knew if I left and went undercover, I would never see my daughter again. How could I escape and leave her there? She would surely become the victim once I left.

My family was a target. If I managed to escape, not only would my daughter be hurt, but my parents would also be at risk. He knew where my parents lived and had hissed on many occasions that if I ever thought of leaving, my family would be history. I believed him.

Just Another Day

Getting my business portfolio together and reviewing my meetings for the day, I wrote a note listing the locations for my sales calls and left it on the counter by the telephone. The designer suit I purchased at the Goodwill Store for $7 was clean and pressed, my stiletto pumps shined. After checking my appearance one last time in the bathroom mirror I leaned against the door and exhaled loudly, realizing Jim had taken my purse the night before and had it in the master bedroom. My heart skipped a beat; my stomach began to tighten and convulse. *I needed my purse.* It had my license and a few dollars needed for the day. If I took off my high heels and stepped into the bedroom, I could grab my purse quickly and be out of the house. I hoped he was in bed alone.

The hallway looked long and dark. I stood at the end of the hall looking towards the master bedroom door, which was open about an inch. All of the blinds were drawn and blankets covered the seams, not allowing a drop of sunlight to enter the room. After years of drugging, sunlight would put him in a foul mood. I nervously glanced at my watch. I had to get the purse or be late for my first sales call of the day.

Without sales, there would be no commission checks. Without commission checks, there would be no money for the house payment or food. . . or his drug habit. Without drugs he would be worse than a caged animal deprived of food for weeks.

Taking a deep, silent breath, I tip-toed down the hallway and crept up to the entrance of the master bedroom. Leaning my hands against the door I pressed softly and slowly opened the door. One of the hinges began to squeak! Why didn't I get the WD40? I held my breath as I heard him move in bed. *Don't move. Please don't*

3

move! Please don't wake up! After what seemed like eternity, I heard the steady breathing of sleep. *Whew, close call!* Quietly, I pushed the door open wide enough and slid into the room. I stood there letting my eyes adjust until I spied my purse on the counter of the bathroom. Why didn't I hide my purse better? Usually, I hid my purse in different places throughout the house so I could easily retrieve it each morning.

Three, four, five soft steps and I reached my purse. The handle was a long strap that hung down along the side of the sink. Looking over, the coast was still clear; he was asleep. Quickly, I grasped the square body of the purse and began to lift. . . a little too quickly. The strap lifted and wrapped around the knob of the vanity cabinet. As I pulled the purse towards my body the cabinet door opened and then swooshed closed with a loud slam! A slurred stream of profanity began to spew from his mouth.

"Where do you think you are going?" he shouted. I could smell the alcohol and cigarettes projecting from across the room. I should have shut up and cowered, but was seething with anger. He raped me the night before, and I was very angry at being a prisoner in my own home. I was despondent, my life seemed hopeless with no way out. I felt my cheeks get hot.

"To work. . . one of us has to earn a living," I said sarcastically. As soon as it came off my tongue, I panicked. Glancing at the dresser, I noticed a hammer. He must have been working with his tools and forgot to put the hammer away. As soon as I spied the hammer, I noticed his eyes on it at the same time. Enraged, he flew out of bed, crossed the room, and grabbed the hammer in one motion. I dared not run. If I ran, he would claw me in the back of the head. I might have a chance if I didn't try to fight back.

I crumpled down by the vanity, crouching on both feet with my hands up in a defensive position and watched in the wall-sized mirror as he filled the room, looming larger than life. I looked up at him and then I saw it as clear as day. He stood above me with the hammer poised to come down, crushing into my skull. His face was contorted and looked like a person possessed by the devil. His eyes were bloodshot and in the darkened room looked like slits of oozing blood. This was it. This was my last moment of life. The hammer started to come down. I saw the scene unfold as if the seconds were all in slow motion.

THE LAST STRAW

CHAPTER 2
FIRST MEETING

Growing up in Southern California in the 1970s was idyllic. My parents were wonderful. Mother loved each of us four kids and raised us with love and encouragement. She prided herself in the role of "housewife," building a comfortable home for our family. Mother was a support-mate and good wife to my father. My father, Domenico Arturo Miani, was the quintessential Italian husband and father—hardworking, loving and moral. He ruled our house with stern discipline; however, he tempered that with embraces, life-lessons and healthy love.

After high school, I began working as a waitress in a local family restaurant near Cypress College where I was taking classes to become a nurse. I moved into a one-bedroom apartment with a roommate who was also considering enrolling in nursing school. It was my first time away from home—it felt both exciting and scary. I loved getting into my '65 Mustang and heading to class, but was often frightened when coming home late after school or work and often ran from the alley parking stalls to my apartment door.

After completing two years of general education and keeping my grades up, I received the coveted acceptance letter into the college nursing program. I knew it would be a great challenge to work full-time and attend school, but my young enthusiastic mind told me I could do it. My body however, succumbed to exhaustion and I stumbled under the pressure of nursing school. I missed too many classroom hours and much to my shock and disappointment, was kicked out of the program.

Weeks later, I finally had the nerve to tell my parents about what happened with my nursing program. They were worried about my future, shared my disappointment, and wanted me to move home. Mother told me that Daddy had accepted a six-year position for the Department of Defense, beginning in the fall. He would be working out of the embassy in Copenhagen, Denmark. My parents had always wanted to live abroad, and now it looked like a reality. An air force couple would be leasing their house and Mother told me that my sister, Debbie, and I could go with them. Go to Europe? I had just enrolled in the nursing program. . . again. If I left, I would never have a chance to finish. If I spent six years in Europe, I'd be twenty-five by the time I came home.

In the meantime, I landed another waitress job at a fancier restaurant, Sunshine Meat and Liquor Company. I hadn't worked there long when I realized the people who worked here were different, much more sophisticated and experienced. Matthew and Rab, the co-owners, were savvy and flashy businessmen, who liked to look at the ladies. I even fell victim to Matthew's sexual advances once, but thankfully, was saved by the appearance of an unexpected bus boy in the locker room hall. Iris, the main hostess, turned Sunshine from a dinner house to a posh nightclub every night at 9:00 p.m. Fellow hostesses, Cathy and Angie, had lived lives I couldn't dream up—they moved from small-town Idaho, escaped abusive family situations, and enjoyed a promiscuous lifestyle. Although these new friends introduced me to a new world—sometimes scary, sometimes exciting – I needed the job and blindly overlooked their dalliances. Sunshine was the ticket to my goal of saving money and getting that nursing degree.

One afternoon, after a particularly slow lunch service, I was sitting at the edge of the dining room tallying my lunch checks when Savage, the lead bartender, came to me from the bar. He winked and asked if I could place a lunch order for a rich, *single* young businessman sitting at the bar. He motioned towards a strikingly handsome man whom I had seen a few times before. I was thrilled at the opportunity to meet a younger wealthy guy. Most of our customers were older than my nineteen years. I figured this guy was in his late 20s or early 30s. Not too old for me, I reasoned. I didn't give much thought to the fact that he was smoking a cigarette and drinking a cocktail during lunch.

I stacked my checks and picked up my order sheet and pencil. I walked over to the bar and stood behind him, waiting for him to finish what sounded like a very intellectual conversation. When he finally faced me, I felt like I was going to faint. He had the most piercing steel blue eyes. They looked right through me. He was captivating with his beaming white smile, tanned skin, and dark brown hair with streaks of sun-bleached blonde. Immediately I noticed the multiple diamond rings, chains and the solid-gold Rolex watch with the diamond bezel. He had more money on his

9

hands than I would spend on four years of college! He was wearing a designer shirt and slacks and had an overpowering presence. I swallowed hard, composed myself, and asked what he would like to order.

He ordered a sandwich; I heard his voice and watched his mouth move, but I wasn't listening to what he was saying. Listen! I commanded myself; I would confuse the order if I didn't concentrate. I nodded, left, and turned in the lunch order. After a few minutes, the food was ready, and I delivered it to the bar. He barely noticed me when I delivered the lunch and quickly uttered a thank you, barely missing a beat of his conversation. Having finished my checks for my shift, I waited patiently until I saw him place his silverware across his plate signaling he was done. His colleague left, and he looked ready to leave. I came over, picked up the plate, and dropped off the bill. I started to leave, but he motioned me to stay while he paid the bill. I stood there smiling at him, trying to look mature and calm. He put down $100, told me to keep the change, and turned and began another conversation.

Keep the change? The sandwich was only $4. . . that would be a $96 tip for a lunch plate? I went to the cashier in back, turned in the lunch bill, and received the change. This had to be some sort of a scheme to dupe me. Men just didn't give girls a tip like that unless they expected something. No way. No possible way. I didn't know what he thought of me. I wasn't *that* kind of girl. Although it had been a slow lunch and I could really use the money, I *had* to give it back. I didn't care how handsome or how rich he might be. I could not be bought.

I'm sure he thought I was crazy when I stood behind him at the bar again, waiting for my chance to tell him what I thought. I took a deep breath as he looked at me standing behind his seat and once again pierced me with those blue eyes. I straightened my posture, put one hand defiantly on my hip, thrust out the tip tray, and started my speech."Hello, I really appreciate the tip and all," I stuttered, "but, there is no way I can keep this tip." His eyes showed the disbelief of my proclamation as he chuckled. I continued my tirade, my chin thrust forward. "There are a lot of girls in this bar; many of these girls would be more than happy to accompany you on a date for whatever, but I am *not* one of those girls." I handed him the tip tray with his change, spun around, and went back to my table to finish my check accounting. I glanced at him a few times and saw him talking with Savage. Maybe I shouldn't have said anything. Maybe I should have just taken the money. But I couldn't. It just wouldn't be right.

I was ready to leave when I looked up to see him looming above me looking like a Greek god. He stood about six feet, four inches tall, and was fit, strong, tanned, and toned. I gulped. At nineteen, I was still very shy around *real* men. The guys at Sunshine were men. They weren't the acne-covered kids I had been friends with in high school. This was the fast lane. These men were investment bankers, plastic surgeons, mega land developers, professional athletes, and agents. I was a nineteen-year-old coffee shop waitress and nursing student with no life experiences. I was way out of my league. He put the tip tray down on the table. I was getting ready for a battle.

"Hey, I wanted you to keep the tip." He stared at me intently, not breaking his gaze. I began to argue again.

"Look, I know you're a very nice guy; you've dated a few of the girls around here, and they all really like you. I'm only working here until I get finished with school. I'm not one of those party

11

girls. There are many of them that would be more than happy to go out with you." He smiled and flashed those perfect teeth.

"Savage already told me they called you the 'Ice Princess.' I wasn't trying to do anything other than give you a good tip." I flushed and felt like a complete idiot. He stretched out his hand.

"I'm Jim. Jim Miller. What's your name?" He smiled warmly. I put my hand in his and felt the world move. Standing up to meet his gaze while feeling like my knees would buckle underneath me, I answered.

"My name is Jeanette." I smiled back, wishing I had changed into a skirt or slacks and had reapplied my lipstick. He motioned for me to sit down and I did. I looked at Savage, who was shaking his head in disapproval.

Jim and I sat at the table and began to share our life stories. Mine was quite simple. Raised in a good family, lived near the college and now studying to become a nurse. His face lit up when I told him I was working my way through school. He seemed impressed by my intelligence as I was with his. He told me he was a doctor of mathematics and showed me his Visa card with "Dr." in the title. No questions asked about what he was telling me; I bought it. I asked him what he was doing now, and he told me he was a master contractor building large industrial projects for corporations. I wasn't really sure what went on in the building trades, but I listened carefully as he spoke. He seemed extremely intelligent, genuine, and real—honest and trustworthy. He was an excellent conversationalist. When I spoke, he listened intently and seemed very interested in everything I had to say.

He told me that if he were to be married and his wife wanted to go to nursing school, he would support those educational efforts by paying for the best education money could buy. From what I had already heard, he was more than rich. He had a house in Corona del Mar on the oceanfront. He had spoken of the Rolls and the Jag, trips to Switzerland and weekends in Vegas. When he opened his wallet to bring out a business card, I saw a thick stack of hundred dollar bills.

We talked for more than an hour, and I became so mesmerized by this wonderful man—I had thoughts of a huge white wedding running through my head. He brought out pictures of his eighteen-month-old daughter. Smiling with pride, he showed me several adorable poses and told me his ex-girlfriend had abandoned the baby at birth. He was raising his daughter alone with the help of a nanny. This clinched it for me. Single, never married, extremely rich, had a doctorate, and was raising his daughter who the mother had thrown out. This darling baby needed a mother, and Jim needed a wife. I was compassionate and could love this little girl like my own. He smiled at me and told me that he was looking for a stable home in which to raise his daughter. I smiled up at him and knew I would be the perfect woman for him. I could finish school, and then we could be married. I would then stay at home to raise his daughter, take good care of our beach mansion, and maybe have a few children of our own. Life would be wonderful. This was my lucky day!

After a while, he glanced at his watch and stated that he had better go. He had to get back and check on the jobsite where he was completing an industrial building. I smiled faintly; he hadn't asked for my phone number. My heart sunk. I stood up with him as he pushed away from the table, and told him I enjoyed meeting him and maybe we would see each other in the restaurant again. He nodded agreement and smiled, flashing those perfect whites at me. In an instant, he was gone. I prayed at that moment, asking God to please let me see him again. I knew we would be right for each other. My parents would love him; I was certain of it. We could be married in the Catholic Church. He could easily convert to Catholicism and escort our family to Sunday mass each week. Now, I had to date him. I was sure he would come back into Sunshine again. Questioning my attractiveness, I argued with myself that several of the "regulars" told me I was one of the prettiest waitresses at Sunshine; maybe Jim Miller would think so too.

Several weeks elapsed and no sign of him. It was only one meeting; why was I so depressed about not seeing him again? I tried to think about other things, but those blue eyes and smile remained in my mind. Wasn't I pretty enough? Maybe I offended him when I gave him my speech. Maybe he was just busy. That was it; he was working hard, taking care of his daughter, and didn't have the time to go out.

In the meantime, I decided I needed to save more money toward college and agreed to move into an apartment with Cathy and Angie. They had a one-bedroom with twin beds and a convertible couch in the living room. Living with the girls would allow me to save an extra $500 a month. So with a little effort, a lot of encouragement from my friends and a quick yard sale, I moved into the small apartment with the girls.

It was a Friday night in early spring of 1978. The weather had already started the typical fog and overcast Orange County pattern. Work had been really busy and I was ready to relax after counting a few hundred in tips. Cathy had run off back to the bar after work, changing into a dress that showed every curve, and in her usual fashion would come spilling through the door after the bar was closed, lucky to have made it home alive.

Angie and I were sitting on our small worn couch, eating take-out Chinese food and watching TV, when we heard a loud commotion outside. We heard obnoxious laughing and chattering and the sound of two very drunk people coming towards our front door. You could hear them tripping, falling, and laughing loudly in the parking lot. Both of us looked at each other. We recognized Cathy's voice right away. She was drunk, again. This was becoming a typical night for all of us. Several nights a week, Angie and I watched TV after work and waited for Cathy to come home. Most nights she was drunk and would get sick. Some nights, she'd bring home a strange man. Angie told me that she had been behaving like that since they left Idaho, sleeping with any man who smiled at her. I couldn't understand it at all; why would she want to give herself to men she obviously didn't love? Angie would usually end up taking care of her in the mornings, making her hot coffee and washing her up after she had been sick.

Cathy stumbled in, falling in the entry and laughing hard, her blonde curls a mess around her face. She was a knockout, but through bloodshot eyes, smeared make-up, and clothes awry, she hardly looked attractive. Cathy looked at us and laughed some more. Angie jumped up and started to rescue her, when a large figure followed Cathy into the apartment. Cathy stood up unsteadily and looked up at her "friend"; she smiled, grabbed his hand and hoarsely told him to follow her.

"One day, maybe she'll wake up and realize that sleeping around will only get her pregnant or a disease. Hope she figures this out before it's too late." Angie took a bite of the Chow Mein, which was almost cold by now. "She drinks too much." She continued her spew of judgment. "If she doesn't stop this behavior, she will regret it for the rest of her life." I was still in a state of shock and unable to speak. Angie looked over at me, her mouth wide open... she suddenly realized who had fallen through the door for a tryst with our friend. Cathy's latest boyfriend was the new man of my dreams, my future husband, the dynamic, handsome, and rich Jim Miller. God had answered my prayer all right! I did get to see him again.

The next morning Cathy woke up late and as usual was sick in the toilet. Angie ran in to help her and held her hair, pressing a wet washcloth to her forehead. Cathy spewed out obscenities as Angie scurried around trying to comfort her. Jim had taken off during the night. This was just another typical "date" for Cathy. Come home drunk, jump into the sack, and the nameless man takes off before the morning light. Angie and I were fine with that; we didn't want to face these nameless men or have them intruding in our lives. But this "date" was different. Cathy had no idea who she had brought home.

Later in the afternoon when I started my waitress shift, Angie and Cathy were hostesses. We had been working a few hours fairly steadily when I saw Jim walk into the bar. He still looked amazing, and I wished my heart didn't skip a beat when I saw him. He was surveying the scene, looking for Cathy, I assumed. I saw him talking to a few people and mulling around. He walked to the main bar and leaned over to get Savage's attention. When you were as good a tipper as Jim Miller, everyone clamored to serve you. Savage left every other patron at the bar waiting and went to serve Jim. Angie walked back to the hostess station with menus, and I pointed to Jim Miller talking with Savage at the bar.

"He's looking for his new girl," I said dryly. Angie nodded and joined me as I looked around the bar for Cathy. In a moment, we both spotted her. With her shift finished, Cathy was enjoying an after-work drink and was sitting on the lap of a very rich businessman. She was wearing a red cowboy hat with matching boots, a very short jean skirt and smothering her new beau with soft kisses. He was laughing and enjoying every minute of her affection!

I watched from across the bar, surveying the scene. Jim's eyes were roving the crowd, and finally fixated on an unaware Cathy, performing her lap-dancing event. I could tell by his body language that he wasn't used to girls not cowering to him and his money. He angrily leaned over to engage Savage again. Angie and I watched Jim storm across the room, looking like a very angry man as he went to confront the "love birds." Cathy was laughing at first, but noticing the angry face of Jim Miller, hopped off her friend's lap and said a few words. Both men shook hands, Jim said a few more things, and stomped off to the main bar in a huff.

This episode felt so wonderful to me. Jim met me, and we obviously had a connection. He knew I wasn't like the other girls; *I* was a good girl. I wasn't Cathy. I wouldn't have done what she did, but he didn't date me, he went after her. Now, the true colors of that type of girl come out. They are not faithful to anyone. I thought very smugly of the entire situation and wondered, was *this* the type of woman Jim Miller wanted? Is this the type of woman Jim Miller wanted raising his little daughter? I think not!

At the end of the night, I changed my uniform and decided to stay and have a drink with Angie. Cathy was already on the dance floor with yet another guy, looking like she had knocked back a few. I put on a pair of skintight jeans, my best stiletto heels, and a white men's dress shirt, belted low across my hips. I appraised myself in the mirror of the girl's locker room. I had thick, long blonde hair, green eyes, and a good figure. Why wouldn't Jim Miller want me? I reapplied my make-up, fluffed my hair, and traipsed across the floor of Sunshine. I could see heads turning as I walked by. Men, who had already been at the club and had seen me as their waitress, were wondering where this girl had come from. One of those men was Jim Miller. I could see him from across the bar as I walked to the table where Angie and a few other friends were sitting. He was tracing my steps. A few minutes later, he was standing by my side, larger than life, holding out his hand for a dance. I was angry and should have said no, but was helpless to do anything except follow him out to the dance floor and dance to a set of the finest disco music in Orange County.

I whirled and twirled my head swimming in the moment, feeling the beat of the music, feeling carefree and happy, and feeling the same wonderful way I had during that first meeting a few weeks ago. This was destiny—Jim and Jeanette. We were supposed to be a couple. I was positive of that. The rest of the night was a blur and went by all too quickly. A few drinks, a few more dances, and the music set ended. I could see the look of affection and gentle pride as Jim escorted me off the dance floor toward our table.

After the last call and the lights turned up, he walked me to my car. Jim smiled and asked if he could have my number and said he would like to take me out to lunch some afternoon. He knew I wasn't Cathy and apparently, the speech I had given to Jim on the first meeting had worked. He gave me a light kiss on the hand and closed my door. My car started and I pulled out, watching him hop into his expensive Jaguar parked in the private reserved space near the limousines. I felt smug, appreciated, scared, and excited at the same time. I was almost twenty years old, and he was almost thirty. Ten years my senior, Jim had seen his share of girlfriends and one-night stands. I felt he was looking for a different type of girl—a girl to love, cherish, and trust; a girl to marry, help raise his daughter, and become the mother of his children. I could feel it.

FIRST MEETING

CHAPTER 3
IRIS

The night with Jim Miller became a distant memory. He didn't call me the next day or the next week. I was growing impatient. I couldn't stop thinking about him; I was certain we had made a deep connection. He had mentioned a job in Palm Springs, but I didn't remember him telling me when he was going there. That had to be it—he was working and didn't have a chance to get away.

One afternoon after the girls and I finished a lunch shift and were eating salads in the vacant dining room, Iris, the food service manager at Sunshine and one of the senior cocktail waitresses, came to our table. Cathy, Angie, and I looked up at Iris as she smiled down, flipping her perfect, long blonde hair. Iris was a beauty, standing almost six feet tall with a naturally toned and built body. We all sort of admired Iris as we watched her pull in hundreds of dollars a night from her regular customers. Iris was almost twenty-eight, and I heard she owned her own house.

"Hey girls, how were tips today?" Iris glanced around the deserted dining room, motioning to the tables as she asked. We all snorted through our noses because it had been slow the past few weeks. We were just complaining about our lack of tips. I was the first one to talk.

"Not too good, Iris, I barely cleared $50 after tipping out." Cathy and Angie joined me in agreement.

"Yeah, and Jeanette made more than we did on our hostess tips," Angie complained. Iris pulled out a chair and sat down next to us. I felt very important. Iris was a manager, right under the owners, Matthew and Rab. All of the rich customers knew her and called her by name, sitting in her station and leaving her huge tips. Iris began to speak to us in a soft intimate manner.

"What are you all doing after work today? Do you want to go shopping at Fashion Island?" I started to shake my head back and forth. Fashion Island was the place where the rich and famous of Newport Beach shopped, not the place where starving students went. Cathy and Angie were nodding their heads up and down, eyes glowing brightly.

"Iris," I began slowly, not trying to sound like a poor punk kid with no life experiences, "I don't think so. I am on such a tight budget, and I don't have an extra dollar to spend shopping." Iris continued smiling at us.

"I know how hard you all have been working. I've watched you here the past few months, working hard for Sunshine, helping to make Matthew and Rab good money on the repeat clients. They see this, and so do I."

I couldn't believe it. I doubted that Matthew or Rab even knew my name, let alone knew that I had single-handedly reformed the restaurant's side-work and cleaning schedules and helped with shift changes that made the staff more efficient. Apparently I was wrong. Iris continued.

"Well, I know you have all worked so hard that I was going to treat you to a shopping spree at Fashion Island. After that, if you guys want, you can come back over to my house for a light dinner and drinks. You can meet some of my friends. It will be fun; what do you think?" Iris was nodding and leaning into the three of us. She was a motherly sort at that moment. I could see my mom taking me shopping and then making me some dinner. It had been a long time since my mother had made me a cup of tea or a sandwich. My parents were in the final throes of packing up their life and moving to Europe. I was already feeling very alone in the world. Cathy jumped in first, then Angie agreed and I reluctantly followed.

Iris took the three of us to Fashion Island on an incredible shopping spree. We tried on sleek dresses, shoes, and accessories with Iris handing over hundred dollar bills to each cashier. After what seemed like a few minutes (but was actually a few hours), we headed towards the valet off to a night of dinner with Iris and company. We thanked Iris profusely. She promised us there was a lot more where that came from as long as we helped her and the business. Sunshine seemed like a wonderful place to work. Iris certainly had made a good living. With the sun going down across the water and boat lights lining up on the harbor, we pulled into the driveway of a very nice single-story house on the hill. Iris had an automatic garage door opener, which she clicked, pulling her Mercedes in next to another smaller convertible. She told us to grab a few things we may want to wear for the evening and leave the rest in the trunk. We happily complied.

After a tour of her four-bedroom, three-bathroom home, we were in awe. This house was so beautiful. I couldn't believe that Iris lived here alone and owned the house. She told us she bought the place a few years ago and had gutted and remodeled the house. It was gorgeous. She opened the blinds on one side of the living room that framed the Pacific Ocean. Although she was on the hill and you couldn't hear the waves, you could see boats passing and the moon shining down across the water. How lucky to live here and live here alone, no husband supporting her. Iris must be doing very, very well.

We quickly dressed into our new party clothes, and Iris invited us into the family room that hosted a full bar. This was almost like Sunshine, with mirrors behind the glasses and stools on one side. Iris handed us tall glasses filled with a pink cocktail, garnished with a pineapple wedge and cherry. I was thirsty from the long shopping trip with little in my stomach but a small salad. The drink was great and before I knew it, I had finished mine and was feeling very heady. Cathy, Angie and I followed Iris into the kitchen to help her prepare some snacks. We giggled while helping Iris put appetizers on an assortment of platters, readying for the informal party Iris was hosting with some of her friends.

The doorbell began ringing and in no time, the house filled with guests, many I recognized as Sunshine's richest customers. Watching Iris smile and kiss her friends as they arrived, I realized we were the only female guests. Cathy, Angie, and I filled our guests' glasses; served shrimp, scallops, and stuffed mushrooms; and assumed roles of friendly waitresses to a room full of much older men. I sipped another drink at the insistence of Iris, making a mental note that I wasn't going to have anything else to drink. Cathy and Angie were already sitting on the laps of several "friends" and were laughing cheerfully while being groped. They didn't seem to mind it at all. I busied myself with cleaning the party room. Every time Iris would look, I smiled broadly; however, on the inside, I was very worried. I felt like something was definitely awry.

The party didn't last much later than midnight and most of the guests filtered out, saying their goodbyes to Iris and the girls. We cleaned the rest of the kitchen and Iris began to tell us how much she enjoyed our time together and how much she wanted us to get together again. Angie and Cathy were red-eyed and weaving around the house. They nodded.

"What did you think of my friends?" Iris asked. I wasn't sure. Although one of her friends told me he was a judge, I had to pull away from his grasp every time he came near me. The others seemed to be rich all right, but the way they grabbed Cathy and Angie, I was pretty sure they didn't seem too nice either. Cathy began:

"They are a wonderful group of friends, Iris. I had the best time. One of your friends asked if I was available to go on a date with him, sort of an escort. I guess he's married, but his wife lives in New York and sometimes he needs to have a date for business dinners." Angie nodded.

"Yeah, I got asked to go to Palm Springs for a dinner date. Can you believe that, Palm Springs?" Angie smiled, shocked that a rich guy had asked her to dinner in Palm Springs. They all looked at me.

"Nobody asked me out, but I was really busy, helping to fill drinks and keeping the food on the platters." Truth was, I had been afraid to sit still. I felt like bait in a tank of sharks. I could feel the leering eyes staring at my body. I wished I would have followed my intuition and refused Iris' offer to go shopping and to her party.

"Well, this is a great way for you all to work and help me out, *and* to make some extra money. It's really very easy. You just go out to dinner with my friends and escort them as a single friend would. They fly into town for a meeting and dinner, and you go with them. I buy you nice clothes for the occasions, and I pay you for your time. There are no strings attached. You can make $500 or more a night for doing a four-hour dinner date."

I couldn't believe my ears – was Iris telling me I could make $500 a night for going out to dinner with one of her friends? One was a lawyer, one was a judge, one a plastic surgeon and another man a land developer. A little old, I guess, but $500 for dinner? Was this right? I looked at Cathy and Angie's eager eyes, ready to sign on the dotted line. Wait a minute, there had to be more small print that Iris wasn't telling us. I questioned her motives.

"Iris, you're telling me that these men will pay us $500 a night for a dinner date?" Iris shook her head.

"No, they will pay me and I will pay you. Just make sure they are happy in private and that you behave like proper ladies in public. You'll get your money from me the next day." Iris smiled. "How do you think I can afford this house and those cars and take you shopping? I date the rich and famous men from all across the United States. They need a smart, articulate, young woman to escort them to important business functions. I fit the bill." She leaned in to the three of us putting her head down and lowering her voice. "So, what do you all say, are we in?" Cathy and Angie were nodding their heads and finding no reason to say no; I nodded my head in agreement. It *was* only a date and I could really use the extra money for nursing school. On the drive home Cathy and Angie chatted about the exotic trips they would take with their extra money. I remained silent in the back seat, fighting the overwhelming feeling that I had made one of the worst mistakes of my life. I prayed a silent prayer, wishing my parents were around and asking God for guidance.

IRIS

CHAPTER 4
THE PARENTS

I waited for days for my future husband to call me. After what seemed like an eternity, Jim Miller finally called to ask me out to lunch. I was so excited it took me several outfit changes to settle on a pair of very flattering white jeans, a light blue sweater, my hair pulled up on top of my head with a clip, and long blonde curls swirling down my back. Since I didn't really know Jim, I was afraid of going with him on a car date. I told Jim I would like to go out to lunch and could meet him wherever he decided. He asked me if I liked Houlihan's Restaurant in Newport Beach. I'd definitely heard of it, but a starving student certainly never went there; it was *way* too expensive for my budget! I was beyond thrilled at the opportunity to date the man of my dreams.

I arrived at Houlihan's early and waited in the parking lot, hoping my old green Mustang looked more like a classic than a jalopy. I met Jim in the parking lot, and in his comfortable and charming manner, he came to my car, opened my car door, and offered his hand. We walked into the restaurant holding hands and chatting, I could see people staring at us as Jim smiled down at me, piercing my soul with his blue eyes. When Jim entered a room, everyone—men and women—stared. I looked back up and smiled nervously. I felt like I was going to be sick. This was my *very first real date*. This was the first time I was actually going out with a man. He looked like a billionaire, and I looked like the lucky princess who stole his heart. I drank in all of the contrasting colors of the beautifully decorated room full of white, green, and soft rusts. The tables were perfectly set and couples were sitting around on large white wicker chairs sipping wine from crystal glasses while engaging in intimate and engrossing conversations.

Apparently the staff knew Jim and immediately escorted us to a reserved table offering a view of a lush tropical garden. The hostess smiled, looked at Jim, and then raked her green eyes over me. Did she know Jim? He smiled, leaned down and said something to her and she giggled. Did he wink at her? No way—I'm sure it was just my imagination. The waiter pulled out my chair, and I sat gracefully as he placed the deep green cloth napkin gently across my lap. Menu in hand, I tried not to stare at the prices, but couldn't help myself.

This was a dream come true. Although I was nervous and could barely think straight, Jim mesmerized me with his dreams and thoughts of the future. He spoke about business and told me at length how he managed the construction of complex industrial projects. I didn't know anything about construction, but tried to ask appropriate questions. The conversation never lagged. Jim seemed relaxed and laughed easily while we ate lunch. I sipped an iced tea and nibbled on my salad, feeling a little concerned as Jim ordered his third vodka drink. I asked Jim about his doctorate, and for a second, I thought he warbled. He told me his doctorate was in math and that he rarely used it. Jim explained that he ran commercial projects for large corporations needing to expand their physical locations or build new facilities. He nonchalantly mentioned he made $40,000-$60,000 in a few months, with bonuses paid if the job came in early. He smiled and boasted he'd never had a job that completed late. Jim had been running his own projects for nearly five years since he left a large construction company where he'd learned the business.

Jim listened to me intently when I spoke about myself, growing up in the southland, my Italian family, my parents, school, and my education plans. He looked at my face and smiled empathetically when I told him about how much I wanted to help my patients. He didn't seem too surprised when I explained to him I roomed with Cathy and Angie from Sunshine. Rushing a little nervously, I told him living alone was lonely and I needed to save all the money I could for school. I was fairly positive Jim didn't remember me sitting in the apartment that night as he stumbled in after Cathy. That night with Cathy must have been a big mistake for Jim. I was certain it was, figuring he was probably drunk, had a weak moment, and was trying to forget it. I would do the same.

The conversation flowed well. When I told Jim my parents were moving to Europe soon, he brightened up. Jim explained he was Swiss and his folks were from Switzerland; they spent a few months a year in the U.S. and much of their time abroad. I was very impressed. He had a doctorate, was European, educated, was bravely raising his baby daughter, and had a wonderful business. This was the best date of my life. I was instantly falling in love with Jim. Jim made me promise to introduce him to my parents before they left for Europe. It seemed a little awkward, as I had only met him and didn't really know him or his family, but since my parents were leaving soon, I agreed. I was positive my parents would immediately fall in love with Jim, just as I had.

The afternoon ended in the parking lot in front of my "classic" '65 Mustang, with Jim leaning down and giving me a soft kiss. My heart was pounding, my stomach fluttering and my head overflowing with dreams. What a wonderful day this was, I was happy and singing inside. Jim told me he would call me tomorrow and would pick me up at my apartment so we could go over and meet my parents.

My car was on fumes again and I called my folks from a pay phone at the local gas station near our place. I enthusiastically detailed my Jim Miller story, telling Mom I had met someone really special and thought he may be *the one*. She asked me a lot of questions I thought were quite irrelevant: Where did he live, where was he from, did he go to church, had I met his parents, had I met any of his friends, what college did he attend, whom did he work for? . . . on and on. I figured I'd let them meet Jim, and later when we were engaged, I would tell them he was dutifully raising his lovely little princess. No doubt this would impress them even more than it had impressed me.

As promised, Jim Miller called and asked me the directions to our apartment. I knew he had been there before, but maybe he didn't remember that night. I gave him directions and in no time at all, he swooped his shiny Jaguar in front of our apartment. Jim rang the doorbell, and I counted to three before leaping across the room to open the door. I floated out the sidewalk and into Jim's car, and in no time, we were weaving through traffic en route to Yorba Linda.

In her usual fashion, Mother put out appetizers and a drink bar. She had an ice bucket with soda and a few bottles of wine and some hard liquor and mixes. Although my folks didn't drink much, whenever they had a little party with friends, they put out the drink bar. These same bottles were recycled for many gatherings as most of their friends had soda or a cup of coffee. Jim entered the house filling the room and I looked at his physical size compared to my Italian parents. He was more than seven inches taller than Daddy and well over a foot taller than Mother. My father leaned toward Jim during introductions and both men shook hands. Mother looked at Jim, nodded nervously, extended her hand and ushered us all into the formal living room.

I could see Mother's disapproving looks as Jim quickly sipped his first drink and got up to get another. I said very little, but Jim chatted quite animatedly with my folks. Dad asked him about his work, and Jim kept mentioning how much money he made. I could see Daddy looking at Jim's gold Rolex and Mom appeared interested and smiled politely, but I could see the worry lines on her forehead. I was relieved when Jim announced that we had to leave; he had an early morning and break-neck pace on the jobsite. Walking out to the car, Father and Jim seemed to be engaging in a conversation about the Jag. I turned to smile at Mother, but looked down into her alarmed face. I couldn't believe what I was hearing. My mother told me to run away from Jim now before I got any closer. What? She whispered intensely she felt Jim had "no character" and was very dangerous. She urged me to break it off immediately. How could Jim be dangerous? How could she hate

Jim after spending so little time with him? We said our goodbyes. I quickly hugged and kissed my parents, not realizing we would not see each other again for a very long time. Jim opened my car door, and I gracefully got in. Daddy and Jim shook hands and Mother nodded stiffly. Jim jumped in and we pulled out of the driveway while I waved goodbye. Daddy and I were so much alike; Daddy seemed to like Jim. Mother was always serious, introverted, and questioned everything in life. With time, she would come to know and love Jim. I was positive.

CHAPTER 5
CLUB ESCAPE

On a busy Saturday night a few days later, Iris told Cathy, Angie and me that she scheduled introductions and meetings for us. She expected us to quickly change after our shift and come to a private booth on the main floor. The girls squealed with delight, while I stood quietly saying nothing. I had to tell Iris that I just couldn't do her "dating" business. It would have worked last week, but I became "soul-mates" with my future husband and was certain he would not approve.

Sensing my reluctance, Iris leaned hard towards me, her face unmoving, and her voice firm and authoritative. "You better not back out on me now, Jeanette," she hissed and squeezed my arm tightly. "You knew the game, took the clothes, and now you're committed! There is no turning back. You *don't* want to mess with Savage or me. You work for *us* now." I gulped and nodded. With a sudden change in her demeanor, she added:

"So, all set, I'll see you at the booth around 11:00 p.m. Please pretty yourselves and Jeanette," she smiled, adding feigned cheerfulness, "please *do* try to smile and be engaging with my friends; it's a meeting and a drink in a public place!"

I pasted on a plastic smile and felt my throat getting dry and hot. Cathy and Angie bounded off to seat a large party in the waiting room. I went back to serving my prime rib and lobster dinners, dreading the night ahead.

It was just after 10:30 p.m. when my section began to slow enough to look up. I happened to glance at the main entrance and locked eyes with Jim Miller. Jim Miller! This was a very awkward time for him to be here. Iris was expecting me to meet with some men in a private booth. How was I going to explain this to him? He beamed a bright smile across the dining room as he maneuvered his way to my side. I felt that lump in my throat and butterflies bouncing around in my stomach. He didn't seem to notice that I had a few food stains on my uniform or that my long hair was up in a bun on the top of my head. He looked into my eyes and smiled.

"Hey there, Jeanette, how are you? Miss me?" he asked, winking and flashing that smile through his perfectly tanned face. I smiled back, wishing I was a million miles away. I wished I was away from Sunshine, away from Cathy and Angie, but most of all away from Iris. Jim was saying something about a drink after work, but I hadn't heard a word he was saying. I looked behind Jim towards the bar where I saw Iris and Savage pointing at me and talking. They looked angry. Savage was shaking his head. Now I was scared. Could I be in some sort of mafia thing? Because I had agreed to the "date" program and had taken the clothes from Iris without giving anything back, could they hurt me? I nodded to Jim and told him I'd be ready to meet him in about fifteen minutes. He went to find a table, and I rushed through my checks and finish cleaning my work station. My next stop was the locker room to change and stuff my uniform in my duffle. What was I going to do?

Iris caught up with me in the hallway and grabbed my arm so hard it swung me around. She clenched her teeth and smiled insincerely.

"So where do you think you're going?" I squirmed out of her grasp, mustering up as much strength and composure as I could and rushed on.

"I'm fluffing up like you told us to." I stood and looked up into her face and began to fabricate my story. "I'm going to change so I look really stunning for our new friends." She smiled and ran her hand down my arm, changing instantly from the wicked witch of the west into my mother.

"That's what I thought; sorry I grabbed you so hard, not intentional," she forced out a little chuckle. "You were walking so fast I just reached out quickly to get your attention. I was coming to ask you if you needed any lip gloss or blush from my locker." I nodded. We both knew the entire conversation was a lie.

"I'll be right out front, Iris. Just let me get into my street clothes. I'll see you at the booth." I smiled and bolted for the locker room. As I changed into my street clothes, my head was a rush of data. I had to get out of this deal with Iris. I had to tell Jim about what was going on. How would he react if he knew that I was making a deal with Iris? He was a lot older than me; he knew Iris and probably knew that she had a "dating" service. What would Jim think about me if he knew I had taken clothes from Iris and promised to escort much older businessmen from around the country? He would probably not want me to be the mother of his children, would he? Here I was, the one they called the "ice princess," the one who didn't date the men from the bar, the virgin waiting until my wedding night, and now I was meeting men and dating them for money! I was such a fool; why had I ever let myself waltz blindly into a relationship with Iris, naively following Cathy and Angie? I could clearly see what she and Savage were. Was I that stupid that I couldn't tell they were prostitute and pimp?

Jim found me as I exited the locker room and was walking towards the main restaurant floor. He looked at me and immediately knew something was horribly wrong. The music had already started, and people were flooding the dance floor. From across the room I watched Cathy and Angie standing in front of the private booth with Iris hovering over them like a mother hen with young chicks. They were smiling and fluttering their eyelashes; no doubt there were several rich older men sitting in the booth salivating at the thoughts of having dates with these gorgeous young ladies. Jim saw tears brimming in my eyes, and he grabbed my hand, leading me out through the service door towards the back parking lot. He leaned me against a car and turned with his back against the deafening blast of the bass guitar leaking through each pore of the building.

"Jeanette, whatever is the matter?" Jim asked. My mind grasped for an answer. I should probably lie right now, I thought, wriggle out of the truth, and try to piece the mess together by myself. No, you can't start a relationship with lies. I just need to tell him the truth, tell him everything and hope and pray for the best. I had tears running down my face as I looked up into a very empathetic Jim.

"Well, this is kind of hard to tell you. . . and I hope you don't judge me too harshly. I feel that it is really important to always tell the truth." I paused and sucked in some air, calming my voice and gathering my thoughts. "I feel that we really made a connection when we met, Jim. I had a wonderful time at lunch the other day and I think we seem pretty compatible." I paused dreading the next information I was about to tell Jim. "Uh. . . do you know Iris very well?" I asked, knowing that he had to know her and probably knew all about her and Savage and the dating game! Jim nodded, listening intently as I rushed out my confession. "Well, before you and I went out, Iris invited me over to her house. She threw a small party, and then told me I could go into business on the side and make some extra money to help me pay for school." Jim's eyes got dark and he began to frown. I kept on explaining, hoping the story didn't sound as bad to him as it now sounded to me. "Well, Iris told me I could schedule a date with one of her friends and be paid quite well to go to dinner. No strings attached!" Jim snorted.

"Are you telling me that you are one of Iris' girls?" Jim spat the words at me, his face changing instantly from one of compassion and empathy to one of anger and hatred. I began to shake my head and cry.

"I've never dated one of Iris' friends, honest; but I did promise her that I would work for her. The money sounded good and all, and I really need to make extra cash for school, but it didn't feel right. When I told her I wasn't sure, she got really mean and threatened me." Jim slammed his hand down hard on the car hood behind my head, and I instinctively cowered and covered my face with my hands. For an instant when Jim raised his hand, I almost thought he

39

was going to hit me. Jim's face was bright red, his eyes black as he began yelling at me.

"Jeanette, are you a complete idiot? Why would you make a deal with the devil? Do you want to give your body to disgusting old men for a hundred dollars? Iris is a prostitute and this is the real world, baby! Are you trying to tell me that you are so naïve you didn't know this? She works for Savage, the wonderful fellow who sells drinks from behind your bar." He continued the tirade as I began crying. "This is great, just great; I really thought you were something special. You really had me with this little miss nursing routine. Oh boy, I didn't see this coming. They all called you the 'ice princess.' They told me you were different. They were so wrong; you're just the same as the rest of those girls. Inside you're nothing but a piece of trash!" he fumed. I looked up at him and pleaded.

"Jim, you have to believe me. I didn't know anything about Iris or Savage. I honestly didn't know. She lied to me and convinced me that there was nothing wrong with the dates she was setting up. She didn't say a thing about being a prostitute, honest. I had no idea; please believe me. I am telling you the truth." I buried my face in my hands and began to sob. I heard Jim stomp off and heard the slamming of the back door to Sunshine. That was the end of it. I blew it big time, and had lost the love of my life.

I didn't know how much time had elapsed, but a while later Jim came running to me in the parking lot. I looked up to see a frantic look on his face.

"You need to come into Sunshine right away," Jim began, taking large breaths. "I had a faceoff with Savage and Iris and the situation is deadly. I told them that you were not going to work for them." I had saucer eyes and listened intently. "You have to go back into Sunshine and look them both in the face. You have to tell them that you are not going to take their job; you are not going to work for anyone else; and that you know you'll forever be blackballed in every restaurant in Orange County." He continued in a stern and controlled manner. "Jeanette, you don't know how dangerous these people are. They kill young girls like you who've seen their dens and try to walk away. You are going to have to run tonight in order to save your life. You will have to quit Sunshine; they know where you live, and you can't go back there ever again. You are going to have to run and hide until things cool off. I know you are scared, but please don't question what we are going to do. Are you able to do this now?" Jim asked.

"Do you think they are going to kill me?" I asked. Jim nodded.

"They are going to give you one chance to leave, but you need to take it now. They are doing this as a favor to me, but who knows, they may change their minds. We need to act now and get out." I shook my head.

"But how am I going to survive? How am I going to live? I need to work to get back to school." I was shaking my head back and forth. This was a terrible situation. I couldn't believe I was living this nightmare. I continued with tears still streaming down my face. "What about my things? What about my clothes at the apartment?" My mind was spinning and in my head I cried out for my parents. They were across the sea and in a foreign land. Why didn't I go to Europe? I was not equipped to live in a world this fast. People wanted to kill me now! My parents' new address was back at the apartment with the rest of my stuff. How could I walk away from the few things I owned? I had to run now; I was certain

41

these people would think nothing about having me murdered. Jim was holding his hand out to escort me back into the club. I didn't want to go, but what choice did I have?

"We go in there. Iris and Savage are ready to talk. We say our peace, and then leave right away before they change their minds." Jim leaned in and looked me straight in the eyes. "Jeanette, this is a matter of life and death." I began to shake; what on earth had I done?

I held Jim's hand as he walked me over to the bar where Iris stood waiting to face me off. Cathy and Angie were oblivious to the turmoil I was going through as they sat drinking cocktails and cuddling with the older men in their booth by the main dance floor. Savage came over, and we all followed him to the storage room behind the main bar. He closed the door firmly and set the lock. Jim looked at Savage and Iris and held me back and a little behind him. I was still shaking with fear. These nice people were killers. I was just twenty years old, and I might be a murder victim. Jim began:

"I've explained the situation to Jeanette. She's agreed to leave right now and will not work for you or anyone else in the business again."

"Is that so, Jeanette?" Savage, the once-joking bartender, now looked like a mafia boss. I nodded my head unable to utter any words. Savage continued.

"Jim, we're only doing this for you; we've gotten rid of little problems like Jeanette for less, you know." I sucked in my breath and kept as still as possible. Jim grabbed my arm, unlocked the door and pushed me out toward the exit of Sunshine and toward a brand new life. Jim turned to finalize the deal.

"She won't be a problem to you anymore, I promise. You'll never see her again." I walked as fast as I've ever walked before without running. I hit the door, with Jim right behind me and walked out into the parking lot. Once I hit my car, Jim urged me to keep moving. He told me to meet him in the parking lot of a coffee shop close by to make our plans. He said it wasn't safe to stay in the lot. I believed him.

On my way to the coffee shop, the reality of the situation set in. I had my bank account with a few thousand dollars in it. No place to live, no clothes to wear; I had my car, but every other possession I owned was left behind. I had a few things in my car and that was it. I didn't even take my duffle bag from my locker at Sunshine. I could never look back or my life would probably be over. I was so afraid they would kill me that night. When Jim pulled up behind me in the parking lot, I flew out of my car and into his arms, sobbing and shaking. Jim stood there until I quieted and stroked my hair, telling me that everything was going to be all right.

"I saved your life tonight, Jeanette. I will take care of you forever. You come and live with me. Nothing bad will ever happen to you, I promise." I looked up at Jim, and he lifted my face. I was completely lost in a soft and passionate kiss. He would take care of me now and nothing bad was going to happen to me. We would be married in the Catholic Church, have a wonderful family, and be together forever. I knew Jim would protect, respect, and love me forever. I smiled up at him, thrilled now at the thought of our future together as husband and wife.

"So we're going to be married?" I asked, expecting an immediate yes. Jim shuffled a little bit.

"Ah yes, yes, we can get a ring now," he answered. I held him closely and knew that things worked out the way they were supposed to. We were going to be married. I was safe now.

We left my car in the parking lot of the restaurant, and I got into the Jag. Jim kept telling me we needed to be very careful and make sure nobody was following us so we drove around for hours to be certain. The night grew very late and we needed to find someplace safe to sleep. As we drove around looking for a place to stay, I figured we were pretty much married now. He saved my life. I owed my life to this man.

After we drove through the streets a few more miles to make sure the coast was clear, we pulled into a motel downtown near Disneyland. I sat in the car feeling very uneasy about the night. How well did I know Jim? What would my parents think about me in this situation? How would I handle myself in a motel room with a man? I was only twenty. The boys I had dated in high school— well, they were boys. We didn't check into motel rooms. We didn't run away from killers. We went to football games and proms and ate fast food at local hangouts. I was way out of my league. My head pounded from crying and it being so late. I watched as Jim spoke with the desk-clerk, smiled and pointed out to the car where I sat feeling very self-conscious. He came sauntering out to the car flashing those white teeth at me. Even in the dark of night I could see those teeth. He hopped into the car and acted like nothing had happened at all tonight.

"So, ready to experience the thrill of a lifetime?" He smiled and leaned over to stroke my hair. I pulled away slightly and stiffened my posture. "Hey, hey, don't act like that now. I just saved your life; you owe me a little friendly gratitude." Jim's voice was not very nice at all. He sounded callous and sarcastic. "Come on," he continued, "let's get into the room. Things will look a lot brighter in the morning."

I followed Jim as we climbed the two flights of cement stairs to the room. I clutched my purse tightly and looked down at my feet, feeling like I was ten years old. My brain kept yelling at me to run, but my feet kept plodding along behind Jim as if I were in a dream. He opened the door and my heart stood still. Old musty smells flooded my brain. The inside of the room had not been renovated in years and the stale smell of smoke and alcohol hung in the air. This wasn't the way it was suppose to be. The first time I was to be with a man was supposed to be special. It wasn't supposed to be in the back seat of a car; and it wasn't supposed to be in a crusty motel room with sagging curtains and a stained bedspread.

Thinking as fast as I could, I tried to make light of the situation and hoped I wouldn't offend Jim. The other girls he dated were not really girls like me at all; they were women. They probably went with him to motels all the time. How could I go through with this? It would be a big lie. I stood by the door as Jim entered the room and set his things on the dresser. I was relieved to see two beds in the room and decided that this was my only salvation.

"So . . ." I began as enthusiastically as I could sound. "Which bed do you want?" I smiled across the room at Jim, feeling my heart pounding wildly in my chest.

Jim looked up at me and began to laugh. "You've got to be kidding, right?" He crossed the room and held me in his arms, squeezing me just a little too tightly. "This should be a very special night for us, Jeanette. We *are* like a married couple now. I saved your life; you've left your past behind. Now the future belongs to the two of us." He kissed me hard and I felt like I was going to pass out. No! Not like this! I pushed away.

"Jim, I do want us to be married and all, I really do, but I can't do it like this. I'm not ready and I feel we should be legal and all." Jim's face turned dark red, and he came close to me and spat the words into my face.

"What do you think you're doing then, playing a game with me?" He continued spewing a string of awful obscenities. I immediately started to cry. "You were fine going off with those old men that Iris was setting you up with, but you won't pony up to a young guy like me?" He held both of my shoulders and shook me. "What do you want, a ring?" He let me go with enough force that I fell back onto the bed. I started to sob and choked out the words.

"Jim, I. . . I. . . am a virgin. I've never been with a man before. I do love you so and thought we would be a perfect couple. Get engaged, have a party, get married in the church, have a family. I didn't want my first time to be like this." I put my head down into my hands and couldn't control my sobs. What had I gotten myself into? I was scared, alone, and I felt like I made a horrible mistake. I had to get out of this room tonight. I had no place to live and no job—the only thing I had was a few bucks and a car. I heard the bathroom door slam hard, and I sat on the bed praying for an answer. God, if you are out there, please, I need you tonight.

After a few minutes, the bathroom door opened and Jim came out. He sat on the other bed and leaned over, putting his hand onto my chin, lifting my face up to meet his. He looked so loving and sincere. He spoke deliberately and softly to me.

"Jeanette, I am so in love with you. If it is marriage that you need, well, let's get a ring and go to the Justice of the Peace. I want to marry you and live the rest of my life with you." I jumped off the bed and onto Jim. I started smothering him with kisses. Thoughts of leaving were quickly forgotten. He was wonderful; I just made him angry. Once we were married, everything would be perfect.

"Oh, Jim, Jim, thank you so much for loving and respecting me. I do love you so much, and I promise I will be the best wife you could ever imagine. I will take care of you until the day we die." I hugged Jim tightly and started thinking about wedding plans.

"What about my parents, will they have time to plan a trip home for the wedding?" I asked. Jim shook his head.

"No, Jeanette, please respect my wishes and let's get a marriage license on Monday morning. You can send your parents a letter to let them know we're married." I knew this wasn't going to make my parents or my family very happy. They would say I was too young and didn't know enough about Jim or his family to get married. They would tell me I needed to wait. I didn't want to wait. I did know how my heart felt and at twenty years old, I was legally old enough to get married and knew what I wanted out of life. I felt that Jim was the one for me. I knew we would be very happy together.

CHAPTER 6
I DO

We stayed in the cheap motel as roommates until Monday. Jim took me shopping at the local mall where I stocked up on whatever I wanted. He pulled out his credit card each time we bought something. After several hours, I had a few outfits, a bathing suit and figured I could always buy more clothes as time progressed. We went back to the motel and swam in the small pool. I felt extremely self-conscious as we met other couples that were traveling with their children; the women always looked down at my hand seeing I had no wedding ring. I knew what they were thinking—me, a young tart throwing myself at a rich young man. A few times there were stares and whispered comments. Jim was oblivious to it as he popped open another beer can, smoked another cigarette, and caught a few Southern California rays.

On Monday, we checked out of the motel and Jim drove me to Fashion Island where we checked into an elegant penthouse suite at the Hyatt Regency Hotel. After settling in, we drove to the shopping mall in search of a wedding ring. We found a very exclusive jewelry store and Jim immediately asked the clerk to clean his three-carat diamond solitaire ring. The salesman eyed Jim's eighteen-carat gold Rolex and scurried around giving us a lot of attention. Jim told him we were looking around for a wedding set and wanted to find the perfect one. Jim pointed to a ring and the clerk took it out, a beautiful, brilliant cut solitaire, set in platinum. I put it on my hand; the size was a perfect five. Jim asked to see three more rings. I tried them all on and Jim motioned for me to let him look at them. He pointed to another ring—a beautiful diamond solitaire, with a circle of diamonds surrounding it and a diamond studded wedding band. I whispered to Jim that I loved that ring the most. He had me take it off and at the same time pointed to three more rings for me to try on.

Jim was in control. I was the blonde babe the clerks were eyeing. I was the lucky girl who landed the rich young construction executive. I was getting a ring. After a few moments, Jim asked the clerk for his ring back and after briskly drying the diamond, he brought it over. I waited expectantly for Jim to say something. He didn't. Instead, he told the clerk we would be back tomorrow and asked about ladies Rolex watches. The clerk handed Jim his card, and Jim smiled that million-dollar smile. "I'm coming back to pick out a ring and would like to put a Rolex on her wrist, as well." The clerk beamed, I felt deflated. We were supposed to get married today. I had a pink silk dress lying on the bed of the hotel, pressed and ready to go. Now I had no ring. I knew Jim was going to marry me, but no ring. They were expensive. I saw one price tag for $17,000. That was so much money! Walking to the car, I sulked a little. Why didn't he buy me a band? I wouldn't have expected him to spend that much money. Maybe things were tight with work, maybe he needed to conserve. I got into the car and was quiet. Jim looked over at me.

"What's wrong? Are you mad?" he asked.

"No. I'm not mad, just a little disappointed, I guess."

Jim turned the corner and pulled into Muldoon's, a very exclusive restaurant and bar in Fashion Island. We walked into the lobby and took a seat by the window overlooking the courtyard. Jim ordered a bottle of Dom Perignon. I was a little depressed and not feeling at all like celebrating. As the waitress poured our glasses, Jim handed me mine and smiled. "Here's to our wedding and a long and happy life together." I took the glass and did a double take. There in the bottom of the glass was the diamond wedding ring I had just tried on at the jewelry store. "Jim!" I cried, "How did you do that? I didn't see you buy this ring." Jim smiled as I quickly sipped the champagne and put the damp ring on my finger, holding my hand out to admire the two-carat rock.

"I bought the ring from Terrence this morning. I called him and had it charged to my account. They know me there. I've purchased thousands of dollars in jewelry from them. When you weren't looking I winked at Terrence and simply slipped your diamond into my pocket. Do you like it?" I came around to Jim's seat and jumped onto his lap, kissing him in public and holding out my hand while admiring my new ring. I didn't care who watched.

"I love it! It's the most beautiful thing I've ever seen in my whole life!" We ate animatedly and happily, the champagne going to my head. With the bill paid, we drove to the county courthouse to get our marriage license. It took about thirty minutes from start to finish to get officially married. There was no white wedding dress; Daddy didn't give me away; there were no invitations; no Italian reception with the whole family dancing the Tarantella; there was nothing but a piece of paper and a few congratulations from complete strangers. Something felt very wrong. The whole afternoon was just a semiconscious blur with me a spectator watching my life unfold.

The afternoon didn't go well. I was nervous, inexperienced and uncomfortable. It was daytime and I felt embarrassed by my nakedness. I could tell by the look on Jim's face I was a real disappointment to him. Maybe he shouldn't have married me? I wasn't a real woman. Afterwards, without speaking, Jim showered quickly and explained he had a business meeting and needed to leave. Reading the look on my face, he huffed a little and then finally asked if I would like to come along. I nodded, quickly threw on some clothes and ran a brush through my hair. I didn't want to make Jim wait. As we left the room, Jim walked in quick long strides with me following behind as we made our way down the hallway of the Hyatt. I thought I heard him mumble something about me being too young and him making a big mistake.

Jim stared hard at me as he gave the claim check to the valet, his face showing disgust. My hair was not curled, I hadn't put on any make-up, and I didn't have time to iron my clothes. I fumbled in my purse, grabbed my lip-gloss, and quickly put some on. I doubted it was much of an improvement. I squirmed under Jim's glare but didn't want to stay back in the room – we were just married. I wanted to be with him, but more than that I wanted *him to want to be with me*.

Jim stopped at a local gas station and filled up the car with gas. I asked him for some change so I could call my brother Tom in

L.A. to tell him the news. He rustled in his pocket and handed me a half dozen coins for the pay phone. I had a new purse that Jim had bought me; it was a designer purse with no money in it. I scrimped and saved and still had money in my bank account earmarked for school, but not a penny on me. I walked across the blacktop and put a few dimes into the phone, feeling desperate to talk to someone in my family. I had gotten married today and none of my family or friends had been there. I felt like used goods and was very confused – a lump was forming in the back of my throat. I heard the phone ring, pinched my fingers together hard and bit my lip to keep from sobbing. The phone rang four times and finally someone picked up. It was my brother Tom; I was so thankful he was home.

I blurted out what happened early in the day and quickly told Tom I was a married woman now. I rushed on telling Tom how I'd met Jim, explaining he was the man of my dreams. I told Tommy Jim was going to put me through school and we would live in his beach mansion overlooking the ocean. The phone had a lot of uncomfortable silences as I tried to convince Tommy what I had done *was* the best decision in my life. Why didn't Tommy sound really happy for me? I heard him suck in his breath and let out a long sigh.

"Uh, how long have you known him, Jeannie?" Tom finally asked. I squirmed hearing the questions as I fingered the metal cord of the pay phone and looked around at Jim sitting in the car. Was he frowning at me?

"Tommy, I haven't known Jim for long, but I feel we are made for each other. I can't explain it. Jim is perfect for me, and he has a darling little two-year-old daughter that I'm going to raise. The mother didn't want her, and I do." More silence, and then I heard Tom let out his breath in a huff.

"He has a kid too?" More silence. "Well Jeannie, you're an adult now and you can do whatever you want. Remember, marriage is forever and you shouldn't just marry the first guy that comes along." I stood up straight and bristled, not responding to the lecture. "Just make sure you call Mom and Dad to let them know. The last time I spoke with them, they told me they hadn't heard from you in months." I was forced to eat that extra portion of guilt on my plate.

"Yeah, I know. I don't have their number, and I sort of lost all of my things." I heard Tom let out another long sigh. He just doesn't understand how happy I am, that's all.

"You lost your things, huh? I guess I won't ask how that happened," Tommy said with condemning words. I asked Tom about a box of my prized possessions I had left at our parents' house before I moved in with Cathy and Angie. He told me he knew where my box of stuff was located and he would keep it until I could pick it up.

Tom gave me our parents' number in Denmark, told me to be careful, and that he loved me and wanted to see me soon. The conversation became difficult over the sound of an irritated driver pumping his car horn. Quickly I realized it was Jim tooting the horn on his Jag, obviously extremely irritated by the long phone conversation with my brother. I waved and smiled as Jim scowled at me. I told Tom I had to go, said goodbye, ran over and jumped in the yellow Jag. This was the beginning of a wonderful life with my new husband. Jim screeched out of the gas station burning rubber and causing a great commotion in the quiet manicured streets of Fashion Island.

"What is your problem? Didn't you hear me honking? Are you deaf? You told me you only needed to get the phone number so you could call your parents! What in the crap took you so long?" Jim hissed. I was surprised. I didn't want our first day as a married couple ruined by my insensitivity. "Couldn't you see I was done pumping gas and ready to go? I have work to do, or did you think a penthouse suite at the Hyatt was free to anyone who wanted to stay there? How do you think I paid for your breakfast this morning? It was from money *I* made. How do you think I got you that diamond ring you begged for? But you wouldn't know anything about working for a living now, right? I'm your new sugar daddy. You don't need to work anymore; I'm the meal ticket, right? Couldn't wait to drop out of school and latch on to the first paycheck that walked by, huh?" Jim fumed, kept swearing under his breath and drove recklessly down the coast highway.

My face flushed hot and red and tears streaked down my face. My stomach writhed spasmodically, and I felt like I was going to throw up. I curled my body into the passenger door, my head barely reaching the window, tears streaming down my face. I *was* sorry. I didn't mean to be selfish, insensitive, or greedy. I really blew it! What an idiot I was! I cursed myself. Next time, I would be aware of what Jim wanted. I had to stop being so selfish. I had to think of his needs too—the last thing I needed to do was to make him mad. I was a married woman now. I had to stop being a young kid and start supporting my husband. He had a business meeting and I was lollygagging with no sense of time constraints. I sobbed angry hurt tears, feeling like a child.

A quiet drive along the curving coastline calmed my nerves and I finally stopped sniffing as we reached the little town of Laguna Beach. The traffic slowed and people walked the main boardwalk, dressed in elite casual clothes. Rich, tanned, beautiful people shopped down the exclusive row of shops, peeking into curio and art studios. Jim growled at me and told me he had an important meeting with a potential client and my thoughtlessness could have cost him the account. During the tirade and explosion of anger, I was afraid at one point that Jim was going to strike me. Several times he had raised his hand and slammed it down into the center console of the car. He kept regurgitating the same information about how stupid I was and how I made him wait. He told me the next time I did that to him he would just leave me there and let me figure out a ride. I was certain he meant it.

I finally calmed down long enough to mumble a soft apology to Jim. I promised I would never carelessly make him wait for me ever again. After about fifteen minutes of the tirade and a few more screeching corners, Jim slowed the car a little, glanced over, and softly took my hand in his. He acted like nothing had happened at all. He started whistling and turned the music up louder. I wasn't sure what to think now. He loves me; he loves me not. My head was spinning. I never remembered Daddy treating Mother like that. I also couldn't remember Mother making Daddy wait while he honked the car horn over and over either. I guess I really needed to grow up. I had to realize what to do to please my husband and what not to do. I doubted Jim wanted to yell at me for causing him to become late. He was frustrated because he had a meeting. He must really love me; he was sincere. Jim reached over and ran his fingers through my long blonde hair. I had applied my make-up in the car, and Jim glanced approvingly at me. I offered a bashful smile. Jim pulled off the highway and parked the Jag in a parking lot behind the bank.

"You wait here while I meet my client." Jim got out of the car and adjusted his belt. I leaned over and nodded but didn't dare question him. Jim assured me he wouldn't be long and I watched him walk through the parking lot, past the door of the bank. I assumed his appointment was with a finance manager or bank customer. I was wrong. Jim reached the sidewalk of Pacific Coast Highway in Laguna Beach and headed south. I wasn't exactly sure where he was going. He didn't offer the information and after the horrible morning, I wasn't about to ask.

I must have fallen asleep for quite a while, for when Jim finally returned the sun was setting in the western sky and the air was getting cool and damp. I jumped, startled when Jim opened the car door. He smelled like alcohol and cigarettes and his speech sounded slurred.

"Hello wifer!" Jim smiled as he got into the car with a thud and clumsily leaned to give me a kiss. I kissed him back and rubbed my eyes, shaking my head to clear my thoughts. "What time is it?" I asked him. Jim laughed.

"I have no clue," he answered happily. "Are you hungry?" I realized I was starving. I hadn't eaten anything since breakfast and must have been sleeping in the car for hours.

"Yes, I am. Are we going to dinner?" Jim smiled broadly and brought out a whole stack of hundred dollar bills. He fanned through them in front of my face. I had never seen that much money in my entire life. Wow. He was rich. Wow, I guess I was rich too! This could feel very good. I always worried about how much money I had, what I was going to buy, how much in tips I needed to earn to make the rent. Those days were gone forever. I felt very secure at that moment and reassured myself it was the right decision to marry Jim. My financial worries were finally over.

"Yepper, we are going out to eat, I guess the treat will be on me." I didn't know where or how Jim got the money. I knew he had a business meeting, and probably walked to the bank to cash his check. At that moment it didn't matter much to me. I was starving and felt a little shaky and lightheaded. I smiled and Jim showed he was pleased with my response. He leaned over and kissed me softly holding the back of my head in his hand. I was so in love, my heart pounded.

"That sounds wonderful, Jim; I don't care where we go, I'm starving!" Jim started the powerful engine of the Jag. We pulled out onto the road driving along the winding bluff-top highway next to the gorgeous Pacific Ocean. The sunset was shimmering across the water and I felt like a princess. Jim pulled the Jag into the valet service area of an exclusive oceanfront seafood restaurant.

Dinner was a dream. Jim was attentive, laughing, drinking, throwing his stack of hundred dollar bills around, and getting a lot of attention from everyone in the place. The waitresses fawned over Jim and then shot quick glances at me. I pushed back the feeling of inadequacy. My clothes didn't look great, my hair wasn't styled... but I had Jim! We feasted on champagne, expensive lobster, and fresh tossed Caesar salad. After eating, we moved to the bar and Jim told riveting stories to anyone who would listen. Jim had the crowd of locals eating out of his hand and everyone was a guest of Jim's generosity. He knew how to play the crowd and was very good at it. I sat there smiling at Jim, watching the faces of the tanned and fabulous Newport rich and famous sharing drinks with my new husband. I was amazed at the power he held over these people. Jim failed to mention we had married earlier in the day. He didn't even introduce me as his wife. I sat there like one of his fans, enjoying the expensive drinks and becoming captivated by Jim, the royal and rich executive of Corona del Mar, the exclusive zip code of Newport Beach.

Walking out to the car, Jim said goodbye to his newfound friends; he opened my door, and gracefully I settled into the buttery leather seat. I watched as Jim tooled around the front of the car and sat behind the wheel. In the quiet of the night, Jim driving and fiddling with the tape deck, I suddenly realized that I didn't have a place to live. It was a queer feeling that made me shiver. I realized all my worldly possessions were stored in a single box. My car was in a parking lot somewhere in Orange County, I had a few outfits and some toiletries at the hotel, I had a new husband sitting next to me, but I didn't have a home. I hadn't had a "real" home since I left my parents' house two years earlier, headed for college. Jim and I would build a new home together soon. We would decorate, plan our family, and create a beautiful life together. My dreams were coming true.

I DO

CHAPTER 7
CORONA DEL MAR

The first few days after we were married and staying at the Hyatt Hotel were very lonely and confusing. I didn't dare question Jim about what he was doing or where he was going. Jim would leave in the late afternoon announcing he had a client meeting, come back in the early morning hours smelling like liquor and cigarettes, sleep most of the day, and then arise, shower, and repeat the pattern. I purchased a few romance novels and spent my days ordering room service or laying out by the pool. One day, when I was out by the pool talking to the lifeguard, Jim stormed over to me, pulled my arm, and scooped up my towel. He led me to the room yanking hard on my arm, ranting about me hitting on the cute, tanned lifeguard, asking if I had "made it with him" in the pool room. Jim pressed me to the bed and painfully forced himself on me while I cried. I didn't move and kept shaking my head back and forth. Did he really think I would be unfaithful? I loved him and was married now. There was no way I would ever dream of cheating on him.

Afterwards I felt extremely dejected, hurt, and abused. I dressed and sat in a chair looking out at the gorgeous ocean view. Jim showered and made some small talk while he primped and began getting ready for dinner. He seemed oblivious to my pain or to the fact that he had just raped his wife. I knew I made him angry by talking to the young lifeguard. The kid was probably still in high school; looking at him as a boyfriend was something I would never do. I wasn't that kind of a girl. . . wouldn't Jim realize I was just making small talk with the guy? I tried to explain I was lonely, striking up a conversation with the lifeguard out of boredom. Jim started to rage again, and I quickly realized I made a huge mistake by starting to explain myself. He heard nothing of my explanation and only stopped yelling when I softly apologized and promised never to talk to the young lifeguard again. Jim told me to order room service and to go ahead and read on the balcony. Jim told me I would be safe in the room and I reasoned he had to conduct meetings when the customers could meet with him. I asked him if he was working a construction project right now but shrank when Jim shot me an angry look and yelled.

"Whether you believe me or not, I am working! Where do you think I keep getting our money? I have clients that need to meet with me, and I meet them on their schedules, not yours!" Jim looked at me, his face red, his blue eyes looking black; he shook his head hard, and then stormed out the door. What was I doing? I was certain now that I had made a major mistake. Maybe I could get to a pay phone and call my brother Tommy collect and have him pick me up. Maybe it wasn't too late to find my car and drive

to L.A. I could get a job and enroll in school. I thought of the lavish lifestyle with Jim and looked at the diamond ring on my finger. I did love Jim and figured he was angry with me because he must be under a lot of stress. I threw my book down and lay on the king bed, thinking about all of my fears and concerns. I didn't move from the bed and began to cry until I finally fell asleep.

When I awoke hours later Jim was standing over me, weaving, smelling of alcohol, and cigarettes. I was certain I smelled expensive women's perfume on his clothes. He smiled down at me and told me he was sorry he yelled at me. Jim proclaimed his undying love and held me tenderly, promising me we would move into his beach house in a day or two. He told me he was proud to have married the best girl out there and couldn't wait to have children together. I quickly forgot our fight about the lifeguard and the abusive afternoon. I loved Jim and wanted to have his baby. Jim was the man of my dreams. Life was wonderful again.

We spent the next two days lounging by the massive pool, swimming, getting tans, having an incredible couple's massage and drinking expensive champagne. Jim was attentive and doted on me observing every detail and treating me like a movie star. I felt like the luckiest woman alive. Jim started telling people at the resort that we were just married, and I was a fashion model. I wasn't comfortable with the lie, but Jim had me convinced because I was crowned the 1976 Sons of Italy Columbus Day Queen and because I had my picture on the cover of their Orange County Newspaper, I was somehow a fashion model. Well, it was pretty much the same as being on the cover of *Cosmopolitan Magazine*, wasn't it? Jim wanted me to look the part of the model and after assessing my wardrobe took me shopping at Neiman Marcus. Shopping was incredible and Jim had me try on numerous outfits and with his approval bought me a new dress, matching shoes and purse. We were going out and Jim wanted his wife to have the best. I took extra care to get ready, put on my make-up, and curled my long blonde hair. Jim glanced at me, showing his approval as the valet helped me into our expensive sports car. I was a model.

We ended up at a hot exclusive disco nightclub named Picasso's in Newport Beach. I had heard my girlfriends in college talking about the place known for its hot disco music, long lines, backgammon games, rich and famous crowd, exotic drinks, and cocaine. You either had to know someone or be someone to get in. My friends and I figured we would never get in and didn't want to wait at the front door as a manager or doorman eyeballed us to make sure we fit the bill.

Apparently, everyone at Picasso's knew Jim because as soon as we walked up to the front door, we were ushered into one of the private gaming rooms. We sat behind curtained windows off a raised mezzanine area, viewing the flashing light glowing onto rhythmically grinding disco bodies. Drinks were flowing, music was pounding, and people were dancing. Several times Jim left me alone at the prompting of a few "potential clients" who popped into our private room. He came back to the table looking a bit odd, sniffing a lot, and having a wild look in his eyes.

Jim smoked a lot that night and drank vodka after vodka, never seeming like he had drunk a drop. I was pretty sure he had been using cocaine like everyone else, but there was no way I was going to ask him about it. Large bouncers escorted us from the dance floor to our private room, each receiving a generous $100 tip. Jim loved the attention, and I sat there with less than $2 change in my purse, wishing I were the server waiting on our table that night.

During the evening, I inquired about going to our new home. Jim smiled and said we would go soon. I wanted to get settled in. Although the past few weeks of our "honeymoon" were idyllic, I was anxious to get on with our life. I wanted to get up early in the morning to make breakfast and a sack lunch for Jim as he went to the jobsite. I wanted to take care of Jim just like my mother took care of my father. The party life was fun and all, but after a few weeks of continual up and down, drinking and lounging, I longed for normalcy. Wistfully, I thought of my parents a world away; I hadn't even called them to let them know I had married. They would no doubt be upset. I would write them and let them know I married Jim, hoping after a few years and a couple of kids, they would accept Jim and learn to love him as I did now. I cuddled next to Jim who was moving a mile a minute, smoking, laughing, chatting, and drinking. I looked up at him and asked if we could go home tonight; he smiled broadly and nodded. We left after a long night of hard drinking, dancing, and partying and drove the few miles back to the hotel to check out.

I carried two plastic department store sacks filled with my clothes, my hair dryer, and make-up, and a few pairs of shoes. Jim had about the same. I floated out to the car paying no attention to where we were going. I was excited to finally have a home. We drove toward the Pacific to Jim's beachfront mansion in Corona del Mar a few minutes from the Hyatt.

When we arrived at Jim's house, I opened the car door, but Jim cautioned me. He had a "roommate" and needed to let him know we were coming in, just in case he wasn't dressed. Jim slammed the door and ran off around the corner. A roommate. . . he had never mentioned a roommate. Why would he need a roommate? He was rich, not like me. I always had roommates. The more people stacked into an apartment, the more affordable the rent. I looked around in the dark, craning my neck, trying to see exactly where the house was. There were manicured shrubs and decorative brickwork. I knew we were on a hill, but because it was dark and I couldn't see or hear the ocean, I had no idea where we were. This wasn't the neighborhood I had moved from, with rows of apartments, rows of second-hand cars; this neighborhood had Rolls Royces, Ferraris, Cadillacs and BMWs parked in carports, garages, and on the streets. Each home looked immense. I couldn't see the entrance to my new home, but if *this* was the neighborhood, I was richer than I had imagined.

When Jim came out to the car, he acted differently and a bit awkward. I thought we were going to *our* home, but Jim acted like he was visiting a friend and needed to make sure he could come up for a visit. It was after midnight, I reasoned, and the roommate didn't expect Jim to come home. He must have been sleeping and no doubt left Jim's house a little dirty, so he needed to quickly clean it up.

"Hey, little wifer, grab your stuff and come on in. My business partner Ken is home and he said it was okay for us both to come in." Seeing the hesitant look on my face, Jim rushed on. "Ken and I bought this place a while back as an investment; we went in on the Vegas place and Swiss Chalet, too. It's a bachelor pad; come on, I'm tired, let's get settled. Remember, I've been gone for a while and I don't think Helga has come and cleaned my room. Don't worry about the mess; she'll come back in a few days to pick up after us." Jim had the bags in his arms and we walked down the immaculate sidewalk and up some very impressive stone steps to the immense entry of the home.

The house was incredible, decorated by someone who loved antiques and had a flair for color and style. Familiar artwork framed the walls, I was positive they were the originals. Each grandiose room was impeccable with attention paid to every detail. The mansion was breathtaking and I envisioned lavish dinner parties in the dining room and could imagine a playpen and baby toys scattered about the floor. The front room had massive windows with floor to ceiling draperies swept open. Looking outside, the only thing visible was the twinkle of a few lights and the vast darkness. I couldn't wait to see the master bedroom where we would now live.

Jim ushered me down the long hallway and into a small room off the side of the house. I was absolutely shocked at what I saw. A cramped guest room with twin beds pushed against the far wall, a small table between the beds, and clothes, bags, trash, cups, dishes, books, and papers piled so high on the floor you couldn't walk through without stepping on something. Jim laughed embarrassingly and quickly scooped the piles aside allowing us to walk over and place our bags onto the twin beds. There was one dresser in the front corner of the room, piled high with books on the surface, the drawers clearly overflowing. There was an extreme contrast between the multi-million-dollar beachfront mansion and the tiny, filthy bedroom that was now apparently my room. I was very confused and pushed all thoughts out of my mind as Jim told me to try to pick up the place a little while he had a quick visit with his partner, Ken. Jim disappeared into the master suite with the door locking securely behind him.

As a dutiful wife "should" do, I cleaned the room, made both beds, and tried to make the room look a little more presentable. I just couldn't hide my disappointment at where I was. It was probably three in the morning, Jim was in the master bedroom with his "roommate," and I was cleaning a dumpy, messy hole in the wall and wishing I was in Europe with my sister, working there and living with my parents. What was I doing? All of this seemed so awkward and wrong. This wasn't the dream I had of Jim and me living in our new oceanfront mansion. I could hear laughing and low voices. I heard someone turn up the television louder, and I could hear many conversations swirling together and leaking out from under the doors of Ken's room. I could make out Jim's laugh a few times. It got a little quieter, and then I heard the water running. It sounded like a shower or bathtub. I put on a nightshirt and lay down on one of the twin beds and finally fell asleep. After what must have been a few hours, Jim came into the room, tip-toed toward the beds, laid down on the other twin bed, and fell asleep. I quietly cried myself to sleep shaking with fear as I tried to figure out what exactly was happening to me.

I heard a car start just after light the next morning; looking over I saw Jim was fast asleep and didn't look like anything would wake him up. Softly, I crept out of the room, down the long hallway, and into the grand room with the large windows. It was just getting light, and I gasped unmoving at the amazing sight: soft purple and blue sky, sunlight beginning to blend with night. The brilliant pastel colors were cascading down from the sky, embracing the deep blue horizon of the vast Pacific Ocean. I stood there for a long time as the light from behind the house started to shine onto the ocean making a glass sheen mirror across the water. Birds flew circles in the sky and sailboats began to emerge from the marina. I felt small as I admired the handiwork of God. If it were any different circumstance, I would have felt like a queen, but as soon as reality struck me, my heart reeled and I could feel the acid rumbling in my stomach. What was going on?

I sat in the easy chair looking out the windows for hours. My stomach kept growling. I looked down at my very, very flat belly. I had never been bone thin, but since I met Jim and moved out, meals were not very regular. I always worked in restaurants since leaving home and had food whenever I was hungry. The past few weeks were much different. I must have lost several pounds and although I looked fairly healthy, could not stand to lose any more weight. Jim arose much later in the day, coming into the grand room and taking a chair across from me without saying anything. He looked like he was very hung over, his hair sticking out, a dark stubble on his face; I was afraid to say anything to him at all. He grinned and gestured waiving broadly at the view.

"Beautiful here, isn't it?" I nodded, not knowing what type of mood Jim may be in. "Hey wifer, are you hungry? Let's get dressed and go to the grocery store so we can have a picnic on the floor." I nodded and rose quickly to dress, throwing on some shorts and flip-flops, pulling my hair into a ponytail. While driving to the local store, Jim rambled on about his "roommate" Ken. Ken this and Ken that. He told me he and Ken worked together on a lot of deals and that Ken was a big time executive for a chemical company. Jim told me he met Ken when building their corporate headquarters in Orange County a few years back, and now they were business partners. I didn't ask a thing about why he was in Ken's bedroom for three hours. I didn't ask why the water had come on. I was scared to death to know why Jim and Ken were in Ken's bedroom in the middle of the night, and I didn't really want to let myself know the answer. No way. It had to be the way Jim said it was. There wasn't anything weird about Jim, was there? There was no way he could be gay. I had seen him with girl after girl at Sunshine. I nodded absently, listening to Jim talk about Ken's deals and about the relationship Jim had with him.

Living in Corona del Mar was beautiful, carefree, and wonderful, and if I was a babysitter and housekeeper it would have been idyllic. Jim finally brought Leah around a few days after I moved in. She was a mixed-up little girl, who behaved badly most of the time and threw tantrums. Only two, she was a discipline problem already and didn't seem much attached to Jim. When I picked up her tiny little frame for the first time, I realized she reeked of urine, her little nails caked with dirt, and her curly light brown hair matted with grease. Jim allowed the biological mother to watch Leah temporarily so we could be married and settle into our new life together. Now that we were married, Leah would live with Jim and me full-time. I guess that meant now *I* was going to watch Leah full-time. I was a new wife and now an instant mother. I watched Leah day and night while Jim went to his meetings all hours of the night and day. Leah and I began to bond to one another. I cleaned her clothes and bathed her, curled her hair, sang children's songs with her, and walked her to the beach. She was a sweet, innocent child and my heart instantly opened up to hers. She responded to me with clinging arms, desperately needing hugs and called me "my GNut." I loved mothering Leah, pretended she was mine and dreamed of having a child of my own with Jim.

CHAPTER 8
FIRST ABUSE

Each day I felt like an emotionless robot, living in the tiny room of *our* luxury mansion. I took care of the house and Leah, and each evening Jim went out and returned home very late. His "meetings" in Ken's room continued several times a week with the same hushed tones, loud TV and running water. One day while Jim was out and Leah was down for a nap, the doorbell rang. I was doing housework, had my hair pulled up and wore an old t-shirt and cut-off jeans. I answered the door with a dusting cloth in my hand and was awestruck by a gorgeous young woman greeting me with a warm smile. From down beyond the front entry, I could see a shiny, white convertible Mercedes parked on the street.

"Hello there, I'm a friend of Jim's. Is he home?" she asked craning her neck to look around me. I didn't know what to think and tried not to feel inadequate – I reasoned that Jim knew a lot of people.

"Uh, no, Jim is out right now; who shall I say called on him?" I looked at this young woman's clothes, tan, jewels, and stunning face, then quickly down at my bare feet, and the strings from my cutoffs. My face flushed and I shuffled. She smiled, flashing her straight white teeth at me.

"Tell him that Lexy, his neighbor from down the street, stopped by." She looked at me and continued explaining. "Jim and I are *very* close friends; he loves my boys so much, they think of him as a second father." I felt the blood drain from my face and I couldn't talk. She continued talking, since I wasn't making a peep. "Anyway, Jim was over the other day; I was dreadfully tired, so Jim took the boys down to our private beach while I stayed back at my house for a little nap, if you know what I mean." She winked at me acting like I knew the secret she was sharing. "When I finally went back into my bathroom I found these." Lexy reached into her purse and pulled out Jim's Ray Ban sunglasses. I took them, feeling the flush rise up my face. Lexy smiled, and started down the steps.

"You *will* make sure he gets his glasses before you are done cleaning, ok love? Or just leave him a note if he isn't home when you leave." I nodded; she waved, slid into her car and eased the convertible onto the street. She thought I was the housekeeper. She thought *I* was the housekeeper. When Jim finally came back later that afternoon I didn't say anything about the sunglasses. I didn't say anything about Lexy, the boys, the beach, the second father comment, or the bathroom. I was quietly moving around Jim and taking care of Leah. I just kept fuming about that lady thinking I was the maid! I guess I did look like a housekeeper – after all, wasn't that what I was now? A live-in babysitter and housekeeper—one who didn't even get paid for it!

Jim was soaking in the large sunken tub and began talking about a job opportunity in Northern California. He had heard about a project looking for a superintendent and someone had dropped his name. Jim was talking about moving, picking up stakes, and relocating in the San Francisco Bay Area. I couldn't concentrate on what Jim was saying, visions of Lexy with Jim, her boys playing with Jim on the beach flooding my brain. When Jim finally noticed I was quiet, he stopped talking for a moment and asked me what was wrong? I felt angry, confused, and brave. So what? I was going to confront him about Lexy. I sucked in my breath and began.

"A friend of yours came by today," I carefully watched his face for any slight change of expression. "Lexy." There was none. Jim kept bathing in the tub barely looking at me. "She said you left these," I thrust my arm out, showing him the Ray Bans, "in her bathroom." Jim nodded. I stood at the door to the bathroom. "Why on earth would you be in her bathroom? Are you having an affair with her? Are you already cheating on me? We are barely married!" With that, something snapped inside Jim and his face changed from normal and nonchalant to a deep, dark red. His eyes looked black, his face contorted, his teeth grinding. Jim rose quickly from the tub, like a huge monster coming out of a cave. His huge body dripping wet, with one move he lunged at me, grabbed me, picked me up, and threw me down the long hallway. I slammed up against the wall and fell onto the floor in a ball. Jim stood over me screaming superlatives, dripping water over my shaking body.

"You never question what I do, you hear!" He lowered himself down to my level and screamed within inches of my face. *"You don't have the right to ever question me, my life, what I do, when I come and go, or anything else. Do you hear me? I took you away*

from Iris. I saved you from being a whore; you are nothing but the street scum she plays with! What do you know? Lexy is a good friend and close neighbor who I knew long before I ever knew your ugly whore face! She is nothing like you! She's gorgeous, rich, and beautiful and has class; something you'll never know about. You... the daughter of ignorant, illegal, immigrant, WOPs! Don't you get it? I have friends, or can't you get that through that thick skull of yours? She is a friend!" I lay on the floor not moving, crying, shaking, bruised, and hurt. My mind screamed and I shook with fear. I had to escape – if I didn't, Jim might just kill me. In one split second, Jim turned from a calm reasonable man to an abusive monster. Marriage or no marriage, my parents would have to understand. Jim's screaming tirade continued for another half hour until Leah woke up and stumbled into the hallway. She began to cry and fuss which finally jogged Jim's mind to the situation. He stopped yelling, stiffened, and looked at me with disgust. I braced myself against the wall and slowly stood up. I straightened my clothes and tried to calm Leah as Jim stomped off down the hallway, got dressed, grabbed his wallet and keys, and slammed out the door. I guess I was babysitting again.

I felt desperate, my stomach rumbling with stress. I was trembling with fear and utter shock at the situation, not believing that Jim had just attacked me, and feeling an overwhelming dread when I realized I made a major mistake. I vowed I would never let Jim hurt me ever again. I would not take this kind of treatment! I scrounged a few dollars in loose change from several places throughout the house and walked Leah to the local store where I could use a payphone. I called Tommy praying to God he was home. The phone rang. I heard Tommy answer in his light and carefree voice.

"Uh, hello," he said with a happy influx. As soon as I heard Tommy's voice, I began to sob in short puffs. Leah was playing with landscaping rocks in the shopping center. I concentrated on remaining calm so I could quickly recover and speak.

"Tom?" My voice shook and cracked; I was a mess. My life was falling apart and I needed my family. Tommy was all that I had!

"Jeannie, is that you, are you all right?" he asked, alarm coating his voice.

"Yes, Tom, I'm ok. I don't have much time and can't do too much explaining, but I need your help. I don't have a ride and need to go pick up my car in Orange County. I need to stay with you for a while. Is that ok?" I sniffed back a few tears and tried to calm myself. My perfect marriage was officially over. No white wedding, no children. Married two months and now getting divorced.

"Sure Jeannie, did that idiot Jim do something to hurt you?" Tom huffed. I answered quickly to get off the phone.

"Tom, tomorrow is Saturday, can you *please* come to 1232 Cliffside Drive in CDM at 9:00? I'm staying there in a house by the bay. It won't take long because I only have a few things to carry in some grocery sacks and that is it. Are you working?"

Tom answered back, "I am off tomorrow and can make it by 9:00. Are you going to be all right until then, are you safe?" I grunted okay, glancing at Leah. Poor thing, she was totally unaware of the chaos in her life. I really had bonded with this precious young toddler. She was a lost lamb who seemed to have two parents who were less than adequate. I wanted to pack both of our things and take off in my car, never to return. I had an overwhelming urge to save us both, to take her and raise her as my own, but how could I?

"Tommy, I'll be looking for you tomorrow morning. There is a private drive behind the house. If you drive around to the side, I'll have all of my things hidden in the bushes back there. As soon as I see you stop, I'll run out." Tommy agreed.

"You take care, Jean. I'll be there tomorrow at 9:00, and don't you worry, I'll take care of you." Tom tried to calm me and reassure me. "Now you stay safe; if things get bad before then, call me from anywhere. I'll come and get you." I agreed, hung up, and took Leah on the three-block walk back to the house. I loved my brother. He didn't ask a lot of questions; he was going to save me. What might transpire for the rest of my life didn't really matter to me at that time. My father had never treated Mother like Jim had treated me. I wouldn't put up with that. I had heard of girls whose boyfriends were abusive. . . that wasn't me.

I fed Leah and put her down, waiting for night to fall. I secretly packed most of my things and put them into grocery sacks, leaving a few items on the bathroom sink careful not to alert Jim. I carried my bags outside, looking all ways to make sure Jim wasn't pulling up the street in the Jag or that some neighbor wasn't out walking their dog. I could just imagine how this looked: me slinking behind the bushes, hiding my worldly possessions in this luxury neighborhood. With my bags hidden, I came back in the house, went into the family room, and turned on the television. Part of me wanted to know where Jim was, the other dreaded him coming back home. I was afraid of what might happen if Jim discovered what I was doing. I was certain Ken was out of town on business; I hadn't seen him in days. After the 11:00 o'clock news was finished, I laid down and fell fitfully asleep. Jim came in after midnight smelling of alcohol, perfume, and cigarettes. Jim began, his voice quivering.

"Hello, pretty little wifer. You are the most beautiful angel in the world." I rolled my eyes in my head, concentrating on my façade. "I am so sorry you made me mad today and that I pushed you a little. I hope you can forgive me." He started to cry softly. Jim was actually crying. My heart began to go out to him. He was hurting inside—that must be why he lashed out. Business must be going poorly for him. He was probably stressed. "I never meant to hurt you. I'd die before I'd ever let anything happen to my little wifer. Jeanette, you mean everything to me. I just don't want to go on without you in my life. I am so sorry; if you can hear me, please don't be mad. Please, please forgive me." Jim leaned over onto me and sobbed. He sounded so sincere I almost turned towards him and hugged him back, wanting to erase his tears. Tommy was coming tomorrow at 9:00 and my things were in the bushes. I didn't move and decided the smartest thing to do was to leave in the morning, a crying husband or not.

After a few minutes, Jim settled into his bed and quickly fell asleep. I was hoping if all went according to plan, I would feed Leah in the morning, put her in the playroom and wait for Tommy to come. If Jim didn't wake up I could slip out quickly. Should I leave a note? I was dreadfully worried about Leah and felt a motherly connection to her, but she was not mine. I was certain she would wake her dad up if she needed anything.

The next morning went as planned. Leah woke up early and I fed her. I showered, dressed, and got ready for the day, nervously looking at the clock. The only thing I had not planned was that Ken came home at 8:00 from his business trip. Ken came in from the garage and I literally jumped when I saw him. Ken made a mention about my nervousness and laughed telling me I seemed on edge. I may have enjoyed Ken if I knew him through another part of my life; maybe if he and Jim didn't have their private meetings and didn't share hours of laughing together, we would be acquaintances.

Ken was an older man, and Jim told me he was a widower whose wife had died of cancer years ago. He seemed very effeminate and rarely engaged in conversation with me, even when I was the only person in the house. Once I mentioned this to Jim and he told me Ken thought I was a "nice kid" and mentioned I wasn't very domestic. Wasn't very domestic. . . what did that mean? I figured I needed to do a better job cleaning house, so I increased my mopping, dusting, and vacuuming and tried to keep Leah's things picked up. Why should Ken complain about me living with him, the house was part mine, wasn't it?

I didn't say anything to Ken; he changed clothes and whistled through the house preparing to wash one of his classic Corvettes. It was almost 9:00 and Leah was playing with a few toys, talking animatedly to them. Ken was outside, proudly washing his car on the long driveway. Jim was snoring in the bedroom. How was I going to grab my things? When Tommy came, Ken would see me pulling my bags from the bushes. Oh well, it wouldn't really matter. I was leaving, never to return. No more Ken, no more Jim, and no more housekeeping and babysitting. I glanced at Leah and felt a pang of guilt. I wasn't her mother! Why should I feel bad about leaving? I know Leah needed a mother, but I was only twenty. I didn't give birth to her; she wasn't my responsibility. I had to admit I really did love the kid. I watched her for a moment as she moved her dollies and played with her toys. She noticed me watching her and ran over, sensing my nervousness. I kneeled down and she wrapped her little arms around my neck.

"I wuf you GNut. My GNut!" My throat closed and I gulped hard. She snuggled her face into my neck and I cradled her head, stroking her soft hair. Leah and I were bonding as mother and child, our hearts intermingling with trust and love. She smelled like baby shampoo, and her skin was soft and clean. Since I had been taking care of her she had polished finger and toenails, clean clothes, and combed hair. Mothering my new child was a role I accepted and took seriously. I only wished she was mine. I released my embrace and Leah bounded back over to her toys to resume her play session.

I looked out the window and saw Tom's car turn slowly at the corner. He was looking at the addresses and trying to make them out. Ken was waxing his Corvette and looked like an old rich guy in front of his beach house. Jim was still asleep. I softly opened the door, and walked out to the sidewalk waving largely until I knew Tommy had seen me. He pulled over and I awkwardly climbed up into the shrubbery and to the bushes while Ken stood there, sizing up the situation. I grabbed my grocery bags of clothes, hopped over the bushes almost slipping on the hose and quickly stepped down the manicured lawn onto the sidewalk. Ken stood with the chamois in his hand staring at Tom and me as if he were a mannequin. Tommy couldn't pull up to the drive as Ken's car was blocking it so he pulled over to the curb and popped the trunk. I threw my bags into the back and had my hand pulling the handle of the passenger door to get in when I heard a looming voice.

"Going somewhere little wifer?" Jim asked, his voice booming and dripping with sarcasm. I whirled around, my heart pounding.

Jim was standing right behind me with Leah in his arms. Tommy stood by his door not getting in the car. I swallowed hard and dreaded this confrontation.

"Jim, this is my brother Tom. I am going to stay with him for a while. Tom, this is Jim and Ken." Both men nodded and said hello. Jim changed his tone once he realized that I was really going to leave. His voice now sounded very sincere.

"Jeanette, you're not really going to leave Leah and me are you? We love you and need you." He looked down at Leah and spoke. "Leah, GNut is going bye-bye, and she is not ever coming back." Leah looked at me. She knew the word bye-bye and a look of panic washed over her face. She began to fuss and cry, getting red in the face and reaching her arms out for me to hold her.

"GNut, no bye-bye." She began to cry louder while Jim tried to calm her. Ken looked on in amazement, glancing around in hopes that none of his rich neighbors would be watching the scene unfold. I tried to calm Leah.

"Leah, I am going for a little while." Jim looked down and I was sure he was crying. I looked directly at Jim suddenly feeling sorry for him, wishing yesterday was only a bad nightmare. "Goodbye Jim, I'm going to stay with Tommy for a while," I said softly as I settled myself into the car, shutting the door, and not looking up. Tom pulled the car away from the curb, neither of us talking, feeling my heart lurching, listening to the shrill screams of Leah fading in the distance.

CHAPTER 9
A NEW LIFE

Life with Tommy was awkward and uncomfortable. Thankful I was safe, living with Tom did allow me idle days of free time to sort out my confusing thoughts and to figure out what in the world I would do with my life. We picked up my car so at least I could drive, but I owned nothing and would have to piece my life together. I did have a few dollars in the bank, so I filled the tiny apartment with groceries and cooked for Tom and his friends. My money was depleting quickly and I hadn't landed a job yet, nor registered for school. I was determined to choose the correct path, moving out of the abyss and forward with my new life.

Tommy's apartment had a lot of beer and ice, a few guys who were responsible for paying the rent, and a few extra guys and girls who were not actually living there but stayed there some nights and on weekends. My bed was a comforter on the floor in Tom's small room—a far cry from the ocean palace I had just left. There were no panoramic views, no chilled bottles of champagne in the refrigerator, no expensive cars in the garage. . . no Jim or Leah. I felt terribly guilty and still hadn't called my parents. I didn't know what to tell them: "Hi Mom and Dad, I'm married, but separated. Didn't have a wedding; didn't tell anyone in the family, and now I've left my abusive new husband and darling step-daughter, and I'm living on the floor of Tom's bachelor pad." That would go really well.

Tommy was very supportive. He didn't ask a lot of questions and didn't point his finger at me. Tommy was busy going to school, working, and keeping up with his social schedule. He really wasn't at the apartment much at all and this left me a lot of time to think. I kept second-guessing myself and replaying my leaving over and over again. Jim *was* crying when I left. I knew he must really love me. . . and what of Leah? Once I was gone, who was going to take care of her? I spent many days and nights crying and wondering if I should drive my Mustang back to the beach and into the arms of my husband. Although it was a very violent act that Jim had displayed, what if *I* crossed over the line? What if I needed to grow up, learn how to be a wife, and not second-guess my husband? If Jim wanted to be with Lexy, he could have married her. She was the perfect family for him: kids for Leah to be raised with and a rich and beautiful woman. Perfect. I shook my head. He didn't want her, he wanted me, but I left. I took off without so much as a note. Had I made a mistake?

One evening over a month after leaving Jim, the phone rang and one of Tom's friends picked it up. I could hear him speaking in a mildly drunken slur repeating louder and louder, "Nobody named Jeanette lives here!" He began cursing until I quickly crossed the room and grabbed the phone from his hand. "I am Jeanette, not

Jeannie like Tom calls me. I am Jeanette!" I explained, pulling the receiver up to my face.

"Uh, hello . . ." I said questioningly, not knowing who in the world would be calling me at Tom's. I heard the familiar voice of Jim on the other end of the line, warm and sincere.

"Hello Jeanette, it's me, Jim. Is that really you?" Jim asked. I immediately felt excited and scared by his voice.

"Yes, it's really me, Jim. How did you get this number?" Jim laughed lightly, sounding confident.

"Jeanette, I have close friends in the Newport police department; they can pretty much track down anyone who has a vehicle registered in Orange County." I was shocked; there was no way to hide from Jim. He had found me in about four weeks, but wasn't that what I wanted? Jim continued.

"Leah has been crying every night and day, asking me where her GNut is and when GNut is coming home." I felt my throat close up and my heart started to pound. "Leah loves you, Jeanette," Jim paused and said softly, "and so does her daddy. Please don't leave us; please don't make Leah lose her new mother. Her real mother doesn't want her, and now you have walked away from her too."

I let out a long sigh, feeling very guilty all of a sudden. Jim continued, sensing that I was wearing down:

"We both need you and love you. Jeanette, please come home."

I thought about the glowing sunsets and the rides along the bluffs overlooking the ocean. I thought about rides in the Jag down the coast highway and sips of champagne. I looked down at my large diamond ring. I should have left it for Jim as I walked out the door, but I didn't. As if reading my mind, Jim added:

"And what about our wedding ring, doesn't that diamond mean anything to you? Did our vows mean anything to you? Do you still love me?" Jim sounded so sincere. Tears started to roll down my cheeks, and I was sure Jim was crying too. But what about the screaming tirade Jim had put me through? There was no way I was going to go back if he was going to treat me like that. I had to make my rules clear. I had to make certain Jim would never treat me like that again. And what about his affair with Lexy?

"Jim, I do love you. I do love little Leah, and I miss you both, but I can't go back to you as long as you have a temper like you displayed that night. You threw me down the hall and hurt me because you were angry." I tried to be strong.

"Jeanette," Jim began softly, "I didn't hit you that night; I did push you a little and I'm sorry for getting upset, but that off-handed comment about Lexy. . . that was way below the belt, you accused me without any substantial evidence. I just happened to be walking by Lexy's house one afternoon. She was in front and asked if I wanted to see her new bathroom remodel. I agreed. I *am* a builder you know. So I went in to see the master bath and must have set my glasses on the counter. Nothing more happened that day, Jeanette, nothing more." Jim explained his side of the story; it didn't sound like an affair. It sounded innocent. Jim was a builder and he was appraising the workmanship of the new remodel. What was I thinking?

"What about the boys? Lexy said you took them down to the beach?" I heard Jim huff a little and let out a loud breath.

"Jeanette!" His voice sounded stern. "Please don't misinterpret what Lexy said! I walked the boys to the beach and stood on the bluff watching them play until their mother arrived a few minutes later. You sound really insecure when you accuse me of being unfaithful." Jim added very sincerely and softly, "How could I have ever been unfaithful when I truly love you and come home to *you* every night?"

Jim was right. He had been home every night. Lexy set me up. She probably knew I was Jim's young wife, and she probably loved every minute of the upheaval a few of her miscast words had caused. I really had messed things up for us. I was responsible for the whole fight! I was still unhappy with our lifestyle and had asked Jim if he could try to get regular day work. I was certain if Jim had a regular schedule and went to work like other husbands, we could be a very happy couple.

"Jim, I'm sorry I accused you and Lexy; it just sounded so sneaky and immoral." I was feeling like a school girl again, not knowing how to act grown up yet. Jim continued.

"Jeanette, Leah and I want you to come home. We have some good news. I was just offered an awesome job building a hotel up near San Francisco, and I am supposed to be starting my new job next week," Jim said and then hesitated, not making a sound.

"You've been offered a new job starting next week up north near San Francisco?" I asked, feeling a flood of relief wash over my body while visions of sack lunches, paychecks, and a little house with a white picket fence danced through my mind. Jim could tell I was softening and continued to explain.

"My mother has agreed to watch Leah for a few months while we get settled. The company owns a mobile trailer overlooking the beach in Half Moon Bay where we can live temporarily. Once we get a house rented, we'll come down, pick up Leah and permanently live up in Northern California. We can finally start our new life together. It's a great job, project superintendent just like I'm doing now, except not freelancing. The starting salary is more than $50,000 a year. It includes medical benefits, gas card, and all expenses paid while we live in the trailer." I couldn't believe my ears. This was what I had been waiting for: Jim had a job; we could get settled; we would start our own home together; no more Ken, and things would be wonderful. I couldn't talk. Jim never apologized to me after the horrible fight. I wasn't sure if it was my fault now or his. Did it really matter? I *did* love him and wanted to start a new life together, Jim, Leah and me—a perfect family.

"Jim, it sounds like a dream come true," I said, not hiding the excitement I felt. I finally looked around the room and saw Tommy glaring at me. Tom didn't understand. I made Jim angry, and it was *my* fault for approaching him the way I had. If I had questions about Lexy, I should have just asked him. Never again – I'm going to be a grown up and I am going to trust my new husband. Who did he come home to every night, Lexy or me? "I can't wait to move up north with you, Jim. I'll pack up my things here and will drive down to the beach tonight – that is, if you and Leah still want me," I said trying to sound sincere. I could hear the smile in Jim's voice.

CHAPTER 10
NORTHERN CALIFORNIA

I readily sold my Mustang to an old friend for $1,000, drained my bank account, and with Jim's promise of a very rich future, handed over all my money. I never dreamed I would sell my car and hand the money over to anyone, let alone my husband, but now it somehow felt right. I was happy to be moving from Southern California. I would be living in a new city, meeting new friends, and starting a new life.

We settled into Pelican Point—a small, quaint, and pristine mobile home park situated high on a bluff overlooking Half Moon Bay. The Pacific Ocean and northern coast were breathtaking: deep blue crescent-shaped bay, sharp craggy cliffs and turbulent waves crashing onto the short rocky beach.

Jim's luxury V.12 XJS Jaguar was parked outside of our humble first home, a slightly used eighteen-foot travel trailer. I was thrilled to move in, and our first few days together were absolutely idyllic. Jim was attentive and calm, looking forward to starting his job the following Monday. I started to nest, enthusiastically decorating our small space.

Our first Saturday night, we decided to go out for dinner, dressing as we would to eat at Picasso's in Newport Beach. When we arrived at Donny's Beach House, the crowd sported jeans, western shirts, and *very* casual attire. Welcome to Northern California, I thought. Jim didn't seem fazed by his polyester wear and my disco dress and high heels, in contrast to the attire of the group.

We enjoyed a good steak dinner. This time I ordered one drink and no appetizer and Jim didn't order a bottle of expensive champagne as I had seen him do on several occasions. I noticed Jim glance into his wallet and for a moment a look of concern crossed his forehead. He was worried about our money, but as soon as he got his first paycheck, we'd be on our way. When we lived in Corona del Mar, Jim mentioned his "family fortune" and multiple Swiss bank accounts. It would be good if he withdrew a few bucks right now, I thought. After dinner, we settled into a small lounge table while the band readied for the "knee slapping" music. Jim excused himself to the men's room while I sat and nursed my drink.

A moment later, a very attractive young man in a black felt hat sat down and asked me why a "pretty little thing" like me was sitting alone in the bar. I smiled, very flattered. As soon as reality set in that I was married and that Jim was close, I looked down and lifted my hand, smiling and pointing to my ring finger. The unnamed cowboy saw the ring and gave a graceful sweep of his hat, stepping back away from the table. He left me with a wink and a smile, apologizing for trying to cut in on another man's dance. I smiled thinking Half Moon Bay was only 450 miles north of Newport Beach, but it seemed like another world.

"So, are you arranging to meet your new boyfriend somewhere?" Jim snarled. I jumped, caught completely off guard. I looked at Jim, shock on my face—new boyfriend?

"What?" I snapped and Jim's face grew red, his eyes getting dark, his brow furrowed together in a straight line. "My new boyfriend... that guy came over and I promptly told him I was married and showed him my ring." I looked at Jim and realized I better keep explaining or he might start yelling at me in the restaurant. "Jim, I don't know the guy. He just walked up. I don't have anything for him, honest," I said as sincerely as I could, looking into his face and praying the hard lines would soften.

"What the crap did he want with you then; couldn't he tell you were married? That diamond shines across the room – any bigger and you'd need a wagon to wheel your arm around!" Jim hissed at me, his anger escalating. I looked around and noticed people turning to look at us, overhearing Jim's angry voice.

"Jim, he didn't mean anything to me, honest. Come on, honey, I love you and would *never* look at another man," I pleaded earnestly.

Jim stood up hard, knocking his chair to the ground, turned and grabbed my arm, yanking me to my feet. He stalked through the bar, dragging me along, looking for a particular cowboy wearing a black felt hat. Jim spied him walking towards us. As the cowboy passed, Jim turned to follow him. I watched in horror as Jim grabbed the back of the man's head and slammed it hard into a thick wooden beam. There were screams from the area as the young cowboy hit the ground hard, not moving. Jim took my arm maneuvering me through the crowd and out the front doors, distancing us from the commotion. I walked quickly to the car, following Jim almost at a run, not saying a word. We drove back to the trailer park not speaking, while the sounds of the turbulent North Coast seeped into the quiet of our car.

The next morning I woke to the soft rays of sunlight coming over the coastal hills, spilling under the short curtains of the travel trailer. I looked at Jim who was still asleep, thankful that he hadn't said another word to me about the cowboy. Had I really seen Jim push that young guy into a pole? Was he hurt? Did he get a concussion? I thought of how angry Jim had become and how violently he pushed the man's head, glad it was *his* head and not mine. I felt nauseated and extremely afraid as I looked at the "man of my dreams," sleeping peacefully in the small bedroom of our trailer. I suddenly felt all alone, realizing I had no one to talk to, no one to protect me or help me in this increasingly scary relationship.

Quietly, I eased out of bed and began to get ready for our Pelican Point Mobile Park Pancake Breakfast. Jim had purchased tickets the night before from the park manager. It was a fundraiser and a chance for us to meet some neighbors. I was certain the elderly residents in this retirement community didn't see young people very often. Although I didn't know many of the residents, the park felt safe and welcoming.

It was after 7:00 a.m., the pancake breakfast was between 7:00-9:00 a.m. There was no way I was going to wake Jim up. If we missed the breakfast, would he be mad? If I woke him, would he be mad? I didn't know and didn't want to take a chance of getting Jim upset, especially after the fiasco with the cowboy. I decided to get ready and if Jim woke up, at least I would be ready. I stepped into the economy-sized shower, hoping I wasn't waking Jim with the sound from the splashing water. As I started rinsing my hair, the shower curtain opened hard, and Jim was standing there looking as mad as he had the night before. I jumped and clutched my hands in front of my naked body, water soaking over me.

"Jim. . . Jim, good morning. Did. . . did you sleep well?" I asked weakly.

Jim didn't answer, but turned and walked out of the small bathroom slamming the door hard. The door didn't latch and swung open and closed, thin paneling not offering much weight behind the handle. I quickly rinsed the soap out of my hair, dried off and wrapped in a towel. I went into the bedroom to get dressed and encountered Jim lying on the bed, not moving, hands clasped behind his head. Blindly choosing a shirt and jeans I dressed in a hurry, aware of Jim watching my every move. Jim cleared his throat loudly. I stopped moving and gave him my full attention.

"Where were you going this morning? Out to meet your new lover?" he asked sarcastically. I was shocked, he was *still mad* about last night and the cowboy. My heart started pounding. I swallowed hard, my mouth immediately dry, my stomach twisting in a knot.

"Jim, no, I wasn't going to meet anyone." Jim lurched from off the bed and started to grab my clothes from the hangers in the closet.

"So, if you want to meet your boyfriend, you better take your clothes." To my complete shock, Jim began ripping my clothes off the hangers, seams tearing, buttons flying, zippers unraveling. I stood by watching Jim destroy my clothes. I stepped back and tried to stay out of arm's reach, tears streaming down my face. I began to speak hoping to defuse the situation.

"Jim, I don't even know that man. He came over to. . . . " As soon as I said that Jim took all of the clothes he'd torn out of the closet and threw them on me. The weight of the clothes and the strength at which they were thrown made me fall through the bedroom door and into the hall, clothes heaped on top of me. Jim continued, grabbing the empty hangers and began to throw them at me.

"Here, you need these, too!" he screamed, throwing the hangers at me as I ducked and covered myself with the clothes. I began sobbing and couldn't talk. I felt like I was going to throw up. Jim stormed by me, his tirade moving to the bathroom. I quickly scrambled up and took refuge in the living room, stepping over clothes mangled with hangers.

"And here, take your hair crap!" Shampoo, combs, curlers, make-up, and hairpins flew out the bathroom door. "You should have stayed with Iris; you could have entertained your cowboy last night and made a few bucks in the process. Why should I feed your face? Why should I feel the pressure to support a whore like you? You just came from one of the biggest pimping operations in Orange County; I saved your pathetic sorry butt! I should tell your big important diplomat father and your pious Catholic mother that they raised a whore! They raised a prostitute. I wonder if they know that? Do you think they know that?!" Jim screamed.

Jim fumed, and I continued to cry not knowing what to do or where to go. I backed onto the foam couch at the front of the trailer, silently cowering, tears streaming down my face. Jim went into the kitchen screaming and cleared the counters with his large strong arms, shattering the few dishes we owned into a pile of glass on the floor. In a furious rage, Jim threw fruit, magazines, dishtowels, kitchen utensils, and anything not nailed down onto the floor. The trailer I scrubbed so painstakingly was a huge mess. My clothes were on the floor, covered in shampoo and hairspray, torn apart at the seams. My dishes were now in piles on the floor, broken and scattered. My little knickknacks were in a pile—bent, broken, and cracked. My heart felt as if it had been broken in two. The pain from my heart felt physical and hurt deeply. I sobbed softly, my muscles shaking, afraid I would be hurt if I were too loud.

"You want this? You want to have this perfect little life? Well, here you go, it's yours!" Jim approached me as I curled into a ball on the couch, cowering below the raging tirade of my new husband. Jim looked scary and dark.

"It's yours. You can have that cowboy, and I am not working to support a cheating wife like you! You take that cowboy, and you can leave right now!" Jim screamed so loud his voice made my ears ring. Jim huffed, kicked aside the mess that sprawled everywhere on the floor and slammed out of the cheap thin trailer door, the screen door waving in the wind.

I stayed on the couch sobbing into my hands, not knowing what I could have done differently, except maybe not smile at the cowboy. I wasn't trying to encourage him; I wasn't. I *was* flattered, and maybe I looked like I was flirting to Jim. Jim was probably watching as the man came over, and he probably thought I arranged a meeting. I wasn't sure if I had been flirting or not. . . I wasn't a prostitute, far from it; my gosh, I was a virgin. I got sucked in and was innocent of the whole thing. I never took a date. I looked at the trailer in shambles, and felt like my life was over. I prayed God would take my life that second. I hadn't prayed in ages and couldn't remember the last time I set foot in a church, but now I started to pray. I asked God to help me, to save me, or to rescue me from this ugly and scary situation. I felt overwhelmed by the unbelievable exhibit of Jim's violence and anger, and at that very moment, I wished I were dead.

After an hour, Jim emerged, filling the small door of the trailer like a huge giant. He walked slowly to the couch where I was unmoving, except for spasms of past tears making me suck my breath in and out uncontrollably every few moments. I looked up at Jim, part of me mad, part of me still afraid. Jim had a soft smile on his face and kneeled down next to me putting his hand on my face, lifting my chin, forcing me to look at him. I didn't want to let him hold my chin, but was afraid of the wrath that may ensue if I didn't. He looked at me sincerely with his blue eyes fixed hard onto mine, not wavering.

"Wifer, you're not mad at me are you? Don't be mad at me; I was just a little jealous, that's all. You know what that means? It means I really love my little wifer. I don't want you taking off with some cowboy!" he said almost laughing. "We are late to the pancake breakfast. I just saw Mr. Phillips. He wanted us to know that the pancakes and sausage are ready and hot right now. Are you hungry?" he asked, ignoring the mess swirled around the floor of the trailer.

"Come on, let's go have breakfast," he added softly. "I love you, honey. Come on, let's go eat, okay? You know I didn't mean to get mad at you. I'm just really kind of a bear when I get hungry." Jim lifted my hand and led me to the bedroom, stepping over a huge mess of glass and clothes. I applied some make-up, brushed my hair and teeth, and finished getting ready for the big trailer park pancake breakfast.

No make-up could hide my tear-swollen eyes and red puffy face. I walked through the food line like a robot with my head down, avoiding eye contact. Jim forged ahead of me in the buffet line, filling his plate high with bacon, cakes, and sausage. I stumbled behind him, my head in a fog, my brain swirling, trying not to think of the unbelievable scenes that kept playing through my head from last night and this morning. Each time something came into mind, I felt a lump in my throat and pushed the thoughts out of my head for fear I would start crying again.

I sat down on a picnic bench across from Mrs. Phillips, the mobile park hostess. She was a sweet elderly woman, wearing a white cotton sweat suit, the top covered in floral appliqués. Mrs. Phillips wore her hair in a 1960s bouffant, silver, tinged with some soft, red highlights. At first she said a perfunctory and cheerful good morning not looking directly at me. I offered a plastic smile and nodded my head. Noticing my still demeanor and lack of eye contact, she looked hard at me over her coffee cup, quickly shot a look at Jim who was smiling and gulping down a cup of juice, and then back to me. My long blonde hair hanging in my face, I did not look up and continued to push the food around my plate, feeling more nauseated than hungry. I lifted my eyes toward Mrs. Phillips and could see the worried look that covered her face. I figured she thought it was a newlywed spat. I doubted she would imagine I was upset because Jim had violently ripped all of my clothes from their hangers and destroyed almost everything we owned in our small trailer.

Jim announced we were leaving, and dutifully I started to get up. Mrs. Phillips grabbed my hand for a moment, softly telling me if I needed *anything at all* to come right over, her door would always be open. I could feel the lump forming in the back of my throat and the tears welling up in the corners of my eyes.

Yes, yes! I wanted to run to her. I wanted to tell her that my new husband was a cruel and horrible man and that I was alone with no family, no money, and I was scared. Yes! Yes! Mrs. Phillips, can you hear me crying out for help? Can you tell I am in pain? Can you feel my broken heart?

Instead, I nodded and swallowed hard, saying nothing to Mrs. Phillips. I looked at her and squeezed her hand back, lingering there, thankful for the soft warm love that felt sincere.

Reluctantly I followed Jim out of the community center and toward our "home." I dreaded walking through the doors into the disaster area. I wasn't sure if it was a safe zone or not. If Jim started to yell, I'd just run to Mrs. Phillips' place. She would probably make me a cup of tea and would no doubt help me with my marital troubles. Jim chatted animatedly while we crossed the manicured sites of the mobile home park oblivious to the fact that I wasn't saying anything. He kept talking about his new job tomorrow and us looking for a real house and bringing Leah up to our place. I didn't comprehend much, but kept nodding to pretend I was listening as Jim orated incessantly.

Jim opened the door and stepped in ahead of me. He looked around and whistled loud, "Will you look at this mess, Jeanette? What on earth happened here?" Jim started to clean up everything while I helped. He took out paper bags, throwing anything that was broken away. Jim put the items that were undamaged back to their original place. In about an hour or so the trailer was presentable. I made a pile of clothes that needed mending. It was just about everything I had to wear that wasn't in a drawer. I figured I had time to repair all of my clothes. Jim emptied the two large paper bags into the park dumpsters making a loud crashing sound, while

I finished sweeping the floor, picking up the small shards of glass on my hands and knees. Jim came in with a big smile.

"Hey wifer, how about a drive up the coast? We can see the site of the hotel I'm building, and then later I'll take you out for a seafood lunch on the ocean?" He gestured big, and I didn't know how to react. I grabbed my purse, make-up, and a sweater, hoping that I didn't do anything to tick him off again.

Driving up the coast toward the site of the new hotel in Pacifica, I didn't say a word, but Jim continued to chat animatedly. The hotel project was impressive, and the men working on Sunday knew Jim was the superintendent. They fawned over him and vied for his attention. A new company truck pulled onto the jobsite. Jim shook hands and introduced me to his foreman, and I nodded and smiled weakly, not catching his name. We all had lunch at the posh restaurant on top of the hill next door to the jobsite. Jim seemed to be in control of his emotions, intelligently discussing the project, telling witty stories and laughing loudly. I ate a tasteless meal pushing my food around my plate, while Jim chatted, drank vodka on the rocks, ate steamed clams, and made frequent visits to the bathroom. I doubted his foreman would believe that Jim had destroyed our house in a matter of minutes earlier in the day. On the drive home, Jim addressed the blow-out of the morning, sounding very sincere.

"Jeanette, I really didn't mean to get bent out of shape today. I hope you understand." He rushed on. "I was a little jealous, and I guess I was hungry. Can we let bygones be bygones?" Jim found my hand and gently held onto it. I didn't say anything, so Jim continued.

"I was thinking the trailer is way too small for us to live in, and we need Leah up here. Next week I'll start the project and we can look for a place to rent over the hill. I heard Sunnyvale is a great place to live. Some days I can stay at the trailer and some days I can come home; what do you think?" Jim fixed his gaze at me and I began to think this made sense. It was a small trailer; I did miss Leah; I worried about her living with Jim's parents, missing her daddy and me. It would be great to have a house of our own. I looked at Jim, and he flashed me a brilliant white smile, blue eyes gleaming, looking very much in love with me. He shook my hand.

"Come on, you can't be mad at me forever can you?" He winked at me. "I didn't hurt you today honey. I just got mad and was really hungry. The house doesn't look too bad now. I cleaned it up, and as soon as I get my paycheck, we'll go out shopping and buy you a whole new wardrobe. Come on, what do you say?" I wanted to have a good relationship. I wanted to be happily married. Maybe Jim *was* just hungry. Hesitantly I smiled at Jim, convinced he really must love me, allowing my memories of the horrible and scary morning to fade into a justification of hunger and lover's jealousy.

The next few weeks went smoothly at Pelican Point, with Jim leaving for the jobsite early each day, working hard, and returning late each day. I made home-cooked meals and after dinners, we took long walks holding hands along the bluffs overlooking the ocean. I was really happy. I prayed to God on many occasions for our lives to remain like that and for a calming spirit to cover my husband so he wouldn't get angry and hurt other people or me ever again.

Each weekend we drove into the Silicon Valley looking for a new place to live, planning on moving Leah up to live with us. The hotel project would be concluding in several months and Jim had already received a good offer for another project starting in Los Gatos. If we lived in Sunnyvale, it would be close when Jim's next project-started.

I rarely saw Jim's paychecks. He would cash them at the local bank every Friday and give me a few dollars. It felt funny asking for an allowance from Jim, even if he was my husband. Jim would hand me $20 or so, while in his wallet there was a thick stack of hundred dollar bills. Every payday, Jim stayed out late explaining it was for morale of the guys; he bought them beer and discussed the project. There were times when Jim came home exceptionally late, and I was certain he smelled like perfume, but I didn't say anything. He seemed to be much more energetic than he had in Orange County, which I attributed to the job. Jim seemed happy and *was* working. It was a good thing.

Mysterious Illness

Almost three months into our life at Pelican Point, I started experiencing a dull pain in my lower abdomen and thought I might be pregnant or suffering an ectopic pregnancy. The pain became so bad that Jim finally brought me to the local ER for an evaluation. I saw the doctor speaking with Jim and laughing a few times before he finally came in to give me the results of my examination. I was glad to be getting some attention; the pain was becoming intense.

"So, doctor, am I pregnant?" I asked. I watched the face of the doctor shake back and forth.

"No, Mrs. Miller, you are not pregnant. May I ask you if you have been monogamous with your husband?" I heard the doctor and certainly knew what he was asking. Why would he be asking me this? Was I having affairs with other men? I was embarrassed and a little shocked by the question. I shook my head.

"Doctor, of course not! I'm married. I have only had one partner in my life, and it is my husband." He looked at his charts and told me I had a very serious infection and would need immediate shots of penicillin to make sure it didn't make me seriously ill.

"What kind of an infection do I have, doctor?" I asked.

"Mrs. Miller, you have a pelvic inflammatory disease or PID. It is a common female infection and very responsive to treatment. With a few shots right now and a prescription you take for ten days, you won't experience any more problems. I do want to caution you that these types of recurring infections can cause infertility."

"Doctor, how did I get this infection and how can I prevent it?" The doctor shuffled as Jim stood by the door. He began slowly.

"As I discussed with your husband, these things can be passed from one partner to another. You both need to be treated and hopefully it will be the last time you get this serious type of infection. The long term prognosis is not good for a person getting recurring PIDs, as I mentioned before." The doctor shot a look at Jim. "Recurring infections like this one can cause infertility."

I was puzzled, infertility. . . what did he mean, infertility? I was barely twenty-one; how could I be infertile? I pushed those thoughts out of my mind, got my shots, and took my prescription home. The doctor also gave Jim the same prescription and when I questioned him, he told me that guys easily caught female infections. Jim intelligently explained that both of us needed to be treated or risk passing the infection back and forth. It made sense to me and in a few days, I began to feel better; the pain, low-grade fever, and sluggish feeling went away.

CHAPTER 11
THE PERFECT LITTLE FAMILY

After looking for several weeks, we finally found a nice condo in Sunnyvale. As we filled out the paperwork for the new place, I was a little perplexed at why Jim asked me to use my maiden name on the application and to use my maiden name for him too. I wrote Jim and Jeanette Miani on the application and only used my social security number. I didn't understand the reasoning behind these small changes, but I didn't care. We were getting the most beautiful condo with a pool, expansive greenbelts with large mature trees, and a modern workout facility. The owners of the property ran our application and we qualified. Since we had no possessions, we bought new furniture on a rent-to-own contract. It was fairly basic: two beds, two dressers, one dinette set, one living room set, and a few lamps. It was basic, but brand new and someday would be ours.

After setting up the house on a Friday night, we left early the next morning to pick up Leah. This would be my first time meeting his folks. I was a little shocked at how small their house was after Jim had explained his father was from Swiss-German aristocracy and his mother had been a famous dancer in Hollywood. The house was lovely, but in a small row of cookie cutter homes on a very busy street in the middle of Orange County—not what I imagined. Jim explained his parents kept a small "cottage" in Orange County when they weren't staying at their Swiss chalet.

We pulled up to the house greeted by the smile of a stately, elegant, middle-aged blonde woman, holding a cigarette in one hand and cradling little Leah with the other. Leah craned her head and squinted against the hot sun to see who was in the car. I jumped out and Leah wiggled free from her grandmother's arms, running to me. I whisked her into my arms and began to smother her with soft kisses.

"Leah, we've come to bring you to your new home!" She hugged me tightly and squealed with delight. She was clean and smelled like Ivory soap. Mrs. Miller had taken good care of her. Jim introduced me to Anne Miller, his mother. She smiled at me warmly and gave the baby and me a combined hug. Behind Anne, I heard a gruff low voice barking something unintelligible. Anne called in to him and said that Jim and Jeanette were here and we would be right in. It must be Jim's father, Emil. From Anne's worried face I thought we had better get into the house and fast before he got upset.

Anne prepared a very nice meal for the five of us. Emil glared at Leah whenever she made a noise, dropped food off her dish, or jumped down from the makeshift high chair. Jim was getting frustrated by his dad's impatience, which made the conversation very stiff between Jim and his father. His dad knocked back scotch after scotch, taking bites of his dinner and getting more obnoxious by the minute. I tried to ignore his racial comments and complaints about every television commercial, the economy, the president, and the traffic. He also started on a long tirade, almost yelling at Anne when he got on a tangent about his "Dego, WOP" ex-partner Al DiNastasio and how he was nothing but a "dirty, cheating Italian." As soon as this left Emil's mouth, he stopped talking, looked up at me from the other side of his scotch glass, and asked me where my people were from.

Where my "people" were from? I knew what he wanted to find out: he wanted to know what nationality I was, where my family had immigrated from. I doubted he wanted to know that "my people" were from Yorba Linda. I was very angry at the inference to Italians, since I was 100 percent Italian and all of my grandparents had come from Italy to painstakingly build a new life in America. I looked at Jim, and he nodded to me. I began softly.

"Uh, Mr. Miller. . . uh, my family is all Italian." I looked down at my plate and as soon as I said that, Jim quickly jumped up and stated we had to hit the road. We had a long drive ahead of us. Emil muttered something disgusting about Italians from under his breath, and I grabbed Leah's hand while walking towards the door, thanking Emil and Anne for their hospitality and lunch. Jim took Leah's hand from me and went out the front screen door, with Emil weaving after them to look at the Jag. Anne gave me a stern look, put her hand on my shoulder and quietly pulled me aside in the small dark hallway. She was clearly once a very beautiful lady, but worry lines deeply etched her face. Anne wore impeccable and very expensive clothes and the diamonds on her hands were stunning! Anne made a quick glance at Jim and Emil and began in hushed tones.

"Jeanette, you seem like a very nice young lady, and I pray that you, Jim, and Leah will be very happy. But I have to tell you this: When Jim was younger I told him I would tell his wife some day about the times he hit me." My eyes just about rolled back in my head. I could see dark spots forming at the corners of my eyes and my throat became dry. Anne shuffled nervously from foot to foot while I felt trapped in a very bad dream. She continued. "Do you see these pictures down the hallway?" I nodded. "On several occasions Jim exploded in violent fits of anger and punched holes in the walls. Emil and I had to have them covered." I sucked in my breath, thankful that he had only hit the walls. She continued, her voice beginning to crack. "I told Jim once he began to hit me that one day I would tell his wife he had abused his very own mother." She now had deep pools of tears in the bottoms of her eyes and the color that once was clear blue now clouded with a watery reddish color. She quickly added under her breath, "He's just like his father." I could hear Jim yelling for me from outside. I thanked Anne again, gave her a quick hug, and ran out the door, waving goodbye to a very cruel, drunken old man and a woman who seemed like she was his prisoner.

During the drive back home at speeds of nearly ninety miles an hour up the I-5, I kept pushing the images of Jim abusing his mother out of my mind. Jim's father had been awful, drinking during the day and speaking in a drunken slur, peppered with vulgar profanities. I kept thinking about how Emil shot Jim a wicked look and then back to me when I told him I was Italian. You'd think I announced I had an infectious disease! We drove home with Leah in the car. I tried to keep her quiet and occupied with small toys and crayons while Jim blasted the tape deck with all of the windows wide open. We were on our way north to our new home. We were going to be the happy little family.

With Leah in the house, we shopped for dolls, toys, and books, and bought her a tricycle for her third birthday. She and I immediately bonded again. Leah flourished with me, quickly learning her colors, numbers, letters, and singing nursery rhymes. The early days were happy days for little Leah and me. Jim was still working long, hard hours each day. Although he seemed very animated and excited all of the time, I wrote it off to the joy of a hard day at work and loving his profession. His days seemed to get longer and he rarely came home before Leah was asleep. Most nights Jim's dinner was in the oven under a wrap of foil, waiting for me to reheat it. I was certain he was spending time around women and maybe going to bars after work, but I was happy being Leah's mom and didn't dare rock the boat. Jim was calm and not angry with me at all. I received a surprise housewarming package from my brother Tom: a few of my personal possessions and a carefully wrapped antique jewelry box I had owned since childhood. My heart warmed and I placed my treasure right on top of the middle of our rented wooden dresser.

Things seemed to be going well until the day I asked Jim if I could use the car to go to the mall with Leah to shoot studio pictures. That evening, Jim came home late from work, parked the car in the garage, and rushed into the kitchen, seeming frustrated and in a hurry. I expected Jim to hand me the keys, wish us goodbye, eat his dinner, and sit down at the table to finish his paperwork while we headed off for the mall.

"Hi, glad you're finally home," I said before noticing that Jim's face looked dark and angry. Jim stormed into the living room in a huff while Leah ran over and wrapped her arms around my legs. I looked at Jim feeling dread in the pit of my stomach.

"Are you hungry? It's after seven. Do you want me to heat up your dinner?" I asked trying to diffuse the bomb I felt was readying to explode.

"You don't need to save me dinner every night. There is food out there in the world, you know? Do you really need the car tonight? I have a meeting scheduled and forgot you wanted me home early. I don't know why you have to go out at night to take those stupid pictures. Now you've screwed everything up!" Jim barked at me so loud and close, it frightened Leah and she immediately lifted her arms and whined for me to pick her up.

"I'm sorry; I didn't know you needed to work late. I could have changed the picture appointment; besides, I'm not sure if I'm actually going to make it." I looked at Jim, immediately regretting what I'd said. He fumed, but didn't say anything. He went into the bedroom, threw his work shirt off, put on a clean shirt, combed his hair, and told me he had an associate from work picking him up. He splashed some after shave on his face and looked at the clock. I knew better than to say anything.

"Don't worry, take your precious car." He threw the keys at me so hard they hit my side, and I winced. "I have a ride." Jim tucked in his shirt and said goodbye to Leah.

"Jeanette, you will stay with the kid and not pick up any guys at the mall, right? If you do, don't think Leah won't tell me!" My jaw dropped as the door slammed and out he went. I was dumbfounded. What did he mean by that? My side hurt from where the keys had hit me and when those hurtful words sunk into my conscious mind, I began to cry. I stayed on the couch for a moment, hot tears streaking down my cheeks, and then feeling a hunch I ran to the back master bedroom. I lightly pulled back the curtains just in time to see Jim jump into the car of a very pretty young lady. He leaned over and I was fairly sure he kissed her; it was dark and I wasn't positive. The car went into reverse and pulled out of the private drive of our condo complex. I felt like I had been punched in the stomach. Now I added anger to my hurt and was completely confused.

Leah followed me into the bedroom, pulling on my blouse to get my attention. She was so excited we were going to the mall and wanted to go out. We didn't have a car at home during the day, so the only places we went were either walking or on the back of my bike. I looked down at this tiny young toddler, dressed up in a frilly red dress, hair curled, black patent leather shoes shined, and tears welled up in my eyes.

"Come on, Leah, let's go to the mall." We went to take pictures. I got Leah an ice cream, but I made sure not to talk to anyone. We went right home. I kept seeing that scene play in my mind of Jim smiling, jumping into a car and leaning over to kiss another woman! I was certain he was with someone else. Who was this woman? I was here washing clothes, cooking, cleaning, and raising his child, while he was out partying with some woman! While I drove back to the condo, I decided I should just let it go and not confront Jim, especially at night when he came home, *if* he came home. It would really make him mad and things had been pretty calm around the house since Leah came to live with us. The last thing I needed was for her to hear her dad in a tirade yelling at her "mom."

I put Leah down for bed and decided to stay up and read on the couch. It wasn't that late, and I was quite frustrated, so I went to the refrigerator and poured myself a glass of wine. The alcohol comforted me and made me feel better immediately. One glass turned into two and then three. . . I vacillated between telling Jim I saw him, and keeping silent. The more the wine went into my brain the angrier I became. I should confront him. Who does he think he is, gallivanting around while I keep his house for him? At that second the door opened – I jumped. Jim walked in whistling. He didn't say a word or look at me and whooshed by, the lingering smell of perfume, cigarettes, and alcohol floating towards me in the breeze of his brisk path. He went into the bedroom. I could hear him throwing things around, obviously looking for something. I couldn't take this much longer. He was partying while I was home, at twenty-one years old, caring for HIS child and reading a book! Jim came into the living room where I was sitting in an easy chair and began to mumble an excuse about a meeting or something. I didn't really hear him and looked up at his face, eyes glazed from the alcohol. I was confident and assured. I knew what I had seen and I was going to ask him about it, that's all.

"Jim . . ." As soon as I heard my words come out of my mouth and watched as Jim stopped to listen, I felt fearful and hesitated. "Um, who gave you a ride tonight?" I asked, looking at his face to see if he had something to hide. Without missing a beat and acting like it was the most natural thing in the world to say, Jim replied:

"My secretary, who do you think? We had a meeting, I told you, and since I didn't have a car tonight, she was good enough to follow me home and drive me!" This sounded a little fishy to me.

"A meeting at 11 o'clock? You went to a business meeting. . . at 11 o'clock with your young, cute secretary, and they served alcohol there?" As soon as I said that and saw the look on Jim's face, I sucked in my breath and was sorry I said anything. He turned red and his face scrunched together in furrows. He began to scream at the top of his lungs.

"Yes, a meeting, a piece of crap meeting at 11 o'clock, and my secretary drove me because I filled your personal request for a stinking car! Who put you in charge of my life? You think you can question me? What, you having porno thoughts about me and my gorgeous young secretary? Well, you little sleazy whore, I think I'm going to have to clean up that filthy little pea brain of yours!"

Looking like a raging maniac and vomiting a colorful array of profanity, Jim ran into the kitchen and grabbed the five gallon bottle of water that was sitting on the water dispenser and slung it over his shoulder like it was empty. I cowered in horror as he held the water over my head and commenced pouring.

"You're filthy, you disgusting pig! Get your filthy mind clean now, you little sleaze! Here is some nice clean water to clean up you and your filthy little pea brain!" he screamed and began pouring the water in huge splashing gushes over my head, my clothes, and my lap. I began to choke and started to sob, covering my head which enabled me to breathe through the gushing stream that was immersing my head. Jim put the water bottle down hard and took a seat across from me, glaring at me as I cried and sat in a puddle of water on my new couch. I felt the familiar sequence of his anger again. He wasn't done. He was going to be cruel and was going to make me pay for my mouth.

"Well!" he yelled from across the room. "Did that little bath clean up your filthy thoughts? Still think I'm out screwing my secretary?" Jim smiled at me with a sardonic look and I only cried harder. "Will you shut up and stop that annoying blubbering, you sound like a little baby!" he yelled. I couldn't stop crying and Jim pounced from across the room grabbing the bottle and he began to pour again.

"I told you to shut your filthy pig mouth up!!" Jim spewed profanity and poured; I gasped, held in my tears and tried to shield myself from the cold torrent of water. "Shut up, you worthless slut, you probably feel guilty about something. What did you do tonight? Did you screw the photographer in his shop after you took pictures? Did he give you a good deal on the package?" After each sentence, Jim poured the water over my head to make a point. I figured I better not say a thing and Jim went back to sit on the couch, looking over at me with his sick smile. "You stay right there and don't move. I want you to hear what I have to say and hear it good. I'm the boss of this home and if I say I have a meeting . . ." He started to scream, coming to me, grabbing the water, pouring, and yelling inches from my face. "I have a very important business meeting! Do you understand? Do I make myself clear?"

I didn't move, but this made Jim angrier. He wanted me to agree. He poured the last bit of the five-gallon jug over my head and screamed at my face, the hot spit covering my wet skin, my ears ringing. "Do I make myself clear? Then nod your idiotic air-filled head, you worthless piece of crap!"

I nodded and nodded and nodded my head, looking down at the water that sat in a huge puddle on my lap, watching the water seep from my lap to the couch to the floor. The carpet was soaking wet and it was making a huge puddle on the floor. I kept nodding. When Jim realized the bottle was empty, he raised it high above my head. I looked up and covered my head, fearful he would beat me to death with the bottle. Jim huffed in disgust and threw the bottle which knocked over and broke a crystal dish I had purchased at the mall when we first moved into the condo.

A few moments later I heard the back door slam, the garage door open and the sound of the Jag pulling into the lane. I held my breath for a few moments until I could hear the sound of the engine fade away in the distance. I let out a loud sigh and began to sob uncontrollably. . . sobbing into the soaking wet arm of the couch, sobbing about my life. . . sobbing for my mom and dad. . . sobbing that I was twenty-one years old and afraid I would be beaten to death by my husband. After a while I pulled myself together and got up. The house was a mess. There was water everywhere and shards of glass from the broken crystal dish. I didn't worry about the water; I figured that could be dealt with later. I didn't want Leah to get up and slice her foot open if she stepped on a piece. So while soaking wet, I crawled around on my hands and knees, picking up every tiny shard of glass. I used every towel we had to try to dry the floor. Finally, I took off my wet clothes, changed into my nightgown, and went to bed. I didn't know what time it was when Jim finally came in, but there was no way I was going to say anything to him. He had scared me a few times when he'd been mad at me, but this time, when I had looked up at his face, I thought he had the look of the devil and that he was going to murder me.

Leah was at my bedside early the next day; she smiled over at me, her shining blue eyes and pink cheeks unaware of the horror her GNut had gone through the night before. She was hungry and started to speak loudly. Her dad began to rouse, and I quickly scooped her up and carried her into the kitchen. I ran back to the bedroom and softly closed the door. I was sure if I woke Jim up, he'd be in a very foul mood.

I fed Leah, and then we went for a walk in the greenbelt of the condo complex. People passed and said hello, a few older women making comments about how beautiful my daughter was. I thanked them politely feeling like a fake, a fake mother, a fake wife, and a liar. "Good morning," I answered back. It was NOT a good morning. My husband had abused me the night before, and I was fairly sure he could have even killed me. No, it was NOT a good morning.

When Jim finally awakened, he used the restroom, and then strolled around the house. As soon as he reached the wet carpet he made a loud whistle, "Will you look at this? This carpet is a mess." He looked at me while I sat at the table finishing some toast with Leah.

"Jeanette, remind me to pick up a dry-vac at the shop today; this carpet needs some attention." He went on like nothing had happened at all. I didn't say a word and nodded, agreeing with a positive uh-huh sound from my throat. Jim sat down and warmly greeted Leah and me.

"Good morning, hug-a-bug and little wifer! Did everyone sleep well?" Leah smiled; she loved her daddy. He was her hero as all dads should be to their little girls. Jim reached over and ran his fingers through my long hair. He pulled back a few strands with his hand and fingered them so they would stay behind my ear. "Are you still mad at me about last night?" he asked, smiling genuinely at my face. "Come on, don't be mad. I had a meeting. You took the car, and it was hard. Things went well. I think I landed the new project." Jim had been talking about the potential for a bonus and the new project starting after this project was completed. I didn't move, and Jim knew I was furious. He reached into his pocket and pulled out his wallet. "I got the bonus yesterday at work because I brought the job in early and under budget!" Jim pulled out a thick stack of hundred dollar bills. I looked over at the money thankful we had some. I watched every penny, was very conservative on every meal and everything I bought the baby, and had not spent a penny on myself. Jim saw me perking up and went for the close. He threw five hundred dollar bills onto the table in front of my plate. "Here you go; I promised you I'd take you shopping when I got my bonus. Let's go to the mall and buy you whatever you want. We can get Leah some new toys, and we can go to the Peppermill for lunch. Would you like that?" I smiled weakly. It had been weeks since I had been anywhere, and I loved the Peppermill. I looked down at the money. I knew I couldn't touch it. Jim would put it back into his wallet and take control like he always did. He reached out, put the money away, and then took my hand in his. "Come on Jeanette; let's not fight in front of the baby. Let's have a good Saturday and go out shopping, okay?" Thoughts of planning my escape from Jim played through my mind. If I had to run away, where would I go? I told myself I had to find a way out, and if he ever tried to hurt me like he had the night before, I would vanish. Instead of acting mad and making Jim angry again, I faked a little excitement about going shopping and having Jim spend time with me. Maybe I hadn't seen him kiss the girl, but he did go out drinking. I couldn't live life this way. Things should be good and my marriage should be happy. Was I imagining things? I hadn't, as the vision of the prior night flooded my brain. The water had been all too real and scary. . . I pushed those thoughts out of my head and rushed around to fix Jim a hot breakfast. As he ate, I cleaned Leah and myself, decided to "go along" with the façade, readying for a glorious day with Jim being generous and buying us both whatever we wanted.

That day was absolutely perfect. We shopped at the mall. Jim spoiled me and bought me whatever I wanted without looking at the price. We bought Leah new clothes, shoes, and toys. And then we had a wonderful lunch at the Peppermill Restaurant. The perfect little family—Jim the breadwinner and protector; me the dutiful, young, and beautiful wife; and little Leah. The package was complete. We were the perfect, little family.

CHAPTER 12
MARRIED?

A few months into living with Leah at the condo, we received mail from Ken Tuttle, Jim's partner from Corona del Mar. It was a large brown envelope addressed to "Jim Miani" and was brimming full of assorted envelopes. Jim perused the contents, flipped through a few things, and paid little attention to it, leaving it on the table. After Jim went to work, I quickly sorted through the numerous past-due bills, opening each one and mentally adding the debt. The amount of the debt totaled more than $150,000. The bills were from jewelry stores, multiple credit card accounts, and a few small bank loans. My jaw dropped as I recognized the meals we had eaten together and remembered the generous tips added to the hundreds of dollars in charges to famous nightspots in Palm Springs, Las Vegas and the Orange County basin. The handwritten note from Ken read: "J-I keep getting the wolves at my door, please make them go away. L.K."

I assumed the wolves were creditors because a majority of the bills appeared to be well past due and in collections. I felt a familiar wave a stress spinning deep in the pit of my stomach and I wrung my hands together in frustration. What on earth were we going to do? It appeared my new husband and I were in financial ruin. How would we ever pay off $150,000? A brand new home in the Bay Area was less than that! I had seen television commercials for a group of consumer credit counselors. This non-profit group would help people like us in this desperate financial situation. There would be only one way to deal with this problem, and that was to deal with it head on. As a young adult, my parents taught me to manage my money, to treasure and protect my credit rating by paying every bill on time and never overdrawing any account.

Jim wasn't the easiest to approach on any important subject, so I waited until he had eaten and consumed a few beers. While washing his Jag one Saturday afternoon, I mentioned the package from Ken. Jim chuckled. I was so relieved Jim didn't get mad I let out an audible tone of relief. Jim didn't notice my worry and explained he had already planned on doing something about the bills. He had contacted an attorney someone at work recommended. I mentioned the ad from television about the consumer program to pay off the bills, but Jim just took another swig of his beer and waved me off with his free hand. Leah was playing in the water bucket, and I wasn't sure if Jim was okay with my recommendation or not.

"Don't worry about it, wifer." Jim smiled, sensing my apprehension about the large pile of debt. "I have it covered; we'll meet with a local lawyer and it will all be solved." Jim looked at me more sternly. I tried to cover the flurry of questions in my head.

"Jeanette, it *will* be okay. Now let's finish the Jag, okay?" Jim said, throwing the roll of paper towels at me signaling me to start on the windows.

The cordless phone rang, startling me. I jumped out of the car to answer it.

"Hello," the voice from the other end was familiar; it was my brother, Tommy.

"Jean, hey, it's Tommy; how are you in Sunnyvale? Did you get the package?" I smiled feeling happy I had one blood relative who knew where I was. I looked at Jim, who was frowning and motioning to me with the bottle of Windex.

"Tom, I'm fine. I got my things and the jewelry box; thanks so much," I said in a rush.

"Good, Jean. Hey listen, I have to get to work, but need to talk to you. Dad called from Denmark. He and Mom haven't talked to you in a long time, and Dad wanted to speak with you about something very urgently. He told me to contact you and for you to call him right away." I became concerned and my face contorted with questions.

"Are they okay?" I asked, worrying about them getting older.

Tom grunted, "Yeah, Jeannie, they are fine. Dad just called me yesterday and told me to track you down to tell you he needed to speak with you right away. I have no idea what he wants, but it sounded important. Hey, I have to go. I love you, Jeanne, and please call me if you need anything, anything at all, you hear?" I looked at Jim who was beginning to glare and had his hands placed firmly on his hips, the anger at me for speaking with my brother showing on his face. I had my parent's number hidden underneath the liner in my bedroom underwear drawer. Jim had told me on numerous occasions that he didn't think a newlywed bride should call her parents very often because it was meddlesome. I hadn't called my parents and missed them terribly; if I did call them Jim would know because calls to Denmark were so expensive.

"Sure Tommy, you bet, love you too!" I said and hung up trying not to let Jim know that Tom wanted me to call my folks. I quickly set the phone back onto the cardboard box and grabbed the Windex, climbing into the back seat with the paper towels hoping Jim wouldn't ask me anything. Jim came to where I was and leaned into the car staring at me with a hard, serious look.

"So, what did little brother want? Courtesy call?" Jim asked fishing for information. I knew I shouldn't be lying to my new husband, but I was so afraid of getting him angry. I didn't look out from the back window and was afraid if I looked at Jim, he would know I was lying. I sprayed more Windex and acted like I had a stubborn spot I was furiously working on.

"Uh, nothing really, he hadn't heard from me in a while, wanted to see if I received that box of stuff he mailed. He told me he started a new job with a large print factory, and he missed me. That was it. He had to get to work." I kept wiping the window and after lingering in the car for an extra few moments, Jim pulled his large frame out of the car and began to put away the washing paraphernalia. I had to call my dad; I'm sure it was very important or he wouldn't have called Tom. Monday morning I could walk across the street to use the pay phone at the shopping center. With the time difference to Denmark, I'd have to call early in order to reach Dad before he went to bed at night. I was broke again, but figured I could pick up several dollars in change from the money Jim left scattered throughout the house.

On Sunday night, I mentioned to Jim that Leah and I were planning on making some special cookies and were thinking of walking to the grocery store across the street from the condo. Jim nodded, not really thinking about what I was saying. I was relieved he didn't start questioning me.

All went as planned and as Jim was chewing through his perfectly crisped bacon and buttered toast, I mentioned that Leah and I might take a walk to the store to buy cookie fixings. Jim nodded, drained his orange juice glass, pecked a quick kiss on my head, patted Leah's hair, and threw $10 onto the table. Jim gave me a stern warning to be careful and stay away from strangers. I knew what he meant by that. He meant for me not to pick up any men at the store and sleep with them today. I smiled and replied we would be careful and watched as Jim left through the garage door.

I froze, breathing shallowly until I heard the door close and the sound of the Jag purring off towards the expressway. I smiled and snorted through my nostrils as I picked up the plates and washed the breakfast dishes. It was just like me, I joked with myself, to find a young guy working in the produce department and have sex with him behind the lettuce counter while Leah played in the shopping cart unattended. What did Jim think of me? He must think I was a whore! I argued with myself – it was my fault that he was worried about me and didn't trust me; after all, it was my fault for cavorting with Iris and the likes of women such as her. But I hadn't really known that Iris was anything other than a waitress. How could I know? I had never met anyone like her before. I realized I had been daydreaming, the dishwater was cold, and Leah was standing by my side, yanking on my nightshirt, repeating GNut over and over again. We had to go and fast.

I quickly dressed Leah and sat her in front of Sesame Street, while I threw on a pair of jeans and a t-shirt. Pulling my hair back would be the fastest. I didn't bother putting on any make-up; the last thing I needed was for Jim to come home and notice I had lipstick on. I grabbed the phone number from the bottom of my drawer, shoved the keys into my pocket, pulled a sweater over Leah's head, and took the grocery list from the table that I had left in plain sight for Jim to see.

We slipped through the divided block wall behind the condo and walked to the intersection. After pushing the walk button, we made our way across the street to the Food Co-op of Sunnyvale. I didn't stop at the first payphone right outside the main entrance of the store, afraid Jim may be watching me. It seemed crazy, but I slipped into the store, and then Leah and I turned around peering through the glass panes in front of the store scanning the entire parking lot for the yellow Jag. I scooped up Leah and stepped onto the black rubber mat of the electric door. I ducked down the strip mall towards the end of the plaza where there was another pay phone outside of the dry cleaners. Upon reaching the phone, I quickly dumped all of the change I had into the phone listening expectantly for the phone to ring. As soon as I heard a ringing, I stretched the phone cord as far as the metal mesh would reach and pulled the phone around the outside of the plastic wall of the phone cubby, using the enclosure to hide behind.

"Hello." It was the warm and familiar voice of my father. My throat immediately closed, my lips pursed tightly together. I swallowed hard, fought back tears, and felt my nose starting to get swollen and hot, my emotions welling up ready to explode.

"Daddy, it's me Jeanette!" I said and immediately bit my lip. Daddy had returned home from work at the Danish embassy a few hours earlier and Mother was probably sewing or reading in their Copenhagen home thousands of miles away. My father was obviously pleased to hear my voice and addressed me in the same loving and affectionate way he had since I was a little girl.

"J for Jeanette! My little Gina, how is my baby girl doing?" I couldn't hold back any more and tears of joy and mixed emotions streamed down my face. I couldn't say anything to Daddy. How could I start? What could I say? I wanted to tell him to come get me, to come save me, to help me get through a very hard time. I wanted to tell him about the scary anger my new husband spewed out every now and then, but I didn't. I smiled weakly only letting him know that I was fine and he needn't worry.

"Fine Daddy, I'm fine. Did Tom tell you I am living in Sunnyvale, Northern California? Jim has a great job, and we have little Leah. She's three now and such a darling." I rushed on, not saying what my heart was screaming. Reality hit me and I began scanning the parking lot for the yellow Jag.

"Jean, Tom told me all about what is going on with you," he said in a disapproving tone. "I heard from Tom that you and Jim got married by the Justice of the Peace back in July, but I checked records with a friend of mine in Orange County. Yes, you *did* file for a marriage license, but the license was never officiated." There was a delay in the conversation due to the distance on the call, but I was very confused and didn't know how to address this new information.

"What do you mean, Daddy? I'm not married?" Things were not getting better for me; they were crumbling down.

"Jeanette, your mother is very upset by all of this. We wanted you to come with us to Europe, both you and Debbie; then you announced you had a boyfriend. Next, we hear from Tom that you're married. No wedding, no family. This is not what we wanted for you, Jeanette. In our family, we don't run away and elope."

I felt deeply ashamed and could feel the folly of my action.

"And no, Jeanette, even if you file a marriage license, you still need a preacher, priest, or other legal entity to officiate. So you and Jim are living in sin."

The words came out harshly and slapped me across the face! Me, living in sin! I had heard my parents' hushed tones when talking about "this couple" or "that couple" living in sin, shacking up together. Not me, I was a good Catholic girl—a virgin until I was married. I was *not* living in sin, no way, how could I? Was this really true?

"Daddy, are you sure? I mean, I thought . . ." I stammered, but I realized my father was a brilliant man and there was no way he would ever lie to me. He loved me and was a wonderful father, always speaking truth, nothing more.

"Jeanette, I am sure. I didn't tell your mother about the legality of this all. You left, you got married and now we expect you to make us proud and to do the right thing. Your mother and I have been married for almost thirty years and we've stuck together, that's what married people do! If you have made this decision to be a wife, you better make it right, capiche?" he asked me, using an Italian phrase. "You chose this path, and made your bed, now you need to lie in it." I knew what he meant. I was a family embarrassment now. . . living in sin, not married, and shacking up with Jim. He didn't tell Tommy, and he wouldn't tell Mother. I should do what my parents did; they made a life-long commitment to be married and to stay married. I needed to do exactly like they had done: work on my marriage. Now I was living with someone and I had to fix it and fast! Now what would I do? The operator interrupted the call and told me I needed to put in $0.75 to continue another three minutes, but I was out of quarters. I sucked in my breath and rushed out quickly before the line cut off.

"I love you, Daddy. I'll make this right for you and Mother, I promise."

Daddy agreed in his warm voice. "Don't worry, little girl. I know you will, and I love you too." The line went dead and I held onto the phone not wanting to hang up. I could still hear my dad's voice over the blank space. I didn't want the call to end, but it had. I replaced the phone onto the cradle and strolled with Leah back into the far door of Food Co-op to complete our shopping trip.

Days after the phone call with Daddy, I wasn't quite sure what to do about the marriage thing. I couldn't keep on the way things were going and had to do something, but was afraid to say anything to Jim. How had I found this information? As if an answer to prayer, another manila envelope appeared in the mailbox from Ken.

"Well, I wouldn't believe this if I hadn't read it!" Jim exclaimed. "Jeanette, will you come in here?" Jim hollered. I came running in with my dishtowel, wringing soapy water off my hands and coming to the table where Jim was opening up the mail. Jim continued. "Looks like we're not really married after all!" Jim let out a laugh. I was both relieved and let the shock show visibly across my face at the same time. Jim looked at my wide eyes and laughed some more, realizing he could use this moment to insult and humiliate me.

"Well, well, the virgin is living in sin with the old man! You are not really married to me, Jeanette. Did you know that?" I gasped at the bluntness and could hear my dad's voice echoing, "Living in sin, living in sin."

"What? Not married? But I was there at the courthouse with you. How could we *not* be married?" Jim explained the letter, similar to what my father had told me a few days earlier.

"Well, I guess we needed to have a judge or someone finish signing off the license to make it fully legal. This letter says we have three more weeks to officiate the license or it will become null and void!" Jim laughed and laughed. My face felt hot and flushed with anger. How stupid; why did I think a piece of paper made us legally married? I became upset and started to cry and Jim kept laughing which made me cry even more. Jim made a quick comment about me finding a preacher to finish the deal, so I immediately started my research.

The next week, I made an appointment over the phone with a Christian preacher and his wife to "get legal." Wearing a skin-tight disco dress and high-heeled shoes, Jim and I had a fifteen-minute "wedding" in front of the local preacher and his wife. It was an empty ceremony. As the preacher read a few Scriptures and spoke of love, Jim kept impatiently looking at his watch. Walking out to the car, Jim announced he had a meeting at 9:00 p.m. and had to leave right away. Jim spoke of work and other job opportunities while I sat in the car not moving, nodding my head and clutching the dry piece of paper. This was the right thing to do, wasn't it? I was now officially married at the ripe old age of twenty-one.

A Legal Matter

Jim called me from work a few days later and told me he needed me to help with an afternoon appointment he'd made for the two of us to see a lawyer. A lawyer—I didn't understand. Jim assured me everything would be okay. I needed to bring the two envelopes Ken had sent to the house, grab Leah, and get onto a bus heading west on Saratoga-Sunnyvale Avenue.

Doing what Jim instructed, I put a jacket on Leah and got ready, being careful not to put on too much make-up.

At the proper stop, we exited the bus, crossed the street, and arrived at Ben Goodfellow's law office. Leah played in the moderate-sized lobby, while I nervously glanced around. Why were we here? After a few moments, a very nice man with graying temples, reading glasses and a warm fatherly voice entered the lobby.

"Mrs. Miller?" I stood up and took Leah by the hand, following Mr. Goodfellow down the long hallway towards his private office. Mr. Goodfellow chatted as we walked together, making polite small talk, and made a few mentions about Leah's beautiful blue eyes. I handed Mr. Goodfellow the two envelopes Jim instructed me to take. Mr. Goodfellow seemed surprised by the large total of the bills, but I figured Jim had already spoken to him about us wanting to make an arrangement to pay these off a little at a time to every creditor. A legal secretary came in and sat down at the adjacent desk in Mr. Goodfellow's office. She took the pile and began typing out a long list of the bills, carefully placing each bill recorded onto a far side of the desk and placing a third pile for redundant invoices. When his secretary finished, she handed the three-page, single-spaced list to Mr. Goodfellow. He perused the list and looked at me over the top of his reading glasses.

"So, Mrs. Miller, I don't see any bills in your name. . . uh. . . only your husband's. Didn't you have any credit cards in your name, or any loans in both of your names?"

My head started to swim. "What do you mean credit cards in both of our names?" I almost died as I began to speak, my cheeks flushing bright red. I looked down, feeling ashamed and sick to my stomach. I added softly, "We were just married last week." I could read the surprise as Mr. Goodfellow raised his forehead in an amazed expression. I saw the legal secretary's jaw drop open and close quickly.

"I see, you were just married last week." Mr. Goodfellow continued looking at the list. "Well, do you have any credit cards or accounts in your maiden name?" I nodded and pulled a Sears credit and Bank of America Visa card out of my purse. I handed the cards over to him.

"I do have these," I said softly.

"We need to add them to the list, Miss Craner." Mr. Goodfellow motioned for Miss Craner to add the two cards to his long list of debtors and handed the cards to her.

"Um, okay, what is the outstanding delinquent balance on each of these cards? Let's take the Sears credit card first."

I scrunched up my face and said, "Let's see, I think zero. I paid the last payment before I came up north a few months ago." Mr. Goodfellow turned his head sideways and looked at me intently. Miss Craner sat poised, waiting for additional information to add to her delinquency report.

"Ok, that's fine. Miss Craner, put down the creditor and list zero balance on the column of debts." She nodded and began swirling her fingers expertly over the keyboard not missing a stroke. "Now, what about the Visa balance?" Mr. Goodfellow questioned.

"Uh, I'd say about $250, give or take a few. . . ." As soon as I said $250, Mr. Goodfellow let out an audible "What?" and my face flushed bright red again.

"Two hundred fifty? You owe Visa $250,000?"

Two hundred and fifty thousand dollars! Did he say thousand? I began to stutter in confusion.

"Yes, two hundred and fifty, no. . . not thousand, two hundred and fifty dollars, under three hundred, I think." Mr. Goodfellow shot a look at Miss Craner, and I wished I were invisible. Leah played with the nearly new box of tinker toys oblivious to the situation. "Mr. Goodfellow, I'm not sure why you need my card information. I'm a good bill-paying citizen. I owe about $250 to Visa, which I fully intend on paying. These bills just came in the mail from Ken in Corona del Mar. I've never seen them before. I don't have much debt, but I think we need to pay these off and start right now, or we'll never get out of debt. You see, Jim and I just got married and well, it's just plain wrong for a couple to ignore their obligation. I know it is a huge sum, but we want to pay these bills 100 percent until they are all cleared." I felt the tears well up in my eyes and Mr. Goodfellow motioned for Miss Craner to leave and close the door.

"Mrs. Miller, now let me get this straight: You just got married last week to Mr. Miller; he has a three-year-old daughter you are now raising as your child; he told you to come here to my office; and you didn't know that he was more than $150,000 in debt? You had no idea he was sending you to an attorney for this? You have excellent credit and will now be forced to file for bankruptcy because you are his wife."

Bankruptcy! What was he saying? I knew what bankruptcy was, but I wasn't going to file it. Jim was in a little trouble, well maybe a lot of trouble, but a lot of folks get into financial trouble. My personal credit was something I revered. I didn't understand why I needed to file bankruptcy; my credit was perfect.

"Mr. Goodfellow, my credit is perfect as you can see. I have no debt. I've been careful not to extend. You see, I've been a working student the last three years and have watched every cent. Bankruptcy is for people who have bad credit and people who have failing businesses."

Mr. Goodfellow added, "And for people like Jim Miller who are way over their heads in debt without a way to conceivably pay it back." I shook my head.

"Well, maybe Jim should file, but not me; after all, I'm not late on any bills." Mr. Goodfellow shook his head and spoke to me like a father.

"Mrs. Miller, now that you are married, you *have* to file with your husband." He paused long and looked at me as I started to cry softly. "I don't normally interfere in people's personal situations, but I am going to give you this advice now. If you were my daughter, I'd tell you to pay for a divorce instead of a bankruptcy. What your husband did to you financially is unconscionable and frankly I find it shocking and unbelievable!" Mr. Goodfellow handed me some papers to sign, told me we would be mailed court dates and that Mr. Miller must sign paperwork and attend the court hearings. I wasn't quite sure what all he was talking about but knew that I had made a big mistake when I went to the nice pastor and his wife and said, "I will."

MARRIED?

CHAPTER 13
THE FIRST EVICTION

It was January of 1980. Jim was now officially unemployed. The bills weren't a big problem, but paying rent was. We received notice after notice of late rent, but without a job, the rent would be delinquent. I mentioned it to Jim, and he said we'd fight it. If we were filing for bankruptcy, they couldn't force us out of our house.

A process server handed us legal papers with a date to appear. Jim prepped me to make sure I said the right things when questioned. A few days later, we found ourselves in a courtroom. I was petrified – it was the first time I'd ever seen the inside of a courtroom. Jim sauntered up with a smile on his face, held his hand on a Bible and swore to tell the truth. The lawyer asked him questions about our lease, and if he physically altered the lease in any way to meet his specific terms. Jim said no. They asked him the same question several times, phrasing it slightly differently, and each time he said no.

They swore me in next and I placed my hand on the Bible, rehearsing the things Jim told me to say. Our landlord was trying to evict us because she claimed we weren't paying our rent and we had altered her new lease agreement. To prove her case, she hired a contract specialist to review the case against Jim and Jeanette Miani. This specialist performed a microscopic inspection of the original lease agreement and a copy that Jim had submitted to the court. The nice elderly man asked me several times if I knew how the contract terms of our lease "mysteriously" changed? I shook my head, flushed bright red, and under oath, while Jim glared dagger eyes at me, I told him I did not know. These were the terms we had agreed upon. The lease had not gone up, it had gone down. Jim smiled at me when I finished my statement. I stepped down feeling like I would faint in the court. I didn't know what I was involved with, but knew it was really illegal.

On the overhead screen the document specialist showed the court the original copy of our lease with signatures of the landlord and Jim and Jeanette Miani. It showed the new terms of six months and a total of $565 per month. The specialist then proceeded to show us the same document; however, the rent now showed a total of $500 per month and a term of twelve months. Under the magnification it was obvious someone altered and erased the lease agreement.

The judge looked at Jim and me sitting in court and began talking about throwing the book at us for perjury. I knew enough from Perry Mason to know what perjury was. Lying in court! I knew what I had done. As I heard the judge rant over and over about a young couple like us doing something very illegal, my head swirled. What kind of a girl had my parents raised? How could I have allowed Jim to coerce me into lying? My ears were buzzing and I could see the judge wagging his finger in my direction and telling us to move out of our condo by the end of the month or we'd be in very serious trouble.

In the car, on the way back to the condo, Jim chatted to me animatedly, exhibiting a cold and heartless contempt for the law. He laughed about being in trouble and swearing into court as *Jim Miani*. *Jim Miani* was in trouble, not Jim Miller, he laughed. I was really scared and felt like our lives were crashing down. We were filing for bankruptcy, Jim had no job, and now we had no place to live.

That night after a quick dinner of cheeseburgers, canned green beans, and sliced fried potatoes, I curled up with Leah on the couch to read to her as Jim prepared to go to another "meeting." He put on his nicest clothes and made sure to splash on extra aftershave. I felt pretty numb. I didn't say a thing to him about the court case or about being evicted; I was afraid of the wrath Jim would spew. That evening, I shivered and shook, although it wasn't a cold night in the Bay Area. I put Leah down and lay down, crying myself to sleep. I never heard Jim come in, and figured it must have been close to dawn.

The next day was Saturday. Leah and I got up early and sat on a blanket in front of the TV watching cartoons and eating toast. Jim woke up and stretched out on the carpet behind us. I knew he was there, but didn't want to acknowledge him. He just came through the door a few hours ago, I thought. Jim tapped my shoulder.

"Hey, sorry I got home so late last night. I made a good deal and think I'll land this job in about two weeks." This was music to my ears. I looked at Jim, not sure what his mood may be. "I have to wait until we move and finish the bankruptcy and then I can start working. If I have a lot of money in the bank when we file, it may look bad. Do you understand?" I nodded my head and tried to act like I was happy about the news.

"We can drive around to look for a new place. We know the area and we will be able to get a good pre-school for Leah. So if you want to work, you can put in a few part-time hours. Would you like that?" I perked up. As much as I loved Leah, it was so depressing and demoralizing to have to beg Jim for a buck here and there. I hated not having my own spending money and brought up the subject of getting a part-time job, promising dinner would be on the table and Leah would be well taken care of. Jim looked at me and pulled out a wad of hundred dollar bills. He smiled. "I won a very large bet last night and collected my $10,000! Let's go out to breakfast and look for a new place!" I jumped up excitedly. Yesterday I lied in court, knew I had filed for bankruptcy, was being evicted from my house, and today I would pretend my life was normal and that I was a happily married woman!

After a very nice breakfast, we drove the Jag around the neighborhoods of Sunnyvale looking for the perfect place to move to. It was almost the end of January and we needed to vacate or become locked out of the condo. Driving down one very nice street, there was a "For Rent" sign in the window of a darling house. Jim pulled the Jag to the curb. Leah quickly bound up the few stairs towards the front door with Jim and me following right behind. We peered in the front window and I envisioned our furniture and how it would look in a real house. A real house with a private back yard! We could have a barbecue and invite our neighbors. I could take a walk and maybe get a cat or dog. We could plant a garden and enjoy a picnic on the back lawn. Just as I started to take down the number a brisk voice came from around the corner. We looked at the short, balding man with a large smile and an outstretched hand.

"Frank Bilbao. Pleased to meet you." Jim shook his hand.

"Jim Miller and my wife, Jeanette. This is our daughter Leah." I shook Mr. Bilbao's hand and smiled as any young wife would.

"You all looking for a place to rent? I've just finished the interior. You see, my wife and I live right up the street and we bought this place from a couple that let it run down. I'm retired and thought I could fix it up, and then rent it. Eventually, this house will be given to our daughter, but she's just in college now and won't live here for several years." I smiled up at Jim and he looked down at Frank.

"Well, Mr. Bilbao, we *are* looking to rent. You see, we just drove up from Southern California the other day." I tried not to look surprised as Jim continued spinning his web. "I have a new job starting up here in two weeks, and my company gave us an exceptional relocation package. I am the construction superintendent for WebCor, the large builder. I'm helping to build the new mall. We are supposed to get established as soon as possible and need a place to rent. We've looked at several places and like this area. " Frank nodded, looking down at Leah, who was playing with a sow bug.

Frank opened up the door to a very lovely little home with new carpet and freshly painted walls. Leah ran from room to room enjoying her own giggles echoing through empty rooms. After the tour, Frank looked happy, Jim was smiling and I was beaming, imagining a happy home.

"It looks very nice, Frank, but how much is the rent and deposit?" Jim asked trying to appear uninterested. I could tell Frank was grateful we showed up to look at the house; we looked like the perfect couple—driving an expensive luxury car, husband, wife and child.

"Well, the rent is $650 a month with a $300 deposit; so that's $950 total up front to move in. Remember, that includes the yard work too," Frank said trying to close the deal. Jim opened his wallet and grabbed 10 one hundred dollar bills, counting them in front of Frank making sure Frank knew there were a lot more where that came from.

"Well, Frank, we don't have a contract signed with you or anything, but since we're living in a hotel, and my wife really likes the place, will this work?" Jim handed the cash to Frank. Frank nodded enthusiastically, while he took the money and put it into his wallet. "I have some paperwork to do and we should get back to our hotel. Do you figure we can start moving in when our furniture arrives in a few days?" Frank nodded again.

"I live in the white house down the block towards the corner. Why don't you come by later to sign the rental contract, say anytime after 5:00 p.m.?" Jim smiled, looked at me and winked, and pumped Frank's hand.

"That will be fine; see you after 5." Jim, Leah, and I got into the car and waved goodbye to our new house and to Frank. Jim started to laugh almost manically. I was quiet and so was Leah.

"We faked him out, huh? The old battle-axe is evicting us under the name of Miani, and now we're renting a terrific home, no credit check under the name of Miller. There are hundreds of Millers out there. They'll never even check our credit, not after I handed the old man $1,000 in cash." Jim continued to laugh all the way to the condo. We pulled the Jag into the garage, and Jim pulled boxes out of the trunk. "Well, we better get packing; we just moved here from Southern California the other day. You better remember that, right, Jeanette?" Jim said that with emphasis making sure I was paying attention. He wanted me to go along with his lie and confirm his story.

With boxes and furniture packed into our small rental truck, we moved into the new house late at night in the middle of the week. Jim wanted to make sure if Frank came by during the move, he would think we had been driving all day. Jim thought a late move would seem more realistic. We dragged beds, dressers, tables, chairs, and boxes into the house, working until early in the morning. We didn't have much, so it went fairly fast, but I wasn't very strong and had to rest a few times when moving the dresser and the new couch. Leah curled up in the closet of her new room as soon as I laid down her blanket and pillow for her.

That morning, tired and happy, I lay back in bed and prayed to God on this late January night of 1980. I asked for God's help and His guidance. It had been so long since I'd prayed; I almost felt God shouldn't listen to me since I had abandoned Him quite a while back. I prayed that God would make our house a home. I prayed that Jim would have steady work and be happy in his work. I prayed I wouldn't do anything to make Jim mad and he would never hurt or threaten me again. I prayed Jim would stay home at night like my father had: playing cards and games, or just talking with my mother and our family. I prayed for God to help me become a better mother to Leah and give me wisdom and patience. I felt a peace and knew that God had His hand on me. I drifted into a peaceful sleep, thanking God for pulling me close even though I was the one who had pushed Him away.

CHAPTER 14
THE NEW JOB

Jim started his job a few weeks after we moved into the little house on LaBella Lane. The job Jim landed was with a huge locally-based commercial construction company. Jim seemed very enthusiastic about the opportunity of running a project: good hours, excellent pay, and four months of steady work. We settled into what most people would call a normal life. For a short time, things seemed idyllic, and I pushed back all of those "episodes" Jim had exhibited. I chalked up his anger outbursts to stress and figured I really needed to be less headstrong and more supportive of him. I kept busy cleaning and setting up our new house, cooking and raising my darling daughter, Leah. I enjoyed reading romance novels in my free time, which kept my mind in a fairytale love relationship with fictional characters.

Knowing I liked to sing and had written a few songs for Leah, when he received his very first paycheck, Jim came home with a cheap acoustic guitar and handed it to me with a big smile and a

141

basic music book. I was thrilled! I had played violin and piano for years, and music was always a part of our lives growing up. Now, I had a guitar. I immediately began to teach myself all of the basic chords and penned my songs onto paper. Leah loved the music. It filled the space in our home with laughter and happiness. The guitar quickly became one of my most prized possessions.

Each day, I would read and sing to Leah and take her for walks in the clean and quiet neighborhood. I didn't have a car yet, but remembered Jim promised me I might be able to get a small part-time job. I desperately wanted a job and each morning, I perused the classifieds under Waitress or Restaurant Work. One morning a few days later, I spotted an ad for a part-time waitress at a local coffee shop. The place was only two miles from where we lived, had a good local reputation, and was a busy store. There was a daycare center only one block from the house. If I landed the job, I could put Leah on the back of my bike, commute her to daycare, ride to work, and pick her up after my shift. It would be good exercise, I'd work a few hours a day, and it would give me some much-needed spending money. I called the restaurant and gave the manager a verbal resume. The manager pleasantly questioned my serving experience and invited me to come into the restaurant after the lunch shift for an interview.

Mrs. Bilbao watched Leah and I walked the two miles to the restaurant in a dress, nylons, and heels with my hair swept into a tight bun. I could have ridden my bike but knew a dress would look professional and feared they wouldn't hire me if they thought I didn't have a car.

The interview went exceptionally well and they offered me the job working Monday through Friday, 8:00 a.m.-1:00 p.m. This would be the breakfast and lunch crowd. I figured I could easily clear $150 a week in tips plus my paycheck. This was a job and schedule made in heaven. Maybe God had heard me and answered my prayers.

After picking up Leah, I rode her on my bike to sign up for the local daycare. It was a very nice place, and Leah bounded off to play with the kids immediately. Everything was perfect, except for one thing: Jim would have to allow me to go to work and Leah to attend pre-school.

I made a very nice filet mignon dinner with a baked potato, fresh vegetables, tossed salad, and a chilled bottle of wine. I figured the wine would help to sell my idea. Jim knew something was up and after his second glass of wine and a few bites into the filet, he asked me point blank what was up. I was afraid to say anything for fear Jim would blow up.

"Well . . ." I began, looking at Jim as sincerely as I could. I began to rush. "I saw a want ad in the local paper for a part-time waitress. I know the restaurant. It is a coffee shop, and it's clean and right up the road and would only be a few hours a week." He wasn't arguing, so I continued. "Leah really could use some other kids to play with. She is three and hasn't gone to any pre-school. This would help her socialize with other children, and she would learn at the same time." Jim took another sip of his wine. I filled his glass, draining the bottle. "I promise you wouldn't even know I was gone during the day, the house will be clean and dinner will be ready before you get home. It's only a few hours a week and I could pay for the daycare with my tips." Jim frowned when I said that. He liked to be the man of the house, but since it was *my* choice, he'd no doubt make me pay for the daycare out of the few tip dollars I'd make each day.

"Okay, only if it doesn't interfere with your main responsibilities of being *my* wife and Leah's mother." I jumped up and hugged Jim, thanking him for letting me get a part-time job. Jim barked loudly at me, making Leah jump down from the table and hide under it.

"It better not interfere with things around here or your job will be short lived, that I promise. Do you understand me, Jeanette?"

"Don't worry, it won't get in the way, I *do* understand," I said quickly, clearing the dirty dishes and putting them into the sink of hot soapy water. "I will keep a perfect house, and Leah will be happy with new buddies to play with, I promise." Jim took another sip and mumbled something under his breath. I didn't say a word but quietly cleaned the kitchen while Jim got ready to go out again. Another meeting, I supposed. I didn't really care. He probably had a girlfriend and was meeting her, I reasoned. Why would he always go out late and come in smelling like booze, cigarettes, and aftershave mixed with perfume? I laughed a little and snorted as I thought about Jim having a girlfriend and me not reacting to it. What would she have, a few hours of drinking and smoking and partying with Jim? That's *all* she would have, right? They wouldn't have sex, would they? I didn't think Jim would have sex with other women and then come home to me each night. Would he?

Each day, I awakened at 5:00 a.m., made Jim a hot breakfast and prepared him a sack lunch. He would perfunctorily kiss my cheek and then tell me the same story: he would probably have late meetings and I shouldn't hold up dinner for him. Jim was pretty much oblivious to the fact I even had a job. He knew I was there from 8:00 a.m.-1:00 p.m. Jim was very suspicious when

144

I first started the job, and drove by several times to make sure I was telling the truth. Once he realized I was running at a fast pace during my shift, and was home with Leah on time when he called, he quit checking up on me.

One day before Jim left for work I told him I was going to use my tip money to buy a few groceries and would be home with Leah about fifteen minutes late. Jim's face turned bright red and he spewed a few obscenities about me screwing the cook in the kitchen. The shock on my face told him I was really going to go to the grocery store, so he capped the conversation off with a warning that he'd kill me if he ever found me with another man. Jim's statement sent a cold shiver through my body.

Across the street from the restaurant was a local bank and since I had filed for bankruptcy, sold my car, and pretty much had no money in my name, I opened up a savings account. My intuition told me not to mention it to Jim, so I kept it my secret. Whenever he asked about my money from work, I explained I used most of it for Leah's daycare and the rest on groceries. Jim would curse at me for being a "stupid idiot," working for peanuts waiting on absolute strangers, when I really didn't have to. But I didn't care. . . I was clipping coupons and saving a few dollars each week. When my savings account reached $400, I was so proud of what I had done. Jim would have been very angry if he knew I had the money stored away. I kept my passbook hidden in the house and was very careful not to make any mistakes.

THE NEW JOB

CHAPTER 15
A WILD PARTY

One Friday night Jim came home early, which was a real switch. Typical Fridays were paydays, and the guys would drink on the site after work. I assumed after the jobsite drinking, they all went to a bar to drink some more. I didn't have transportation and couldn't drive the twenty miles to the site, so I didn't have a clue what went on. I had dinner ready, and as usual, was getting ready to wrap Jim's plate in foil and leave it in the oven. Leah was fed, bathed, and in her pajamas, reading books and playing with her doll house. Jim came bursting through the garage door and told me to dress up; we were invited to a big party.

A big party—I wasn't ready to go out; my hair was clean, but wasn't curled. I looked at Jim, wondering what I needed to wear. Jim excitedly rushed to explain.

"Skip and Betty Lowry have a mansion on top of the hills in San Jose. Skip is the vice president of West Coast Operations for the company, and he wants us both to come up for drinks, food, and a party. Apparently he has a gorgeous view with a complete bar and professional discothèque in his home! Come on, put on that blue satin dress I bought you with the short jacket. Get the lead out of your butt, the party starts at seven, and it's almost 6:00 p.m. I don't want to be too late. This is a great thing for my career, and you need to look fantastic!" Jim was running through the house, pulling off his t-shirt and briskly filing through hangers in order to find his white polyester vest, pants, and black shirt. It was the perfect John Travolta outfit and Jim wore it well. He was a very handsome man . . . at least on the outside.

"Jeanette, you have to hurry, do something nice with your hair and would you try to put on a little make-up? I told Skip about your modeling career, and he and Betty can't wait to meet you. . ."

"A model! Well, where did you tell them I worked?" I asked, realizing it was the wrong thing to say. Jim stopped rustling with his clothes, bounded across the room, and grabbed both of my arms tightly, lifting me off the ground. He shook me hard and spat in my face.

"You stupid whore, you were a Cosmo model. You did petites for them. You better not ever forget it, whore! Now!" Jim thrust me back hard, making me land on the bed with a thud. "Get ready, or I'll leave without you!" Jim stomped outside, slamming the door. He went to ask the girl next door to baby-sit for Leah. I tried not to cry but tears began streaming down my face. I put the hot curlers into my hair and started dressing as fast as I could. The last thing I needed tonight was a fight with Jim. I grabbed my make-up and figured I could put it on in the car to save time. Jim came back in and announced the babysitter would be here in ten minutes and I had *better* be ready to leave.

I sucked in my stress, pulled the curlers out of my long blonde hair, put one side of my hair up in a blue and gold hair clip, and dabbed a little pink gloss on my lips. I hugged Leah and told her to be a good little girl, promising we'd be back soon. The babysitter was playing with Leah as we pulled out of the garage, the yellow Jag going about fifty miles an hour through the quiet suburban lane in Sunnyvale.

Twenty minutes later, we parked on the long impressive driveway in front of a gorgeous mansion in the San Jose hills. While we stood at the large outside entry, in front of two enormous dark wooden doors, Jim pulled me tightly towards him, leaning over and approving of how I looked, a leering smile painted on his face.

"You are beautiful tonight, little wifer. Has anyone ever told you that?" I smiled a perfunctory smile and was not looking forward to being at this party. My husband had just grabbed me, cussed me out, and thrown me back onto our bed. I had nothing to smile about.

"Thank you Jim, you look very handsome too. I'm sure you'll be the most attractive man at the party." No matter how he looked on the outside, Jim was ugly on the inside, I thought. Jim flashed that white-toothed smile, the smile that caught my attention almost two years ago. The massive door opened and a nice looking middle-aged man with wavy salt and pepper hair welcomed us to his home. Jim shook his hand vigorously and introduced me to Skip Lowry. Skip took both of my hands into his and whistled.

"Well Jim, when you told me your wife was a model, I had no idea she would be this stunning. Welcome little lady, the party is just beginning." Skip left Jim behind and took my hand leading me through their long entry, huge living room, and formal dining room and finally to the back of their home where double doors revealed an in-house disco. This was the real thing. There was a long bar with room for twelve or more patrons. Small intimate tables surrounded a huge parquet floor with a disco ball hanging in the middle from the vaulted ceiling. A mixer panel and DJ booth completed the room. I was awestruck. This was as big and fancy as any high-end disco I'd ever seen. Skip asked me if I liked it, and I nodded my head, observing the few couples and singles that had beat us to the party. Skip escorted me to two large sliding panels, which opened to an expansive deck with multiple tiers. Down a few tiers was a huge lighted Jacuzzi. Steam was rising from the water and a light reflected rich aqua-colored bubbles. This was some house, I thought. These people must be filthy rich.

"What do you think?" Skip asked as I absorbed the beautiful landscape. "Do you and Jim swap in the spa?" Skip winked at me and took my hand, leading me back inside to the bar. "I kept asking Jim to bring you here. He's been here a hundred times with no wife! Glad he finally brought you up! You're so gorgeous, why was he hiding you?" Jim had a drink and cigarette and was already talking with a few of his buddies; fortunately he could not hear Skip's comments. I smiled and watched as Skip raked his eyes over the clingy blue satin dress. I never felt comfortable in that dress and wished I hadn't worn it. Jim liked it and it did look good, but it was tight and clung to every curve. Skip put one hand slowly around my waist, feeling my side all the way down, and held my hand while leading me towards the bar. I took a seat on top of a tufted black leather barstool complete with high back and arm rests. They spared no expense on this bar, I thought as I made a mental list of the skimpy cheap furnishings we had on a "rent-to-own" plan.

A few minutes later, a stunning trim and tanned blonde entered the disco. Skip immediately rushed over to her side and brought her over to introduce us.

"Betty, this is Jim's wife, Jeanette Miller. Jeanette, this is my precious and gorgeous wife, Betty." Betty smiled and immediately reached out to hug me. She seemed genuine and took the chair beside me, while Skip ran around the other side of the bar to get her an ashtray and a drink. Betty asked me about myself, the move, and the modeling. By the time it was 10 o'clock or so, the place was bursting at the seams. There were people snorting cocaine openly on the bar and all of the tables. People kept offering me some, and I smiled holding up my drink—the same drink I had started with three hours earlier. "Drug of choice," I said, taking my cue from another guest who said the same thing every time someone offered him the mirror. It worked for him. Betty was one of the first people to bring out the white powder arranged neatly into lines. She approached me. I held up the drink. Betty smiled a gorgeous smile, with perfectly capped white teeth, spun around, and went right over to Jim. Jim took the mirrored square and sniffed up a few lines of the powder, looking wild-eyed almost immediately. I suspected Jim used drugs, now I had proof. I didn't like it one bit. Skip mentioned Jim was always at his house, but Jim never said a thing or brought me before. Now I knew why. I knew Jim had smoked pot on occasion. At first I argued with him about the drug, but when I saw that it totally calmed him down and made him like a little kitten, I didn't say a thing. But wasn't cocaine addictive?

Betty grabbed me by the hand and led me into the bathroom. She told me I was the prettiest girl she had ever seen and Jim was a fool to look at all those other bar flies. She gushed on while fixing her make-up in the large, expansive powder room. She mentioned the spa and asked if Jim and I swapped. Betty laughed when she looked at my face.

"You don't, do you?" She laughed a hardy laugh fueled by the alcohol and drugs.

"No, I don't . . ." I said meekly. "Does Jim?" I asked.

"Well, little princess, that needs to be between you and Jim; I would just be careful if I were you. Some of those other flies out there can have very dangerous germs." With that she flushed the toilet, finished checking her hair and led me out down the long hallway towards the blaring disco music.

I immediately found Jim with his nose down onto the mirror, sniffing more of the powder. He looked at me and lifted the drug tray to my face. He smiled looking both drunk and high.

"Want a hit?" he asked. I shook my head back and forth. Looking at the wall clock, it was almost 11 o'clock; we told the babysitter we wouldn't be very late.

"Don't you think it's getting kind of late? It's almost 11," I asked as Jim did another line, not noticing I wanted to leave. At that moment, one of the sliding doors opened up and a naked man walked into the disco, across the floor, right by us, and out into the house. I couldn't hide my surprise. I urged Jim again.

"Jim, honey, it's getting late. I can drive us home. We told the sitter we'd be home before midnight." Skip entered from the hot tub next; he had a towel slung over his shoulder and that was it. He walked to Jim, grabbed the coke tray, and took a big sniff. He slapped me across my bottom.

"Hey little lady, get those clothes off. The water is fine. Betty is getting ready now; she has an extra towel if you want one." Skip crossed the bar stark naked and fixed himself another drink before bounding out the door to the hot tub. I stepped out to glance through the door and could see the outlines of bodies laying about everywhere. I shook my head and marched over to Jim.

"Jim, we have to go. These people are. . . are. . . are. . . naked and doing sex in the hot tub. This is probably an orgy!" At that Jim started to laugh with a cruel and mean squint in his eyes. He stared right into my eyes and started the low hissing tirade. "Miss Priss!" he spat. "Now you're turning into Miss Priss the prude. You worked for the best madam in Orange County, and now you're developing a conscience. I should have never married you! I should have left you at that dump of a bar where you could have sold yourself for a few bucks a john. Okay Miss Priss, let's go back to the dream house!" Jim grabbed his coat, yelled goodbye to a few guys who were buried in their powder and stormed out the door. I just about sprinted to get my purse, following Jim out the door and down the long sweeping driveway towards the Jag.

Jim yelled at me during the entire high-speed car ride back to Sunnyvale. Jim's anger kept escalating. He began cussing at me, tires screeching, while I sobbed, slumping low in the beige leather seat. He was yelling that I was a whore and a slut and an unfit mother to Leah. He told me I was the biggest mistake of his life and he was tired of playing house with me! When we got to the house, he barely slowed down long enough for me to get out. With one foot on the ground, he spun the tires out away from the curb, causing me to lose my footing and fall hard onto the pavement. My knees went down and I skidded across the bumpy pavement skinning them and tearing huge holes in my nylons. I could see the babysitter open the front drapes, wondering what all the screeching car sounds were about. I quickly got up and smoothed my dress, picked up my purse, and hoped the blood wasn't ruining my dress. I had to pull it together; I didn't want the babysitter to think something was wrong.

As I opened the door, the young girl gasped – blood was running down both of my legs and the palms of my hands were full of road particles and small cuts. I tried to laugh and made up a story about how Jim dropped me off on his way to get a gallon of milk for breakfast, and I had tripped coming up to the porch. I grabbed a paper towel to keep the blood from dripping everywhere and told the sitter to fish $10 from my purse. She kept asking if I was okay, and I said I was fine. I explained the cuts looked worse than they were, adding a few comments about not wearing spiked heels again. As soon as the door closed, I locked the door and went limping into the bathroom, locking the door behind me, tears welling up in my throat. If Jim came home I didn't want him to see me bleeding and humiliate me for my clumsiness, so I quickly doctored up my bloody knees.

I cried myself to sleep again and prayed hard to God. I prayed for God to give me a sign that He loved me and would always protect me. Feeling a sense of peace, I was startled at four in the morning when Jim plopped hard onto the bed. He smelled like perfume. Jim was angry when he came home and I tried to pretend I was asleep, but he woke me, telling me that I needed to fulfill my wifely duty to him. This was the way things were most of the time: Jim forced himself on me and then rolled over and fell fast asleep. I was angry with God for the answer to my prayer; I prayed for protection and my husband had raped me. Did God hear my prayers?

A WILD PARTY

CHAPTER 16
A TEACHING OPPORTUNITY

Jim knew I was upset the next morning as I did my chores in a perfunctory manner and did not offer any niceties to him except for a bland greeting. I was a mess, had cuts and bruises on my legs which were hard to miss. I was going to start breakfast, but Jim pulled out a stash of hundred dollar bills and announced to the house we were going out to breakfast and to the mall shopping! Leah jumped up and ran to her daddy, hugging him on the legs. Jim approached me as I was standing in the dining room, frozen, unmoving.

"Hey, you know I didn't mean to hurt you last night; it wasn't a good scene and I am under a lot of pressure at work and all. . . " Jim lifted my chin and I couldn't bear to look at those eyes. He had a really sincere look on his face and spoke lovingly and softly to me. "Jeanette, you are the love of my life. I couldn't live a day without you. You know how much you mean to me." He paused and added what I really needed to hear. "Hey, I promise I will never hurt you again. . . ever." I felt my defenses weakening and was lonely, hurt, and wanted so much to be loved. Jim stroked my long blonde hair and tried to get me to agree with him. "Come on, Leah's already putting on her clothes. Let's get ready, and I'll take you to the Peppermill for a nice breakfast. We'll go shopping at the mall; I'll get you those earrings you liked so much!" Jim flashed that white smile and looked really sincere. He *was* my husband, and although I didn't want to respond, I was lonely and craved true affection and honest love. I wanted to hate him and make him pay for hurting me! Why did it have to be so hard? Why did he always get so mad? I agreed, and Jim lifted me off the ground, spinning me around. "Let's go!"

We had a wonderful breakfast. I once again pretended I was happy, imagining our life as a carefree young couple. At the mall, Jim selected the gold earrings I had eyed and handed the clerk $200 for them. I put them on immediately once in the Jag and smiled at my reflection in the mirror.

After getting home, Jim flipped on the television, and Leah and I went for a walk. We walked down the street and stopped in front of the local Catholic Church. I read the information bulletin board mounted close to the sidewalk of the neatly manicured lawn—Mass and confessional times. Confession, that's where I needed to be!

Guilt about not having a relationship with God was striking a hard chord in my heart. My parents had always taken us to church each week. It was a part of our family traditions and heritage. I owed it to Leah to raise her in a faith. Jim didn't have a religion, and he mentioned before, he didn't care if I took Leah to church. They had a late Saturday afternoon service; Leah and I could walk there and be home before I had to feed Jim dinner. He would no doubt go out because it was Saturday night.

We came back home quickly. I didn't want us to have a long walk and worry Jim. The last thing I needed was to be irresponsible and make him angry. I pushed back the thoughts of being a prisoner in my own home. Not having a car or much money, I didn't have close family or any friends. It was a poor quality of life, but it was *my* choice that got me here. I had an obligation and would make my parents proud, doing my best to keep peace in my marriage.

I made Jim lunch as he sat in front of the TV drinking a beer, eating sunflower seeds, smoking a cigarette, and flipping through a newspaper. After he'd consumed a few beers, I figured he'd be feeling a lot better. I carefully approached Jim during a commercial break from his show and asked if I could take Leah to church later in the afternoon. He laughed out loud at first, and then after asking me the regular interrogation questions—what time it started, how long it would last, was I meeting anyone there, and when I would be home—he said sure.

During the service, I looked with great envy at the wholesome, young families. Although I wasn't using birth control and had not tried to prevent a pregnancy, and somewhere deep inside of me I longed for a baby and a perfect marriage, I was thankful at the same time that I hadn't gotten pregnant. I figured something must be wrong. But I was only twenty-two now; how could there be something wrong with me? I scrutinized these families who all seemed to have a common thread; the families had genuine Christ-loving husbands and fathers, and the mothers looked really happy as they cuddled their young children. I felt the empty hole inside my heart each time I looked at them. It would no doubt shock each person there and probably the priest as well, if they knew what my life was like.

I happened to flip through the church bulletin prior to rushing out of church. There was one particular ad that caught my eye. "Help Wanted: Computer Lab Teacher. Our Catholic school is looking for a computer lab volunteer. Must be willing to learn the new Apple computer program and be willing to work (two) one hour classes a week teaching the programs to our Junior High students. No experience necessary, will train." This caught my eye. I had heard a lot about computers and a new company called Apple, which was about three miles down the road. The area I lived in was nicknamed "Silicon Valley" and I had read something about Sunnyvale and San Jose becoming the center of the global computer revolution. I was very interested and thought computers would be the future, and I should inquire about becoming the teacher. Why not? They would train me and I was always good in typing, science, and physics. The ad told any interested person to fill out an application in the church hall after Mass.

After Mass, I took Leah and meandered past the donut-eating parishioners and toward the booth where a young man sat, going through a manual. I approached and when he looked up, our eyes locked. I felt a familiarity and thought I may know this man.

"Uh, hello," he said, seeming a little nervous. I smiled and let go of Leah's hand allowing her to play with a little girl she had seen in church. I looked down into green eyes and a warm and genuine smile. I was sure I knew this guy.

"Hello, I'm Jeanette, uh Jeanette Miller," I said in a quiet voice. "I've come to get information about the computer lab teaching job?" He nodded.

"Hi there. Yes, I'm Rick. Rick Hansen."

That was it, Ricky Hansen. I was certain it was him! This was *my Ricky Hansen* from Our Lady of Peace Catholic School. He and I chased each other around the playground as kids and held hands under the desks when the nuns weren't looking. One Christmas Ricky gave me a silver ring in a real jewelry box and I gave him a realistic rubber knife. When I moved away, Ricky told me he'd never forget me and would write me in Orange County every week. I received two letters and that was it. My life went on and so had his. I was positive this was him.

"Rick Hansen, did you ever live in Sepulveda or Mission Hills before?" The surprise on his face showed he had. A flash of recognition crossed his face, and he stood up, came around the registration table, and smiled big and broad. He reached out both hands to take mine in his.

"Jeanne! Is it really you! Jeanne Miani in the flesh right here in front of me! I thought you moved to Yorba Linda and I would never see you again." I squeezed Ricky's hands together and looked up into sincere eyes and a genuine smile. I smiled and nervously glanced at Leah and quickly dropped Rick's hands, stepping back away from him. At the same time, he looked down at my hand, noticing the wedding ring and then saw Leah playing a few feet away.

"Yes, Rick, it is me, Jeanne Miani *Miller*." I emphasized the Miller and Rick's face looked suddenly somber.

"Oh, I see, you're married and is that your daughter?" he asked, sounding very disappointed. We were the same age. I could see the wheels counting, figuring I would have been pregnant at eighteen to be twenty-two and have a child turning four. I started to explain.

"Well, I met a man two years ago and he had a child from a previous relationship; things progressed, and we eloped to Northern California," I said with thoughts of my horrible home life flooding into my conscious mind.

"Are you happy?" Rick asked me point blank, watching my lip quiver and my face grow serious. I looked down at the ground.

"Marriage isn't the easiest thing, it takes two people to work on it," I said trying to put some enthusiasm in my voice, "for better or worse." I smiled weakly and Rick stepped back behind the table looking defeated. He took out the registration form and handed it to me to fill out.

As I filled out the form, I began to share my journey with Rick, and I listened as he told me about finishing college and fulfilling his dream as a computer engineer. He now worked for Apple and was one of their first employees. The company was doing well and he had afforded a home. He told me he never forgot me and times when business brought him down to Orange County, he thought of me. We exchanged polite information with me sharing few graphic details of my life with Jim. The beatings had not gotten *really* bad, but pushing, throwing, and verbal threats were commonplace. The conversation stalled and felt strained as I handed Rick the job registration figuring I better start walking home before Jim came in and found me talking to a man. As I said goodbye and started toward the door, Rick rushed over and grabbed my hand pressing a note into it.

"Jeanne, you don't need to say anything, but if you ever need a friend to talk to, please give me a call." I kept the paper but jerked my hand away. What was I thinking? I was married. How insane was this taking a phone number from another man? I felt nervous and looked up at the clock, realizing Mass had ended over thirty minutes ago.

"Rick, I need to go." Rick looked at me and held his gaze without flinching.

"Call me, if you ever need anything or just want to talk." I tucked the piece of paper deep into my purse, grabbed Leah, and bounded quickly down the street. We were home in a few minutes and the TV was still blaring. A row of five beer bottles lined the coffee table in front of Jim. He barely noticed we were home. I tried to usher Leah into her bedroom, taking out a few toys from the closet to occupy her and keep her quiet. I was hoping Jim didn't ask about the service. I put on a pair of jeans and a t-shirt, readying myself for a riveting night of *Dallas* and a glass of wine. As I came out and passed through the living room Jim was obviously drunk and getting belligerent.

"Well, how is Saint Jeanette doing?" he asked sarcastically. I wasn't quite sure how to answer. If I said okay, he'd be mad. If I didn't answer, he'd probably be mad. I answered.

"The Mass was good, a little long. . . some priests will go on," I said holding my breath. I clanged a pan onto the stove a little harder than I needed to. I was going to make burgers and pork and beans for dinner. Jim hollered from the living room.

"Shut up in there, all that clanging around. Can't you do anything right? You stupid or something? Shut up, don't you know that I'm trying to watch a show?" He paused, and I could hear him taking a long drag off his cigarette. "Hey, make dinner. I said you could go to church. I didn't say you could be gone all night. It's almost dark out, and Leah and I are starving. What's for dinner?"

he asked, slurring his words. I rolled my eyes and wanted to spit in his food.

"Burgers and beans, honey. You know you love hot cheeseburgers," I said drippy sweet, feeling trapped and angry. Why was my life like this? I heard Jim let out a growl.

"Well now, I'm hungry! Quit sucking up to me, you stupid whore. Make me and my kid some dinner!" he yelled. The undying love that Jim had professed earlier had quickly dissolved and my love with it.

"Coming honey, I know you're hungry. Dinner will be ready in twenty minutes." I focused on cooking, but remembered the phone number in my purse. I wanted to start over. I wanted to end this awful marriage and at the same time wanted to make it work. I wanted to experience a happy marriage with Jim. I didn't want to be an abused wife and called horrible names. I was married; I took my vows and knew I would never consider another man. I could never lose my precious Leah and knew if I ever left I would never see her again.

I served a nice, hot plate that looked like it came fresh out of a fancy restaurant. Every meal included two side dishes and garnish, just like a regular restaurant. I called to Jim and Leah to please come to dinner. Jim stumbled and just about fell over the chair as he sat down. He mumbled something and I recognized his request for a beer and I rushed over to get one. I prayed quickly, as Jim dove into the hot cheeseburger and sweet pork and beans, served with home-fried potatoes. Jim raised an eyebrow and spewed some obscenities.

"You go to church once in your life and now you think you are Mother Teresa." He let out a very ugly laugh. I would not let Jim bother me tonight. I felt better because I had gone to church and met an old friend. I felt closer to God and encouraged, thinking I might learn how to use a computer and give myself a better chance in life.

As I was cleaning the dishes, Jim got ready as usual and told me he had a meeting. I knew better than to say anything; so he did his usual kiss on the head to Leah and me on the cheek and out the door he went. I put on *Dallas*, curled up with a glass of wine, and enjoyed the peace, at least for a few hours.

I thought about Rick and the phone number. I wanted so much to call him, but knew that would be wrong. If I took the job and learned the basic Apple computer programming, Rick would be the teacher. There was some talk in the news that personal computers would be a reality and Apple Computer would be the company to revolutionize the world. Apple Computer actually thought people would have a computer on every desk in every office and someday people would have computers in their homes. What would they think of next? I wasn't sure, but I felt learning computers would be a great thing. It could possibly open doors for me in the future and may have a positive impact on my life.

The only thing computers would change in my life at this time was negotiating working at the restaurant and juggling classes. The church wasn't far from my house, but it would be two hours a week. If I snuck around to try to take a class and Jim found out, I'd pay severely for my deception. I decided the best thing would be to tell the truth and ask if I could take a class at church.

I got my chance a few days later when Jim came home early from work and began rushing around getting dressed up. He must have a hot date, I mused. I think I had another female infection and started feeling poorly again. I mentioned this to Jim and he told me to call and make an appointment for next week, and he'd take me. Jim approached, holding two shirts; he asked me to choose one of the shirts to match his black slacks. I chose one wondering if his bar fly girlfriend would appreciate my taste. As he was pulling the shirt on, I mentioned a class at church I saw in the bulletin, not telling Jim I'd be learning Apple computers. Jim quickly agreed not paying me much attention. It would be okay, as long as. . . now the warning came again. . . it didn't interfere with me being *his* wife and taking care of *his* kid. I thanked him nonchalantly and breathed a sigh of relief.

I was supposed to work on Tuesday morning, but felt terrible. I had a fever and a dull ache in my lower abdomen. I told Jim I made an appointment to see a doctor, and felt I should go right in because I had bad discharge that looked serious. Jim took me to the doctor, and I experienced the same treatment I received from the doctor in Half Moon Bay. Am I married? Am I monogamous? Do I have other partners? Jim took the doctor aside again as the nurse prepared me for dual shots of penicillin to be injected into both hips. This time they sent us home with two bottles of penicillin pills and a sharp warning by both the doctor and his nurse for us to take the pills and make sure we took the whole bottle. Another infection? Jim accused me of not being clean enough and made a comment in the car about me getting him sick all the time. Jim's comment really hurt because I was positive I couldn't have given him an infection so serious that we both needed medication. I remembered Betty Lowry's comment about the bar flies and their "germs" and cringed. If Jim was unfaithful, he was probably giving me these horrible infections. I took the pills and after a few days, felt better.

I went back to work at the restaurant and contacted the church to let them know I would like to enroll in the computer training classes as soon as possible. I knew they were desperate for a new teacher, and I wanted to be one of the first volunteers.

Rick stood outside the training classroom on the church grounds as I rode up on my bike, gym shorts showing underneath my uniform skirt. I set the kick-stand and walked toward the room. Rick frowned.

"You don't have a car, do you?" he asked, and I flushed and looked down towards the ground avoiding his face.

"Uh no, I uh. . . sold my car before moving to Half Moon Bay last year and haven't had a car since." I could feel Rick's disapproval. He didn't know what I had gotten into with Jim, but I think he had a good idea. Rick led me into the classroom and introduced me to the other students who were there to learn how to use a computer. The computer class was fascinating. We studied how the big box and monitor worked, and then Rick demonstrated our instructor workbook, one lesson at a time with our class. We would learn how to enter basic commands into the computer to make different shapes. In our advanced classes, we would enter commands that would show us how to make the shapes move on the small screen. I shuddered when my mind wandered and I thought of life with Rick instead of Jim. If Jim knew I was taking a computer class from an old grade school sweetheart, he'd probably murder me.

CHAPTER 17
THE 25K GIFT

Nearing Christmas of 1981 I completed my computer classes and looked forward to teaching a class of students immediately after the New Year. I continued to work like a dog each day, clipping coupons, saving my tip money and paying for daycare. The frantic pace didn't dull my enthusiasm; I felt an overwhelming excitement and victory with my secret knowledge of programming and using a computer! I tried to get into the spirit of the season and mentioned to Jim that maybe Leah would like to decorate a Christmas tree. He grumbled as usual and said we only threw them away so why bother. Jim mentioned his mother had called and left a message at the office; apparently his parents wanted to come up before Christmas. Jim began to swear and badmouth his parents.

"I don't know why they want to come up. Suddenly in the Christmas spirit. My mom wants to bring up some nice gifts for you, Leah, and me." Jim paused, and took a long drag off of his cigarette, blowing a thick blue stream of smoke in my general direction. I had gotten so sick of the smell of smoke in the house. The house had ashtrays everywhere and a stale yellow haze continually loomed inside. Mr. Bilbao did not know Jim smoked. Jim hid that fact and outright lied when he wrote non-smokers on the application. Jim continued the tirade about his parents.

"My dad is a filthy man. He drinks too much and will probably hit on you or anything else in a skirt after a few bourbons. My mother will chain smoke and pretend she doesn't drink, but I'm sure I'll have to carry her to bed; hopefully they won't get sick." It didn't sound too appealing, but these *were* Leah's grandparents and maybe a nice visit with family would do Jim some good.

"I think it might be a good idea if they came up, Jim. It would give them a chance to get to know Leah and she would have a chance to spend time with her grandparents. How long did they say they were going to stay?" I asked from the small kitchen, getting a broiling chicken ready for the roasting pan. Jim came into the kitchen and scowled.

"You really don't want to do this! I'll bring them up, but I'm warning you, it will be a bad idea." I nodded my head.

"Tell them that you have work commitments, and maybe they'll only stay a night or two," I suggested, craving a "normal" family Christmas holiday. Jim acquiesced.

"Okay, I know my mother would love to see me. I *was* always her favorite," Jim said smugly, warming to the idea. I thought of the wall of pictures in the small dark hallway, and the warning Anne had given me when she had thought we were already married.

"If you decide to invite them let me know when they're coming and I can sew some curtains and get the extra room ready." I began to get excited. It had been so long since I had seen my family; any family would help my deep homesick feeling.

About a week before Christmas, the Millers arrived as planned. Emil and Anne Miller pulled up to the house. Emil walked up and Jim greeted his father stiffly. Jim helped Emil with the bags and chatted about the drive and the new car they had just purchased. Anne didn't get out of the car. At first, I thought she was getting something and would get right out, but as I approached her side of the car—door slightly ajar, window down—I looked into her face, stained with tears and smeared make-up. She shook her head, leaned over, and began digging into her purse searching for a tissue.

"I know I must look a mess," Anne apologized, embarrassed. "Emil was a wreck last week, and the drive was horrible." I didn't know how to react, so I shook my head and placed my hand on her shoulder. As soon as I touched her, she began to sob and shudder, spasms wracking her body. I didn't know what to make of it. Emil had gone into the house like nothing was wrong.

"I am so sorry, Mrs. Miller. It sounds like an awful trip." Anne started to sniff and pulled down the car mirror, quickly glancing up at the house to track her husband's whereabouts. She rubbed her face hard and fast, moistening the tissue with her tongue and cleaning up the telltale make-up stains.

"You don't know the half of it. These Miller men. . . they are crazy. They're possessed, I tell you!" She began spewing anger and tears. "Last week, Emil got mad at me because I hadn't used enough starch on his shirts. He pulled the shirts off the hangers tearing each one and every button flew onto the floor. After he made a complete wreck of the bedroom, he grabbed the hangers and began beating me over the back with them. I started running as fast as I could. I ran into the backyard and towards the pool. Emil was right behind me and pushed me into the pool with all of my clothes on." I listened in horror and complete disbelief and shock.

"I started to climb out, and as soon as I looked up, there was Emil. He had a hammer in his hand and was swinging wildly at my head, trying to push me down under the water. I was pretty sure this would be the end; he would finally kill me." Anne looked like she was reliving the fear, her blue eyes brimming with tears again, her face wrinkled in an awful frown. "After a few moments, he looked at me and laughed, telling me I wasn't worth it. I was only a. . . a. . . a. . . whore." With that, Anne burst into tears again. "Can you believe it, a whore? I'm sixty-six years old and a whore!" I stood still, not saying anything, but kept my hand on her shoulder, trying to comfort this poor woman whom I did not know. Anne continued and expertly applied a coat of Borghese lipstick to her trembling lips. "Well, I didn't speak with Emil for days; I cooked and cleaned, but he knew I was more than mad. So this time, even though he kept bringing me perfume and flowers, notes and letters declaring his undying love for me, I would not budge. I wasn't going to give in that easily. He almost killed me!" Anne fidgeted in her purse and pulled out a gold-beaded cigarette case. After lighting one and taking a long drag, her tears slowed and her shaking ceased. "I know I shouldn't be burdening you with this. You are new to the family and all, but I just couldn't take the car ride. He was horrible again."

She looked up at the house, not seeing anyone, and continued, "A few days later, Emil came home with this." Anne held up a thick gold chain from around her neck, a Liberty gold dollar mounted in stunning setting surround by a bezel of quite large diamonds. She watched my jaw drop. That was easily worth a nice down payment on a house! "It's appraised at $25K," Anne said triumphantly.

"Wow, that's a fantastic piece," I said admiring the necklace and silently thanking God that my father never bought anything for my mother to apologize for violent or abusive behavior. Anne smiled and then quickly remembered the trip.

"After Emil gave me the necklace I acted like I always do— kissed him and hugged him, thanking him for the generous gift. Emil smiled and went back to life as it always was. But the car ride was awful. He was cussing at all the other drivers. I was the navigator, and Emil made me so nervous I didn't do a good job. We got lost a few times. He hates it when I smoke in the car, so I was a mess. The last time we got lost, he slammed on the brakes, dragged me out of the car, and left me on the side of the road. About an hour later, he came back for me. I was sitting on a metal highway barrier, on I-5 in the middle of nowhere, sobbing! Emil found a bar somewhere and had a drink. This was good; it calmed him down. He finally picked me up and we drove over here—without getting lost! I've been crying all afternoon. I just couldn't stop."

Some noise was coming from the house – it was Emil. He was calling sweetly for his "Snoogie Lumps." Anne rolled her eyes and gathered her composure. "Honey, can you please help me get out of the car?" Anne looked up and extended her hand. Even with the puffy face and tear stained cheeks, she was beautiful.

I prepared a very elaborate and expensive appetizer tray, using imported cheeses, meats, and exotic European delicacies. Emil looked up as I added fresh ice and poured bourbon into his glass.

"Bring it on, girlie," Emil said with a twisty tone, already sounding a little drunk. "I like it when you keep my glass full." Jim was right; he did drink too much. Raised the daughter of Dominic and Mary, I was trained to be a gracious and accommodating hostess. I would do my very best, so I smiled and tried to pretend life was perfect.

The rest of the two-day visit before the Millers left was uneventful. Emil was really edgy most of the time, but as long as we kept driving to the mall or keeping a schedule, he didn't get angry. He was very aloof and indifferent to little Leah. It was heartbreaking. Leah would see her grandfather sitting on the couch reading a newspaper and would approach, trying to get some attention. Each time Leah attempted to connect with him, Emil would yell, tell her to be quiet, or to stop rustling his paper. Leah finally quit trying. On the other hand, Anne was genuinely loving and gracious, taking Leah for short walks down the street and reading her stories. She interacted with Leah and played dollies with her on the floor. Anne seemed to love Leah and was very good to her. Leah adored her Grandma Anne and climbed up on her lap any time Anne was sitting down. How did such a nice woman like Anne get stuck with a cruel and hateful man like Emil? I kept thinking about the pool and hammer—that would be me someday, I mused. I breathed a sigh of relief when the Millers' car pulled away from the curb en route to Orange County.

CHAPTER 18
A BOX EXPLODES

After Christmas break, my computer classes picked up again. Rick would drop into my class to check on how things were going and offer assistance if needed. I was very self-sufficient and knew Rick used helping me as an excuse to say hello and see how I was. Tutoring was a breeze, but things at home were not good and many days I craved Rick's friendly smile and warm greeting. January was cold in Sunnyvale, but out of necessity, I continued to ride my bike everywhere.

More frequently Jim would stay in bed after a late night out and wouldn't mention work at all. I attributed it to poor winter weather. I would never wake him for fear of the wrath that would ensue. My paychecks at the restaurant were paltry and the joint checking account that Jim and I shared was overdrawn. I just didn't understand it; Jim was bringing home a paycheck and seemed to have a lot of money. I was paying house bills with my restaurant checks and buying groceries and paying for daycare with tips. I rarely used the account, yet Jim seemed to drain it every week.

It all began to make sense one Saturday morning in January of 1982. Jim was awake when I got up. When I entered the small dining room, he was sitting in a cloud of smoke playing cards set up for solitaire. He had a frighteningly wild look on his face. Leah was sitting on the floor with her blanket, about four feet in front of the television. The volume was down so low you could barely tell the TV was on. I walked by Jim and he waved to me with the back of his hand, cigarette burning in his fingers and another one lit and burning in an overflowing ashtray. He mumbled something unintelligible without looking up. I was startled, feeling the hair prickle on the back of my neck as I viewed the collection of drug paraphernalia scattered in front of him next to the ashtray and the line of beer bottles. There was a glass water pipe, a small mirror with chunks of small white rocks on it, a razor blade, and a Bunsen burner type glass bulb with a flaming wick. I didn't say anything and went around the corner and into the kitchen where panic set in.

He was doing some kind of drugs, heroin or something. I wasn't quite sure. Jim looked very scary. He didn't seem to care the baby was sitting right near him, smoke filling up the small room. I put water in a teakettle as I always did and decided I'd start making eggs as if nothing were happening. I poked my head out of the kitchen and watched as Jim held the pipe up to his lips, put the burner underneath the pipe, and sucked the smoke deep into his lungs. His eyes rolled back in his head. I decided it wasn't a good time to ask him anything. He was a drug addict; this explained his erratic behavior and hours away from the house. I had some suspicions; now it was confirmed. A drug addict! I was married to a drug addict! How did this happen?

A moment later, I heard Jim saying something to Leah. She ran next to him to snuggle near his side. He wasn't really talking, but was mumbling. I figured it would be a good time to ask about breakfast. I sucked in my breath and tried to sound normal.

"Honey, are you ready for eggs, tea, and toast?" I asked cheerfully and watched as Jim shook his head in disagreement, putting the pipe back up to his lips.

I started the breakfast as Jim sat there, smoking up his supply of white rocks from the mirror. As I served Leah the eggs in the living room, a loud whining from an engine sound startled me. Frank Bilbao was in the back yard with his lawn mower. He was there promptly at 9:00 a.m. each week. I was certain Frank could see through the curtains easily, observing Jim abusing illegal drugs in his pristine rental house, but apparently not. Frank finished mowing the back lawn and started out to the front, pulling the yard waste receptacle to the curb. There was a knock at the door. Jim looked up and shook his head, warning me not to open the door, but Frank knew we were home. What could I do? I couldn't open the door. Jim was like a zombie and there were drugs and smoke everywhere. I quickly ran out the back slider and down the side yard path to the front door.

"Good morning, Frank!" I said as cheerfully as possible. I startled Frank causing his head to whip around. "I heard you in the backyard and came out to say good morning. I guess you were coming round the front." Frank smiled and nodded, his face suddenly turned serious.

"Jeanette, I think you and Jim are great kids and all, but as of last week, you're exactly two months behind on rent. I have your deposit, but need to get at *least* one month payment, or I'm going to have to ask you to move out." Frank looked like he hated telling me we weren't paying. I had no idea Jim wasn't paying the rent and had to think fast. We had about $40 in the bank; adding my next paycheck of $115 or so wouldn't come close to the $650. Was Frank going to evict us? My heart began to pound as I started telling Frank an outright lie.

"Frank, things have been a little slow at Jim's work with the weather and all. I promise we'll try to have the rent this Friday." I smiled weakly. Frank looked worried. I felt he was thinking I looked a little thin and was probably lying.

"Is Jim home? I'd like to ask him when he could bring over the rent. Can you please get him?" Frank asked peering through the front windows as he asked. I panicked hoping Frank could not see Jim with a drug pipe to his lips, and feeling overwhelming guilt from lying to this nice man.

"Er, Frank. . . uh, Jim's not feeling well this morning. Maybe by lunch, he'll feel better. I promise I'll have him go over and talk to you about the rent." Frank nodded, said goodbye, and pushed his mower down the street back to his house. I waited until I was certain Frank was gone and went back into the house the way I had come out.

Jim was still sitting at the table staring down at the solitaire and reshuffling every once in a while. Three or four cigarettes sat burning in the ashtray and the little white rocks were all gone from the mirror. Jim looked up with a crazed, wide-eyed look. He asked me in a very slurry voice about Frank.

"Frank said he wanted to talk to us," I examined Jim's face to see if he would react. No reaction, so I continued. "He said we were two months behind on rent." I kept looking at Jim, no reaction, but an empathetic nod and grunt. "He wants you to bring him the rent later today, okay?" I asked. Jim nodded, mumbled, and guzzled the rest of the beer sitting in front of him at the table. It was weird, if I had ever said anything to Jim about the rent before, he would have exploded. But now, with the drugs, he took it in and grunted in agreement to my urging.

I was confused, scared, and unsure of what to do. I had to get my head together, calm down, and figure out a plan. No money, a child to support, an abusive husband who was apparently using drugs, and a landlord threatening eviction. My mind kept reflecting back to my parents' marriage; my father and mother mentioned to all four of us kids throughout the years how they worked to make a good marriage. They *made* their marriage work, but there was no abuse, no infidelity and no drugs or alcohol involved! Jim spent the rest of the day locked in the bathroom. I figured he was doing more of his drugs in there. What if he had a heart attack and died. . . that would be a Godsend, I thought.

A few hours later, Jim emerged looking less wild-eyed. He had a towel around his waist and was getting ready to go out. I was so glad he was leaving and taking his illegal drugs out of our house! Performing his usual schedule, Jim dressed in his best clothes, while I watched television and Leah played. Jim mumbled goodbye, gave me a perfunctory kiss, and patted Leah on the head.

I was extremely unhappy, very angry and resentful at that moment and I wanted to be somewhere, anywhere but where I was. I loved Leah deeply and I wanted to break free, but knew

179

Jim would never let me leave, never let my life go on without him. Leah needed a mother and my heart was hers; Jim had crushed my heart and controlled it. After tucking Leah in bed, I struggled guiltily with wanting to call Rick, justifying he was just a friend and I needed a friend tonight. I relented and finally decided to give Rick a call, knowing it was wrong but feeling lonely and desperate.

I grabbed the cordless phone from the kitchen and walked into my bedroom, feeling like a huge sneak as I rustled into my drawer and found the small piece of paper with Rick's number. I couldn't shake the eerie feeling that someone was watching me. Glancing down at Rick's number with shaky hands, I dialed carefully holding my breath as the phone rang on the other side. I heard Rick's voice and could feel my heart beating wildly. Slowly, I began to speak:

"Rick, hi. . . it's me, Jeanne. . ." I continued. "You told me I could call you anytime just to talk," I said and realized telling Rick the truth about my husband smoking drugs in front of me today would sound surreal. I sucked in my breath and rushed on not waiting to hear Rick's response to a married woman calling him. "Rick, you know I'm married and I'm not really sure why I called...." I felt an overwhelming rush of emotions and held back tears, realizing my life was a total mess.

"Hey Jeanne, I *am* glad you called. I told you to call me anytime. I've wanted to reach out every time I've seen you teaching, but I've been unsure of how to approach you." He paused and then added, "Is everything ok with you, are you ok?" Thoughts of Jim flooded my mind, I shook my head hard. My life was awful. I thought about telling Rick the truth but couldn't.

"Yeah, I'm fine Rick, I shouldn't have called you. It was a terrible mistake... I am a married woman and really need to hang up," I lied, wishing my life was very different than it was and not really wanting to hang up. There was a long pause on the other end of the line and Rick huffed a little.

"Jeanne, I'm not sure what is going on with you, but like you said, you are a married woman. I won't keep you, but remember if you need anything, call me, I mean it. Good luck with your classes *and* your marriage. Good-bye, Jeanne," Rick said abruptly.

"Good-bye, Rick." I heard the front door slam as I hung up the phone. I spun around quickly as Jim burst through the bedroom door, my mouth instantly dry. . . His face was dark red with anger and with one giant move he grabbed my antique jewelry box from the dresser and raised it over my head readying to crush it into my skull. I dove onto the bed and watched in horror while my jewelry box crashed down onto the ground, slivering into a million pieces of mixed jewels, glass, and lacquered wood. My jewelry box was destroyed! Jim pounced on top of me crushing me onto the bed. He was angrier than I had ever seen him. I clutched my hands in front of my face to protect myself. Jim spat hatred and anger; his breath smelled of stale cigarettes and beer.

"You worthless whore! Who were you talking to?" he demanded as his hand rose above his head threatening to hit me. I shook my head from side to side not answering and felt my face sting like painful needles as Jim's hand slapped the side of my head. My ears began to ring and blood began to pour from my nose. He must have heard me on the phone! Jim slapped me hard again, and I felt like I was losing consciousness – this hit was so hard I lost control and wet the bed. "Who... who... Who in the world is Rick?" Jim screamed, spitting into my face. "Tell me, you worthless piece of dog crap! Is this the guy you're sleeping with every day while I'm out at work, paying for your sorry slime? Give me that idiot phone, you pig!" Jim jumped off the bed and grabbed the cordless phone hitting the redial button. I didn't move and prayed that Rick would not answer the phone. Jim held the phone up to my head, pushing one large hand over my throat and pressing hard, cutting off my air supply. He hissed at me to ask for Rick. I began to see black spots and nodded quickly, hoping to catch a breath. Rick answered and Jim let his hand off of my throat and I gasped a deep intake of air. Jim held his hand high poised to hit me if I didn't comply, as he heard the phone ring on the other end. I knew what to do.

"Rick?" I asked meekly.

"Jeanne?" Jim grabbed the phone and started in.

"Who are you, Rick? You sneaking piece of worthless crap, are you out sneaking around with my wife? You stay away from her from this day forward, or I'll kill you, do you understand me? If I ever find you two together, I'll pour acid on her face so no man will ever look at her again and I'll dice you into a million pieces, they'll never find a trace of you! If you so much as look at my wife again you are a dead man! I've done this before and I'd be happy to do it again! Do I make myself clear?!" Jim screamed, and I heard Rick answer yes.

After Rick hung up the phone, Jim slammed the phone onto the ground shattering it into a hundred pieces joining my antique jewelry box. "That will teach you to stay away from your boyfriend. You'll get the both of you killed." I gulped hard not moving from the bed. Jim continued his rampage, ripping my clothes off the hangers and pulling them out of my drawers and onto the floor. He grabbed my framed senior high school picture, broke the frame, took the picture out, and began ripping it into little pieces, laughing as he heard me cry.

"You are a slut! I knew I should have left you at Sunshine. You Italian pig, you are nothing but a whore who can't be trusted. You're a broken worthless hole too, two years no birth control and you can't even give me a baby. But it probably wouldn't be mine anyway. How many others are there, huh? Long list I guess . . . that's how you keep giving me VD! Is this how you're making your money on the side, screwing guys in the parking lot at work? Do you serve sandwiches and a side of sex?" Jim accused, getting angrier as he yelled and deciding he would make me pay for my crime. He stormed into the living room and I heard him open my guitar case. The guitar had been my prized possession and he knew it. Jim came into the bedroom and raised my happiness over his head, smashing it down into a pile of strings and wood. I just cried more. First my jewelry box, then my senior picture, my clothes torn to shreds and now my guitar – my heart was crushed into little pieces. How could Jim have ever really loved me if he treated me like this? I was nothing to him. I didn't move from the wet bed and tried to offer a lame apology, explaining that I really didn't know Rick, had just met him at the restaurant, and he had gotten my number from the manager. It was an outright lie, but I had to say something. I was afraid of what he would do to Rick, and I was really afraid I'd be hospitalized tonight or would end up in the morgue! Jim continued his tirade, screaming at me and then in a final display of his dominance and anger he flung himself on top of me, tearing off my clothes.

Jim then raped me violently, calling me filthy names. I lay there, tears mixing with blood streaming down my face, pain exploding through my body. After he was done, he screamed a few obscenities at me, punctuated by hits and slaps and punches on my sides, chest, arms, and stomach. I reeled with the pain and gasped with each hit. Jim finally seemed to tire of the game and jumped off me. I just lay there on the bed, partially naked, blood and tears still coming down my red, puffy, and swollen face. Jim straightened his clothes and warned me if I ever tried this stunt again, he'd kill me. I believed him. He told me he'd killed others for less. Jim looked down at me crying and laughed, called me a few more choice names, and slammed out the front door. I heard the car drive away but lay unmoving for a few moments to make sure he wasn't coming back through the door.

After a few moments, I got up and limped into the bathroom, feeling agony with each move. I dreaded looking into the mirror and rinsed my face and mouth, bright red blood splattering into the sink. When I finally looked up, I was indistinguishable. My eyes were almost swollen shut, my lips cut and bruised, and my nose was twice its size. I sobbed as I blotted the blood from my nose and stuffed toilet paper into my nostrils to prevent it from bleeding. After taking a quick, hot shower, fearful Jim would come back, I dutifully cleaned the entire room, throwing away glass, wood, and metal pieces into large paper bags, tears streaming down my face. I picked up clothes and put them somewhat where they belonged, stripped the bed, changed the sheets, and then went to bed. I would never talk to Rick again. I couldn't. Jim's threats were real. I was pretty certain he *could* kill me and would kill me if I provoked him.

I lay in bed and cried for a long time feeling very depressed and fearful. The only thing I owned, the only thing I had that represented my family, the only piece of my childhood, my prized jewelry box was gone. Every time I kept thinking about what had happened, I cried all over again. I cursed myself for being so stupid, talking to Rick on the phone by the window. I shouldn't have done it, I was married to Jim! I wanted to escape that night. I was now a prisoner in my own home. I doubted I'd ever have a chance to escape my prison alive and get out of the living nightmare. As I lay in bed crying and cursing my stupidity for ever calling Rick, I felt desperate for God to help me, to hear my prayer. I began to pray to Him as I curled up in the fetal position, pulling the covers tightly over my head as if protecting myself from anything bad.

Lord, I don't know if you're up there, and I don't know if you can hear me tonight, but Lord, please, I'm crying out to you. I'm scared God, and I'm hurting. I know I've made mistakes, and I am so sorry for what I've done, but Lord, I'm afraid I'm going to die. Lord, I need you to help me, to save me. Lord, I need you to let my parents know where I am and to keep me safe. Please Lord, please . . . answer my prayers. I finally fell asleep and woke to the birds singing in the trees. Jim had not come home and I was relieved. The next day, he still didn't come home. I couldn't help but feel anxious about the next time I would see him, but loved my life without him around. Days went by and still no Jim.

I worried not knowing where Jim was and felt overwhelmed, angry and stressed with the responsibility of overdue rent and a pile of red-stamped bills. The house was quiet and serene and Leah seemed happy, so I continued my life as if nothing was different. I lied to the people at work about a bike accident and nasty fall. Some of my co-workers gave me questioning looks, but I laughed and told them I was a real klutz sometimes.

I took Leah to daycare each day and taught my Junior High computer classes, scared to death I would run into Rick. Even though it was weird not having Jim at the house and I felt like I was in a trance, it was a needed break and allowed me time to clear my head. If Jim didn't come back, I would have no place to live. I certainly didn't make enough to pay the bills or rent. Maybe Leah and I could rent a room from some older couple and I could get a full-time job. How in the world could I even consider taking Leah? Wouldn't that be against the law? If I ever left and took Leah, I couldn't imagine the nightmare I'd have to endure once Jim found me.

CHAPTER 19
RECONCILIATION

The following week, Frank Bilbao came by, knocking for a long time on the front door while I hid in the house, warning Leah not to make a peep. He left a notice on the door with a very official final warning to "Pay Rent or Quit." I was shaking as I read the note. Each time I left the house and took Leah to daycare, I looked up and down the street to see if Frank was coming. I would have to do something soon; I figured Frank may come and change the locks any day.

Feeling overwhelmed I headed for church. I always felt a sense of peace when I was connecting with God. As I got closer to the parish on my bike, I saw Rick walking towards the sanctuary. This was the last person I wanted or needed to see. I parked my bike as he walked up. I looked down towards the ground, not making eye contact.

"Hey, I'm really sorry if I got you in trouble the other night, are you okay?" Rick asked with concern. As soon as he spoke I felt a lump in my throat and wanted to confide in him telling him what happened that night, telling him about my awful predicament. Instead, I sucked in my breath feigning a confidence that I certainly did not feel.

"It was my fault for calling you. I *am* a married woman, Jim was rightfully upset." I thought of my wedding ring and decided I could probably get $150 or so if I could find a pawnshop. I slowly lifted my head and looked into Rick's eyes and knew that I should never contact him again. Rick reached in his pocket and held out a piece of paper.

"Hey, I thought you could probably use an opportunity to get a good job, now that you know computers and all." I thought I saw Rick's mouth quiver a little as he spoke and realized this must be very difficult for him. I took the paper from Rick's hand and looked at the paper as Rick explained. "I have a good friend; he's an electronics engineer at Motorola Semiconductor. They have a sales office not far from here, and he mentioned they are looking for field sales associates. It would be a great job: pay is great, benefits, and it offers commissions too. You would be qualified because," Rick offered with emphasis, *"you know computers!"* My eyes lit up. Rick knew if I landed the job, this would be a much-needed boost for my life.

"I can't guarantee anything; all I have is a name and number of who to call for an interview. You'd have to get a resume typed out," Rick added. "You could type the resume in our church office before you leave today, and if you interview well they may hire you. It's full-time and maybe Leah could go to school. It's worth a shot, huh?" Rick was trying to help. I think he had an idea of my situation, but doubted he could imagine the wrath I endured that night.

"Thanks, Rick, that would be fantastic. Do you have a template I could use?" I looked up at Rick and smiled meekly. Although I was petrified Jim might catch me, I went ahead and followed Rick to his church office and in no time, I held ten copies of my first professional resume.

As I walked from the office, I thanked Rick sincerely, told him goodbye without even a shake of the hand, and felt the lump in my throat again. I knew that would be the last time I would ever see Rick. As I was riding my bike towards Leah's daycare, my resumes carefully tucked into my book bag, I thanked God and felt He heard my prayers for help that night.

Later as Leah and I were eating dinner, I heard the garage door open. Leah jumped off her chair excitedly chanting "Daddy, Daddy," and I swallowed hard not knowing what to expect! Leah ran to her daddy and hugged his legs, moving with him as he came towards me. I froze. . . looking down at my plate and seeing through the corner of my eye the looming dark figure that was supposed to be my protector and lover enter the dining room. Jim was holding a beautiful bouquet of two-dozen red roses in a crystal vase, festooned with a large pink bow. Jim sat down and looked at me, sliding the roses towards the middle of the table in front of me. He placed a small black velvet case beside my plate and arranged an oversized pink greeting card against the vase. Jim looked dashing, was wearing new clothes and smiling broadly at me.

"Hey there, my love," Jim said, speaking to me with admiration and love as he had when we first met. "Did you miss me? Sorry I've been gone a few days, but I have great news. I have a new job!"

Jim announced. I kept looking down and pushed the food around my plate. Jim ran his hand through my long blonde hair and kept professing his admiration for me. "Jeanette, you know you're the only one who knows me the way you do. We can't throw this away and try to build this with other people, right?" I turned towards Jim, but couldn't bring myself to face him. I was angry, hurt, and very confused. Yes, yes, I wanted a good marriage, but I wanted a safe place to live. I wanted a husband who loved me. I wanted a "normal" life.

Jim continued, "Wifer, you know that you shouldn't call other men. Any guy would get mad about that, right? You know this was your fault, I never meant to hurt you." Jim kept his gaze on my eyes. I knew I was wrong taking Rick's number. I never should have called him. It was wrong; I knew it was. I *was* married, but so deeply unhappy. The horrible night flashed into my mind reliving Jim the abusive monster attacking me. I looked up at Jim and tears started coming down my face. I was confused. I only wanted a good marriage. I didn't want a divorce and a new husband. I wanted a man like my father, a man who treated me with respect. I needed a good man to love me and protect me. Jim kept caressing my hair and ran his hand down the side of my face cupping my chin in his large hand. "Let's give it a shot. I love you so much and don't want to live without you. Leah needs a father and a mother. Let's have a baby and make a go of this." Jim had tears in his eyes. I felt my heart soften, desperately craving human attention and love.

Jim knelt down in front of me, a tear running down his cheek. He handed me the small velvet box and smiled up at me. "Open it, my love," Jim said sincerely. I opened the case and inside the box was the hugest diamond ring I had ever seen. I figured it was at least three carats and made my wedding ring look small. "Put it on. You know, I love you and never want us to fight again. . . deal?" Jim asked standing up and lifting me to my feet. I put the ring on, moved by the moment, and we embraced in a perfect hug. At that moment, I lied to myself and pretended I had the perfect marriage and that everything was normal—everything was perfect.

Jim excitedly told me about his new construction job, told me he was putting down the drugs, and some of his guys were coming tomorrow morning to put our stuff in storage until we moved into the new house we were buying. I couldn't believe my ears. We were buying a house? I quickly forgot all of the last scary episodes and started dreaming about the wonderful news, buying a house! That was every young couple's dream!

The Homeless Family

As we loaded the Jag, I told Jim I would call and quit my restaurant job. He agreed that this would be a good idea, since we were moving to San Jose. It would be hard to get to work with the bike and all.

"Jim. . . hey. . . uh, I heard about another job from a customer of mine today. You think I might put in an application? I think it's in San Jose," I said while putting hanging clothes into trash bags, tying the bottoms to prevent the clothes from falling out. Jim looked up for a second, and I held my breath. He kept focusing on quickly getting his things together.

"Why don't we move into the house first, and then we'll talk about another job for you, okay?" Jim asked. I agreed.

Close to midnight, we checked into the Cozy 8 Motel. The hotel was on a busy boulevard in San Jose bordering a fairly seedy area. The room had two double beds and a small bathroom.

Each morning Jim went to work, while I tried to keep Leah quiet and occupied. She needed to start kindergarten in the fall and I hoped I could get her enrolled before it was too late. I wasn't exactly sure where we were going to live, but I was trusting Jim. We were moving to a new house, and it was going to be ours! Jim was working each day and acted happy and calm, not argumentative at all. He didn't seem to be smoking much, and although he still stayed out late just about every night, I didn't think he was doing any drugs.

Jim had a wallet full of hundred dollar bills, and we had money for food and for the motel. Leah and I ate a lot of sandwiches and had an ice chest for milk, cheese, and deli. We weren't the only family living at the Cozy 8. Next door was a family of four: a father, two grown sons, and one teenage daughter. They all lived there while working a temporary project in the family construction business. Apparently, their home was in Seattle and they had a few more weeks to finish a job in Sunnyvale before going back home.

A few weeks into the stay at the Cozy 8 Motel, Jim came through the door of the room looking wild-eyed. I took a quick breath and held it, feeling frightened immediately as Jim mumbled something unintelligible and retreated to the locked bathroom where he remained for the next three hours. Drugs! My heart sank, he was on drugs again. We were trying to buy a house and now Jim was on drugs again. Leah was fast asleep when Jim finally came out and with a low and stern tone in his voice, demanded I turn off all the lights and the television. I quickly complied. I watched in horror as Jim lay on the floor creeping on his hands and knees toward the door and two sets of drapes. Once under the drapes, he used a hanger to pull the drapes out to see who was walking by the room.

"They're out there. I just know they are," Jim said with slurred speech. I didn't know who he was talking about. Did this have something to do with drug dealers or the eviction notice?

"Who's out there, Jim? Are you in trouble?" I asked becoming as flat as I could and not moving from the bed. Pacing from one side of the room to the other, Jim continued to peer out the drapes looking for his enemy. He shushed me and to my surprise said:

"The Russians. . . they are out to get me. I see them outside – they are coming to get me!" He was hallucinating! Jim continued to look out the windows for several hours while I lay still, realizing he was experiencing some kind of drug paranoia. I fell asleep, and in the morning Jim was sleeping hard. What a strange night. I hoped when Jim woke up he would be himself again and would not creep across the floor on his belly. I wanted to walk to the little store up the street to buy some more milk and bread, but was afraid to open the door without Jim's approval. I kept Leah quiet by reading books and coloring with her.

It was close to noon when Jim finally woke up. He seemed back to himself as he hugged Leah and me and then took a shower. When dressed, Jim announced he was famished, he was taking us all to lunch and then we'd swing by to see the new house. I was excited and felt a sense of relief with this information. I was getting worried we would be living at the Cozy 8 forever. After lunch, we drove a few blocks and stopped in front of a darling white house with soft blue trim. The house was in a nice suburban neighborhood and right across the street from an elementary school. It was perfect.

Although we couldn't get in, I peered into every accessible window and was thrilled when I saw a pool in the back yard. What a wonderful home, I thought, imagining summer cookouts and pool parties. I was walking on cloud nine, Leah was bouncing around and Jim seemed happy and content.

"So honey, when do you think we'll move in?" I asked. Jim frowned.

"Well, it's a little complicated . . ." he began, and I started to feel dread in the pit of my stomach. "I have a business partner. Since our credit isn't the best, we're making the payments, and he's signing on the loan. After a few months, he'll quick deed the property to us." I had never heard of this before, but there was *no way* I was going to question it. I nodded my head showing enthusiasm and approval.

Two weeks later I met Bill Steward, Jim's partner. We arrived at the new house, the Jag stuffed to the gills. A moment later, a handsome, well-groomed man in his fifties, driving a shiny black Mercedes and sporting a gold Rolex pulled into the driveway. Leah and I stayed in the car while Jim ran and greeted him with an exuberant handshake. Jim and Bill talked quietly for a few moments, while I looked on. Jim finally waved me over and introduced me to Bill. I nodded uttering a polite greeting. Jim opened the front door to our new home and we all toured the house together.

When Bill saw the master bathroom, he said in a voice that sounded shockingly effeminate, "Oh my goodness, Jim, would you just come here! Don't hate me, I absolutely love the wallpaper in this bathroom!" Jim leaned close to Bill and viewed the wallpaper, nodding in agreement, not seeming to sense my alarm. I felt my stomach constrict tightly as my mind replayed the scenes with Ken Tuttle in Corona del Mar. Bill was obviously gay. He was Jim's "partner"? Is this where Jim spent all those days away from Leah and me? I pushed down disgusting thoughts. I was so happy to be moving into a real home and out of the Cozy 8; I forced myself to forget any thoughts of Jim and Bill Steward. We had a house, Jim had a job and things were looking up.

We moved into our new house without any major life disruption. I mentioned to Jim again how much I was hoping to get a job. A few days later, I called the Motorola office. The receptionist told me they were still interviewing for the position and to come by and drop off a resume or mail one. Since I lived two blocks away, and didn't have a car, I decided to walk and bring my resume. I wanted the job.

When I reached the office, a very welcoming receptionist named Valerie smiled, explaining she would see if anyone might be available for an interview. When Valerie looked down and realized I had a little girl with me, she pulled out a pad of paper and some colored pens and handed them to me. I leaned over expressing how I really needed the job and my daughter would be starting school soon. Valerie nodded, reading my desperation, smiled, and buzzed the boss to see if I might have a chance to interview. She winked and told me she'd keep an eye on my daughter while I interviewed.

When Lou Givens came out, I was thankful she hadn't noticed Leah sitting quietly on the lobby chair coloring with Valerie's pens. I quickly stood up, extended my hand, without breaking gaze, and confidently introduced myself. Lou ushered me into her private corner office where she perused my resume. I was extremely nervous and tried not to let it show; I needed this job. She asked me how fast I typed and if I took dictation. She seemed impressed when we discussed my computer skills and understanding. There were few employees who had ever used word processing programs and fewer who knew how to use a computer. I knew basic programming and computer functions. I knew this skill would give me an edge over the other candidates.

"Well Jeanette, I have two really great applicants. Although you do have excellent computer skills, you don't really have a proven sales record." I smiled genuinely at the petite, middle-aged woman, and figured if I wanted to land this job, I better sell Lou on myself. I mustered all of the self-confidence and composure I could and then began.

"Lou," I started out sounding as sincere as I could. "First, I want to thank you for taking the time to meet with me today. I am certain you have excellent candidates; however, *I am confident I would be the very best choice of any candidate you could hire.* I'm a quick learner. I already know the computer, and I'll make it really easy for you. Give me a month. If after a month, I don't *exceed* your expectations, we can part friends." I smiled and paused for a moment, and then asked: "What is the expected start date?" Lou smiled, acknowledging that I had just given her my best sales pitch.

"All right, I'll give you a chance because your pitch was pretty darn good. Bring the completed packet, and if this works out with your schedule, you can start next Monday." Lou handed me a new-hire packet and salary information, shook my hand, and then saw me down the hallway and towards the lobby. I prayed Leah wouldn't come out yelling, and that Lou would turn around and go back into her office. She did, closing the door. I walked back through the lobby, new-hire packet in hand, with a huge triumphant smile. Valerie nodded at me, and I thanked her profusely. Motorola Semiconductor hired *me* as a field sales associate. My base salary would be $19,500 and I would make commissions! Now, my challenge was how to get Leah into school and tell Jim I had a full-time job.

RECONCILIATION

CHAPTER 20
GUNS

Landing the job at Motorola was the best thing that could have ever happened to me. They offered a comprehensive training program on electronics and semiconductors. I easily understood the technology and became the technical assistant to three electronics engineers. The engineers met with large clients like Hewlett Packard and Memorex, selling the technical benefits found by designing Motorola semiconductors into their products. My sales activities increased as well as my technical abilities. I was almost always number one in sales for the entire western region.

As capable as I was in the office, I was nothing at home. Jim was working sporadically and I was certain he was using drugs again. Every time I deposited my paycheck in the bank the money quickly disappeared, causing my checks to bounce. I began cashing my checks and hanging onto the money so I could pay bills and buy groceries. The predictable cycles of abuse escalated. Jim would get agitated, become violent and tear down doors and punch holes in the walls. He would leave for days at a time and then come home with gifts and empty apologies. I would forgive him to keep peace, and then it would start all over again. When he was home for any length of time, he was restless, became rude, and abusive. Many nights when he came home late and drunk, he would force himself on me.

One Friday night in the spring of 1984, Jim came home at about 9:00 p.m. with the "wild look" on his face. Leah was bathed and in bed. I was doing what I did most nights—sitting alone on the couch and watching television. Jim murmured something about being in a lot of trouble, and he fled to the back room. After emerging from his cocaine freebasing party of one in the bathroom, Jim came into the living room waving a gun around my head.

"Get your idiot head down and turn the lights off now!" he commanded, eyes bulging, mouth open wide, head snapping from left to right in a spasmodic movement. Jim flung the gun towards me gesturing for me to shut off the television. I wasn't sure if he was going to shoot me, or if the gun was going to go off. I quickly responded to his demand and turned off the lights and television. I took refuge in Leah's room lying down on the twin bed next to her. I shook violently with fear, not knowing if I would live through the night. For the next several hours, I lay there praying to God for protection, not making a sound while Jim crept around peering through each window, holding the loaded gun up with both hands ready to shoot a dangerous perpetrator.

The next morning, I awoke to Leah's little seven-year-old hands on both of my cheeks, oblivious to the crazed terror her father put me through the night before. I put a single finger up to my lips and gave her the warning with my eyes. She knew the drill. Daddy was probably asleep, and we shouldn't make a lot of noise to wake him. I tiptoed by the master bedroom and saw Jim hard asleep, fully clothed, gun by his side. I softly closed the door and grabbed Leah, escorting her to the kitchen to make breakfast.

I left a note and we walked hand-in-hand across the street to the playground at the school. A few hours later, I saw Jim walk through the gate of the chain link fence. He approached, and I didn't say a word. What could I say? He was a drug addict, and we both knew it. Things had always been bad, but the episode with the gun was over the top. Jim seemed to know I was shocked and dismayed at his behaviors. He came over and stood next to the wooden bench where I sat while Leah climbed up the ladder and cheerfully slid down the metal slide.

"Hey, last night was a bad scene," Jim shuffled and continued. "I've been having so many problems at work, with the guys and all and I made a mistake, it won't happen again. I promise. This time it will be different. I'm putting down . . ." I bristled when he leaned to kiss my cheek. I was in the power position now, and in the weird and twisted relationship of the cycle of abuse we had, this was my role. I had to make him pay for scaring me, using drugs, and walking around the house with a gun like a mad man. I had a short time being in command until the cycle started again. Would I stay and be hurt again or leave and be murdered? My choices were not good. I needed help. *God can you hear me? I need help!*

"Hey, come on, Jeanette. Don't be mad at me. Things are going to be fantastic. I made a lot of money last night on another bet. I have over $10,000, and I have to go to Hawaii for a business meeting. After a few days, I'll send for you, okay?" My mind did flip-flops.

Last week we couldn't make the rent and now this week Jim is going to Hawaii and asking me to go? Every promise Jim ever made me was broken. I was mixed-up and not sure where to go and which way to turn. Did I love Jim at all? I highly doubted it. There were so many hurtful words and so many punishing tirades that I felt little but fear, anger, and indifference most of the time.

Jim continued to tell me about his business trip and tickets to Hawaii as I internally rolled my eyes in disbelief. He had my attention and in a loving union or happy anniversary celebration I would be thrilled at the thought of going to Hawaii, but now I smiled and responded as I knew Jim would want me to, wearing the mask of the perfectly happy wife.

"So... when is your flight to Hawaii?" I asked, half unbelieving, half knowing it might be true.

"My flight leaves tomorrow afternoon, and I promise I'll call you in a few days with a ticket waiting at SFO." I tried to shoot holes in his plan, ignoring the fact that Jim was in one of his "apology moods" trying to woo me back. Jim held my face in his hands and locked his eyes onto me.

"Jeanette, honestly please, I will try. I really blew it last night, and wow, bad night. Can you please forget that and start thinking about what you need to bring to an island paradise?" Jim let go of my face and smiled at me, that beaming white smile. I desperately wanted to believe Jim was sorry and I wanted a happy life with a good man. I doubted this would ever happen and challenged what Jim promised.

"It sounds too good to be true. *We* have the money to go to Hawaii?" I asked, and as I said that, Jim pulled out a thick stack of hundred dollar bills.

"Yes, plenty." Every time he ever showed me this kind of money, I wished he'd give me a stack to put away. But as quickly as he flashed it, he stuffed it back into his pocket to blow on drugs, women, booze, or whatever. Knowing Jim had enough money for us to go and feeling that whatever relationship I had with Jim was gone, I agreed to meet him in Hawaii.

I asked a neighborhood family if they could keep an eye on Leah for a few days, offering to pay a few hundred dollars. They were nice folks, parents with three teenage kids who had already watched Leah on occasion. I left contact information and packed a small bag for Leah. Jim called five days later and told me my ticket was at the United Counter at SFO and if I didn't have the right clothes, he had plenty of cash to buy me whatever I needed. Within a few hours a bellman at the Hyatt Regency Hotel, Waikoloa Maui, escorted me to my ocean-view suite.

Jim wasn't there, so I put my things away, desperate to pull my long hair into a ponytail. Opening the outside zipper pouch on Jim's suitcase, I swished my hand back and forth, searching for a ponytail holder. I did locate two identical boarding passes: Jim Miller and Bill Steward. So that's who Jim went to Hawaii with, Bill Steward! Horrid visions of Jim with another man ran through my head. A sudden wave of nausea rose in my throat and I ran into the bathroom to throw up. I was positive Bill Steward was gay, and he went to Hawaii with my husband! I was disgusted and knew Jim would be furious if I said anything.

I carefully put the boarding passes back exactly where I found them. Jim probably forgot they were in the luggage. A moment later, the door to the suite opened and Jim emerged with a tan, a new designer shirt, designer sunglasses, and a tropical drink in his hand.

"Hey, little wifer. Aloha!" Jim said as he enveloped me into his arms, kissing me passionately. I faked affection, feeling betrayed, and hoped I was convincing. "Are you ready to go out for a walk, do some shopping, and then go out for a drink and dinner?" Jim asked. "First stop can be the boutique downstairs where I've already told them to expect us." I smiled trying to push down thoughts of Jim being intimate with Bill Steward.

After shopping for a very expensive dress and sandals, and feasting on a sumptuous lobster dinner, Jim and I had after-dinner drinks and walked along the wet sand. I pretended I was a newlywed in love with my mate. For a moment I accepted the façade and lied to myself and any other that saw us that Jim and I were happily married. He certainly was attentive and not angry or rude. For the moment things were different, just like I had always wished. As we walked down the beach a local Hawaiian approached us and sold Jim a few joints. I was not going to have any part of the pot, but Jim wanted it. And as usual, I shut up and went along with it.

Jim and I continued down the beach not talking while he smoked his pot, making a few crazy statements about the universe. We continued back towards the hotel and stopped at the bar to get Jim another Mai Tai. After taking the elevator back to the suite, Jim filled the large sunken tub and got into a very hot bath with his drink. Jim was really loaded, seemed loopy and began to act very strangely. He wasn't mad so I decided to get ready for bed and began taking my make-up off in front of the large vanity on the other side of the elegant bathroom. I heard him begin to ramble in a loud voice.

"Well, Jeanette, by now he's probably dead," Jim said matter-of-factly. What did Jim just say? I asked to clarify, wondering what he was talking about.

"Who's dead, Jim?" I put down my cotton balls and walked toward the open door of the bathroom. Jim began a long drugged confession, and I listened in horror, not certain if he was hallucinating.

"Well, you know Bill, right? Bill Steward. Well, you see, uh, he's probably dead by now. He was really in love with me, you know. . . kind of weird, kind of gay, you know? But I told him we had business only now, and I was married, you know." Jim took another long drink of the Mai Tai and continued while I stood leaning against the door jam, feet glued to the floor. "We both needed to make a lot of money, so we decided to make some. We took all of his jewelry, pictures, valuables, my parents' stuff and yours and had it appraised by his jeweler, pretending it was all his. A few months ago, we planned for me to break into his house and steal all of his things. He called the cops and the insurance paid him back an *obscene amount* of money. I got my fair share, you know; you got a house, right?" I listened not moving. "Well, the deal was we would split the rest of the money in Hawaii and when he got here... I guess he wanted me to dump you and Leah and to stay with him, you know. That would be really hard. So he was pretty addicted to coke and couldn't handle it anymore, you know. I taught him how to use the stuff, how to smoke it. . . met him in a gay bar. Uh, he really liked the coke. . . like to stay up all night, you know what I mean? It worked too," Jim laughed a filthy laugh and took another long drink. "Well, I guess he got pissed at me and was depressed that I had a wife. . . crap. . . a wife. . . and so I told him how to do it, you know. . . how to use a shot gun and pull the trigger with his toes. Poor bastard, he just couldn't go on anymore; he was distraught. I guess I showed him how to smoke coke. . . made him fall in love with me. . . broke his heart. . . and told him how to off himself. But I got my money. Poor bastard. . . he's probably dead by now. He just couldn't go on without me. There is only one problem though, we never signed the house into our name and might have to move at some point. . . maybe in a few days. . . or so. Guess he didn't use his money to pay the payments. Bill was pissed because I kept promising to make the payments to him, but crap, I never seemed to have the cash. . . and you don't make much money, so crap, how could we pay him?" Jim relit another joint he pulled out of his wallet and took a huge toke, coughing hard as he choked on the irritating smoke.

When we got home, life went on for the next few weeks. I didn't mention Bill Steward, the house payment, or the insurance fraud story. I kept a growing stash of money in my little savings account and when I had enough for a small down payment for a car, I began asking Jim if we could look at cars for me.

The next Sunday afternoon, we went to a Ford dealership, and I inspected many of the affordable used cars, eyeing the gorgeous new ones. I watched silently as Jim filled out a phony credit application using a fake ID, plunked down a thousand dollars in cash, allowing us to drive off the lot in a brand-new 1984 Ford Mustang Convertible, red with a white top.

One evening, I received a disturbing call from a woman who introduced herself as Jan Steward; she was looking for Jim Miller. I told her he wasn't home and asked if I could please take a message. *She told me in a threatening voice she knew Jim had killed Bill, and that he probably had all of her family heirlooms and original artwork. She wanted them back or Jim would pay.* She told me she'd hired a detective to follow Jim, and knew he had pressured Bill to kill himself and had committed insurance fraud, keeping all of her family possessions. I just listened, copied her number on a piece of paper, and threw it in the trash. If the police found him, so be it.

A few weeks later we found a notice on the door: the bank was repossessing the house since no one was making payments. Again, we moved all of our things into a storage facility and back to the Cozy 8 Motel, this time with a Jaguar *and* a brand new Mustang. Jim told me he had some friends who would let us stay with them a few weeks until we had the money together to get into a new place. We would stay at the Cozy 8 a few days, contact the Hutsills and if they agreed, move in with them temporarily.

GUNS

CHAPTER 21
THE SHAMEFUL DISEASE

Moving into a "real home" with Burt and Karen Hutsill in Santa Clara was fairly easy. Leah was thrilled with her new living arrangement, and I had to admit, it was a welcome change of pace from the Cozy 8. The house was immaculate, had basic furnishings, and the schedule Burt and Karen adhered to helped me reestablish some semblance of normalcy in our lives. Jim and I stayed in a small guest room; Leah shared the girls' bunk beds and loved having new-found siblings. Jim started a new project and our bank account finally had a balance above zero.

Each weekday, Burt and Jim left for work. Leah and I piled into my new Mustang and I drove her to school in the old neighborhood. Each evening we came home to Karen's wonderful home-cooked meal on the table, hot and ready for us to eat when we arrived. The kitchen was a gathering place for the Hutsills. Each Friday night after Burt received his paycheck, he'd hand it to Karen, and she would give Burt a few dollars for himself.

After dinner each Friday night, the ritual would begin: men and their wives, a few kids or singles would file in, bringing six-packs of their favorite beers and assemble at the long, welcoming table to talk, play cards, or tell a few jokes. Some Fridays there would be ten to twelve adults at the table, and I loved being a part of the group. My new friends asked me questions about being from Southern California and my job at Motorola. The women all eyed Jim and told me how "lucky" I was to have landed him. I agreed and then silently added: "If they only knew." I was safe living with the Hutsills; even though Jim got angry a few times and looked like he was going to back-hand me, he stopped because of the watchful eye of Burt and Karen.

One Sunday afternoon a few months after moving in with the Hutsills, Jim awakened after a late night out and announced he wanted to take Leah and me to a movie. I hadn't been feeling well for about a week and thought I was running a low-grade fever. I tried to explain to Jim that I had a headache and a few cramps, but he found a bottle of aspirin. So Leah and I jumped into the Jag and headed for the movies. Throughout the movie my symptoms worsened. Jim seemed to be enjoying himself; however, I felt worse, my head felt hotter and the cramps in my stomach throbbed painfully. Finally not being able to endure anymore, I told Jim I thought I was extremely sick and asked if he would please take me to the hospital. Reluctantly we left. Jim drove recklessly and complained the entire way. Pulling into the local ER, Jim dropped me off so he could park the car.

I felt lightheaded and when I approached the counter thought I was going to faint. The nurse quickly called for a wheelchair. After taking my temperature, she rushed me back to the exam room. My temperature was 103.5. The doctor came in and gave me a cursory examination, asking me a lot of questions about my lifestyle and my symptoms. When pressing on my stomach, I cried out feeling excruciating pain. Dr. Palsano explained I was probably having an appendicitis attack. Dr. Palsano recommended performing an appendectomy; my head was foggy with fever and I was in so much pain, shivering with the chills, that I couldn't respond. Jim came in and chatted with the doctor telling him about *his* "appy" and how he walked out of the hospital the next day bringing a cute nurse home with him. I winced, but could really care less; I was in so much pain. I only wanted to feel better.

They immediately prepped me and wheeled me into the operating room for the appendix surgery. I awakened in recovery, my stomach wrapped with a large dressing, an IV with several types of bags hanging from a metal extension attached to the gurney. A few hours later, time lapsing between pain medication and nurses coming to take my vital signs, Dr. Palsano talked to me about my condition. Jim was nowhere around – I assumed he went back to the Hutsill's with Leah.

"Mrs. Miller," the doctor began looking at me over his chart. "How are you feeling?" I nodded, my stomach feeling very tender and painful and my mouth parched like the Sahara Desert. "We went in to do the exploratory and found your appendix to be healthy and in perfect condition. We removed it proactively. The problem is not with your appendix, Mrs. Miller, but unfortunately with your fallopian tubes." I was listening, but not fully understanding what the doctor was telling me. "Most fallopian tubes are quite narrow; however, yours are abscessed and are the size of. . ." Dr. Palsano looked around for a comparison and held out his hand, gesturing with a fist, thumb extended. "Of my thumb. Your tubes are extremely enlarged, full of puss and abscesses; with a high fever you are at great risk of your tubes bursting at any time. If that were to happen the infection would spread quickly throughout your body, you would most likely develop a systemic infection and possibly not survive." I was disgusted and angry. Another pelvic infection!

"Doctor, is this why I can't get pregnant?" I asked. Dr. Palsano looked at me and frowned, explaining my reproductive organs had a raging pelvic infection and were severely damaged and abscessed.

"Mrs. Miller, you have pelvic inflammatory disease. Do you understand what I'm telling you? This is a sexually transmitted disease passed from one person to another; it is an STD. You probably didn't get very sick the first time you got an STD; many women don't even know they have it. A disease with symptoms this severe are a result of recurring infections and scarring in the tubes that lead to chronic problems like the tubal abscess, cervical cancer, hysterectomy, and in some cases, death. You are extremely sick, Mrs. Miller, your condition posing life-threatening complications."

I must have shown the shock on my face because the doctor didn't rush off like many doctors do, but stayed to answer some of my questions. I had recently been to the doctor for an annual gynecological examination and mentioned a few concerns. The doctor told me my issue was "normal" so I ignored the worsening symptoms. Dr. Palsano confirmed these chronic infections were sexually transmitted which made me fall deep into a pit of despair and depression. My mind calculated all the times I hadn't felt well, the times I did go to the doctor. Why didn't I know when I was infected? I was angry and did know Jim was the source of my shameful disease.

"We will be monitoring you round-the-clock, watching your temperature and making sure you are responding to our IV antibiotic treatment. Mrs. Miller, if one of your fallopian tubes burst before you got to ER, you probably would have died." He had my attention. "Hopefully the IV antibiotics will get the infection cleared up. If we get the infection to respond, we still may have a chance for your fallopian tubes to heal." Dr. Palsano patted my hand as he saw the tears in the corners of my eyes dripping down my cheeks. I wanted my mother next to me, to hold and comfort me, but I hadn't spoken with her in a very long time and wouldn't dare have anyone call her.

Later that night during nursing rounds, Jim appeared. I couldn't tell what time it was, but I assumed it was the middle of the night. Jim looked like he was wild-eyed and high. He said a few unintelligible words and whoosh. . . he disappeared. Nurses came in and out checking my vital signs and giving me round-the-clock antibiotics.

Ten days later, Dr. Palsano came in with the worried look on his face. It didn't look good. "Mrs. Miller, I was hoping you would have responded to our aggressive treatment, but it is difficult to treat and cure an infection as severe as yours. I would like to give it forty-eight hours. If you are not responding to the IV antibiotics, we must consider another surgery." I wasn't sure what the doctors could do during a surgery... clean out the infection?

"Dr. Palsano, what do you mean? Why would you do another surgery?" I asked. Dr. Palsano came over to the side of my bed, and with compassion on his face told me the possible outcome.

"Mrs. Miller, if you get worse over the next few days, we will operate to remove your fallopian tubes or may be forced to perform a complete hysterectomy in order to save your life." My mind was spinning with confusion and fear.

"What! A hysterectomy? I'm twenty-five!" I blurted out. Dr. Palsano nodded.

"Yes, but this will be a life-saving procedure if we perform it." I began to cry. Dr. Palsano folded his charts, said we'd hope for the best and left the room. I prayed hard, crunching the sheets up over my head.

God, if you can hear me; it's me again, Jeanette. I'm hurting, I'm lost, and I'm sick. Lord please, please help me. Help me right now. Please help me get through this terrible disease. Please help me, Lord.

I fell into a fitful drug-induced sleep, the pain in my stomach not abating, but increasing. A nurse came in and took my temperature at 11 o'clock; it was 102.3 degrees. My body was burning hot, shaking with chills; I worked in a hospital before and knew my elevated temperature wasn't a good sign. At midnight, another nurse came in and began taking my vital signs again. I was shivering so violently my muscles were contracting, and I couldn't respond. I felt like I was in a dreamlike trance and saw people working around my body as it lifted up above the bed. I heard tense voices and the nurse pushed a panic button, calling a team of people into my room. People were rushing in and out. It seemed like a second later; I heard voices talking about me, saying my temperature was 105.9 and rising. The next thing I knew, I was floating and people were standing all around, lifting me and turning me, while pulling a circulating cooling bed under my body. I wasn't in pain and didn't

FROM PRISONER TO PRESIDENT

feel much of anything but saw a lot of bright lights and thanked God for helping me. Everything else went black.

Two days later, Dr. Palsano came back looking more worried than before. This look was not welcoming to me, but I was so weak, still hot, and in pain, feeling extremely sick, I really didn't care. Dr. Palsano came to the side of my bed holding a clipboard. I knew what he was going to say. I grimaced and my throat closed tightly, fighting to hold back tears.

"We have to operate again, Mrs. Miller. The IV antibiotics are not impacting the infection as I hoped. On Sunday your temperature spiked hitting 106; this can cause permanent brain damage. If your tubes burst, your body has no resistance; you won't make it." The doctor placed the clipboard next to me on the hospital bed, pointed to words I couldn't read, and began to explain the procedure he was going to perform. "We're going to surgically remove your fallopian tubes; we'll try to clean up any additional infection. If the abscess is in your uterus, or infecting your ovaries, we'll perform a complete hysterectomy." Dr. Palsano added a small consolation. "Mrs. Miller, I know you are young, and you've told me you want children; if we can save your uterus and your ovaries, we will. There are some new fertility procedures out there allowing women to conceive babies without functioning fallopian tubes; it's called IVF." He paused. "And you know if a couple really wants children, adoption is a viable option as well." I was so weak I could barely hold my hand up to sign the agreement. Dr. Palsano left the room and I cried as the surgical staff wheeled me alone to the operating room for the second major surgery in two weeks. I prayed fervently for God to hear my prayer and not let me down. *I need a miracle,*

Lord, I'm in the worst possible condition, I said, tears running down my cheeks.

I awakened in my room, stricken with searing pain through my abdomen. This time, the bandage was huge and there were drainage tubes coming out of my side, filling with awful blood and fluid. I had the usual IVs with multiple bags of fluid filtering down into my veins. At least I was alive, I reasoned. Still no sign of Jim, and I hadn't seen Leah one time since I left her in the car at the ER. It seemed like ages ago. I thought of Leah and cried again. My emotions were running high and the nurses were acting like I was a dirty and disgusting person.

Dr. Palsano finally came into my room. I didn't want to hear what he had to say. I looked up at him with pain making my face contort.

"Hurting?" he asked. I nodded. "I'll have your nurse come in and give you another shot of morphine." I looked up, dreading the next part. None of the above was the right answer... bottom line, no matter what Dr. Palsano told me, I couldn't get pregnant. I couldn't carry a baby. I was now permanently sterile. What man would want me now? Jim? Rick? Nobody.

"Well, I think we took care of the infection. We removed your fallopian tubes, but the ovaries and uterus looked okay. You have a lot of local infection and scarring, but because of your age, I think you'll recover and eventually heal without any additional surgery." I nodded, hot tears streaming down my face, not saying a word. Dr. Palsano quietly left the room.

Great, I thought. I only had my fallopian tubes removed. I still have my ovaries and my uterus. That's wonderful. Now how in the world would I get pregnant without tubes? In 1984, there were very few infertility centers and fewer babies born to women who had serious issues like I did, like missing a few key parts. I had vaguely heard about IVF and it cost more than $50,000. It didn't really matter if it cost $5,000, I would never have a dime to afford a baby.

My doctor discharged me after seventeen long days in the hospital. I careened into a serious depression, not caring about anything. Jim managed to pick me up in the Mustang, saying something about selling the Jag to a friend, rushing around, telling me he had an important meeting and quickly dropping me off at the Hutsill's house.

Great, I thought. . . no car again. The tiny guest room bed was stripped and didn't have sheets. I walked slowly into the room figuring Karen must have placed the clean folded sheets on the chair for me. I was certain Jim hadn't done the wash. Karen was being nice trying to help out. I was as weak as a kitten, hurting and limping around hunched over like a ninety-year-old as I made the bed. Two major abdominal surgeries within fourteen days had made a mess of my body. Each time I pulled the sheet over a corner I had to sit down or pass out. I was faint and weak. I fretted. . . so weak I couldn't even make my bed.

THE SHAMEFUL DISEASE

CHAPTER 22
THE GARBAGE DISPOSAL

A few days later, I was limping around the house recovering when Jim came in looking like he was in a foul mood. He demanded answers about Leah's school and the daycare fees, and then barked about me hiding my checks. He accused me of telling Valerie at work not to give him my paycheck so he couldn't cash them. I didn't know what he was talking about, but the next thing I knew, Jim loomed over me and struck my face with the back of his hand, knocking me across the room to the floor. I didn't move. I had fresh incisions all over my stomach and didn't want to end up back in the hospital. Jim screamed something about having to sell his car to support me and that we were probably losing my car too. He then turned and stormed out of the house. I sat on the floor clutching my stomach with one hand and my face with the other, tears streaming down my cheeks. "Lord, are you out there?" I cried out. I crept back to the small room, lay across the bed and wept.

Soon my body healed, and I went back to work with Jim driving me in the Mustang. Life at the Hutsill's continued like clockwork. The only difference was that I was a very unhappy woman feeling my young life was over. Two of the single gals at work, Amy Anthony, an MIT grad and electronics engineer, and Helen McHale, a young sales rep, befriended me. They lined up a few get-well cards on my desk, and after I returned, took me out to lunch to cheer me up. I couldn't mention the serious depression I was fighting, my homelessness, and my embarrassing and life-long sentence of sterility. We escaped reality for an hour, drank margaritas, and ate Mexican food. The girls invited me over to have a few drinks on Friday night. Sure, I thought. That was going to happen.

Friday after work Karen picked me up and gave me a ride home. I planned to approach Jim with the invitation to my friend's house for a few hours, but decided against it. Burt and Karen took the kids out for burgers and when Jim came home from work, there was no one home but me. This was frightening because it seemed Jim was angry with me all of the time now. When we were alone, he used any excuse to hurt and threaten me. He stormed into the room where I was putting laundry away into the small bureau.

"Where is your worthless little paycheck?" Jim demanded. I shook my head.

"I. . . I. . . don't have a paycheck yet because I didn't work the last two weeks before the checks were…" I didn't have a chance to complete my sentence before Jim raised his arm and backhanded me across the face, sending me spilling backwards across the bed.

"You lying worthless piece of dog crap!" he spat at me. "Where's the money?" Jim demanded, screaming filthy profanity at the top of his lungs. I began to cry.

"I don't have any!" I answered putting my hands up to protect my face. I prayed he wouldn't find my small savings account passbook hidden in the bottom of my drawer. I had less than $1500 saved now and it had taken me years to squirrel away a dollar or two from my earnings. Jim punched me hard on the thigh, smart enough to hit me where people wouldn't see the bruises. I winced from the excruciating pain.

"Where is it?" he yelled. This time I didn't answer; I was numb and curled up on the bed with tears running down my face. Jim continued. "Oh, what's the use? You're a used up hole anyway. Can't even have a baby! What a worthless piece of crap you turned out to be!" With that Jim spun around, cruelly laughing at me, and left the room. I lay there sobbing, convinced he was right. I *was* worthless; what man would want me now? I heard the door slam and the car start. The feeling of pity soon turned to anger.

About fifteen minutes later with tears quieted, I got a really good idea. The girls wanted me to come over and I had Amy's number hidden in the lining of my purse. I went to the phone in Karen's kitchen and dialed.

Amy answered as bright and happy as always, "Hello!"

Hesitantly and feeling like I was making a huge mistake I began, "Amy, hi, it's Jeanette. You. . . uh. . . still having a few drinks at your house with Helen?" Amy said yes and urged me to come over and stay the night so we wouldn't have to drive after drinking. I didn't even have a car to drive and no money to catch a cab. If Amy picked me up and Jim arrived, he could hardly accuse me of having a boyfriend. He'd probably still get mad if he saw me in the car with a girlfriend, I thought feeling rebellious. "Amy, I am not supposed to drive yet, uh. . . do you think you could come by and pick me up at my house?" Amy cheerfully agreed.

I shoved a few toiletries and some clean clothes into a grocery bag, wishing I could leave for good and never come back. Amy picked me up and once at her house, I felt liberated by a few drinks and thoroughly enjoyed conversing with my colleagues. I shared a few *choice* things about Jim, leaving out several graphic details. Both the girls looked at me like I was nuts. They drooled over Jim when they were introduced; he was so charming and debonair. Neither of them believed my story of escalating abuse and after a few drinks and more conversation, I wasn't sure I believed my story either. After several hours of laughing and blowing off a little steam we fell asleep in front of their wide screen TV. The next morning, sunlight blazed through the window and I awakened in a panic. I hadn't called home and had not told Jim anything. I left Leah without as much as a goodbye. I was dead.

I nervously endured a quick continental breakfast waiting for Amy to drive me back home. She brushed her long dark hair into a ponytail, pulled on her MIT sweatshirt, and off we started, heading for the Hutsill's. A few minutes later we stopped in front of the house. I nervously thanked Amy, told her I'd see her at work on Monday and walked into the Hutsill's like a death row inmate.

The house was eerily quiet which was very strange because kids were typically everywhere and noise abounded. As I crept down the hallway, I felt like a twelve-year-old kid sneaking home after running away. Quietly I put my things away, hearing low whispers coming from the kitchen. Karen and Jim were talking in hushed tones and when I walked into the room they both stopped talking. Jim glared at me with huge eyes. I pretended to ignore him, swallowed hard, and walked past them both toward the kitchen counter where Karen had been cutting up vegetables for dinner. I washed my hands and began to help prepare, finishing where Karen had left off.

Before I knew what was happening, Jim exploded towards me, picked up the knife, and held me in a headlock with the blade pressing lightly into my throat. He screamed into my ears.

"You worthless whore! Not even out of the hospital a month with a rotting female disease and you go out whoring again!" Jim shook me hard with each word, squeezing my arms down at my side. I looked up in the kitchen, my eyes pleading for Karen to help me. Her eyes locked in a frozen stare, smirking, with no compassion on her face. She looked pleased and not a bit surprised that Jim was holding me at knifepoint. Karen met my wide eyes imploring her to help me with a glare, and then nodded to Jim in approval.

"Jeanette, now I don't normally take sides, but when I saw that guy drop you off, I had to tell Jim the truth!" Karen looked at me with disgust and added. "You'll finally get what you deserve. Jim's been telling me all along you have been cheating on him, whoring around. I didn't believe him until today. You sure had us all fooled with the innocent Catholic crap. I really believed you were like me, but you're not! You're just a no-good cheat! I felt sorry for you not being able to have a baby and all, but not now. You don't deserve a good man like Jim!" Karen huffed, turned and walked out the sliding glass door closing it with a slam. I swallowed hard and felt bile rising in my throat. Jim loosened his grip on me and threw down the knife. I pulled away from Jim and rubbed my hand across my throat, blood dripping down onto my shirt.

Quickly, I backed out of the kitchen and into the living room with Jim following, still screaming at the top of his lungs. How could Karen have lied to Jim? I was with my friends. Amy dropped me off right in front of the house. If it *were* a man would I be so stupid as to let him drop me off in plain sight of everyone? I tried to explain to Jim that Amy had dropped me off. I had to do some quick talking or I was certain I'd be back in the hospital... or the morgue.

"Jim, Jim, please listen. Please, I wasn't with a man. Karen saw wrong. It was Amy. . . Amy Anthony from work. She's an engineer. She's. . . a. . . ."

Jim crossed the room and slapped me hard on the side of my face sending me sprawling across the wooden floor sliding onto the oval braided rug. I clutched my stomach with one hand, wobbling and trying to right myself up. My face stung and my ear rang. Jim continued his tirade.

"A man. . . Karen saw you with a man! You whore! How stupid, you brainless pig! Do you think we don't look out the windows when you bring your used-up whore body home like the tramp you are?" Jim hovered over me, and I looked up, afraid to move. I learned a long time ago that if I acted broken and didn't move or try to escape, Jim wouldn't hurt me as badly. The minute I fought back, Jim would go insane with anger. I tried to apologize and lied to Jim.

"Jim, please listen, I only love you. I would never have another man but you. Please, please, Karen saw Amy. She had on a guy's MIT sweatshirt and had her hair pulled back in a ponytail. Please,

---

please, don't hit me again. I swear to you it wasn't a guy; I swear." Jim looked down at me and started to yell again.

"You used up worthless piece of crap! You're not worth the money I gave the hospital to get you out! Now give me your rings, you slut!" he demanded. "Give me the diamond and your wedding ring now!" I wasn't sure why Jim wanted the rings, and was hoping to keep them as a last resort if I desperately needed money. He leaned low and screamed within inches of my face. *"Give me those rings!"*

Jim grabbed my hands, pulling me across the floor on my back while he twisted my fingers hard, ripping the rings from my fingers. Both rings came off causing me to hit the wood floor with a hard thud. The next thing I heard was the sound of the garbage disposal and Jim laughing hysterically as metal clinked and grated against the sharp blades. My heart sunk, my priceless public display of unending love was crunching and grinding in the disposal.

A second later it was quiet. Jim slammed out the back door to join Karen and the Hutsills in the backyard. I ran into the bathroom and quickly locked the door, standing in front of the mirror to access my injuries. I was shaking and sobbing, unable to stop. My neck had a shallow four-inch cut and my fingers were bleeding from where the rings once were. Both of my cheeks were bright red and my nose and eyes puffy and swollen. I splashed myself with cold water and tried to use soap and toilet paper to tend to my cuts. I sank onto the hard toilet seat and sobbed feeling desperately scared and lonely, holding my neck and listening to the sounds of Jim, Burt, Karen, and the kids enjoying a lovely spring barbecue and a few cold drinks in the backyard.

A few days later when Karen and I were alone, I asked her why she told Jim I was with a man. Karen told me soberly she saw a man drop me off, and she knew what she had seen. I tried to reason with her to no avail; she swore she saw a man. She began to treat me with disgust and was short with Leah. Karen treated me rudely whenever she had a chance and Jim would smile, enjoying the treatment and the punishment Karen continued to dole out.

Work was progressing and I received another promotion. Each time I heard of a new product I devoured the information enabling me to excel in my technical understanding. During a national sales contest, I sold more electronic semiconductor components than any other sales associate in the entire western region and received a high commendation from a vice president of Motorola. At work I was a hero; my colleagues spoke highly of me, and I had loyal appreciative clients. I was the golden-girl in sales and treated politely and with utmost respect. In contrast, at home I was a worm, a used-up hole, a whore, and a worthless piece of crap. The more Jim and Karen told me I was a liar and a cheat and a no-good, the harder I worked to get accolades in my professional life. Management appreciated me; I was *worth* something to them.

One day upon entering the office, it appeared as if someone had died. People were speaking in hushed tones. I watched a constant stream of people coming out of Lou's office carrying manila envelopes and looking like they had lost their best friend. It didn't take long to figure out the office was having a major lay-off. Lou called me in, and with earnest sincerity apologized for having to tell me I no longer had my job. I felt the tears welling up in my eyes as I listened to her explain she had no options; there were eighty-five people in the office and fifteen would remain. With two years,

I was low man on the totem pole, and people who had more than twenty years seniority lost their jobs.

I cleaned out my desk and stood outside the professional offices with a box in my arms feeling like another part of my body had been excised. When Jim picked me up in the convertible, I quietly told him I lost my job, waiting for him to say something nasty. I looked down at the scraped up wedding ring he'd given back a few days after the garbage disposal incident and thought if desperate I could pawn it.

Jim smiled and whistled an old tune, oblivious to my despondence, top down in the Mustang, my long blonde hair flying wildly.

"So, guess where we're going?" Jim asked. I knew I had better sound excited and animated.

"Where, Jim? Tell me where?" I faked the role of the loving wife and fawned over Jim, rubbing my hand through the back of his hair, smiling at him, hiding my hurt, anger, resentment, and despair. Jim responded and smiled at me, taking a new route back to the Hutsill's. He turned the corner passing the house we'd vacated a few months back. The weeds were growing in the front yard, a lock box on the door. We continued driving deeper into the same neighborhood, turned and then pulled up in front of a vacant house: clean, manicured, with a "For Rent" sign in the window. I began to light up. Leaving the Hutsills might be a reality.

"Welcome home, little wifer. It's a new home and a new start for us," Jim said beaming, running around and opening my door. I couldn't believe it. A new home and Jim held up the key. "My new boss owns the place. I negotiated the house as part of the salary. I start my new job on Monday. We can move in tomorrow." I couldn't believe my ears. A new job and a new house! I couldn't stand to look at Karen another day and felt so depressed on the little bed that had become my life. A new house! I pushed down my despair and put an enormous band-aid on my pain.

We easily moved into the house with usual drill, Jim's workmen appearing with a rental truck filled with our possessions. It felt like a million years ago that I left the memories of Bill Steward, Hawaii, the suicide, and the house we had abandoned. I wasn't working and swallowed my pride to collect unemployment. I lied to Jim about the amount of the stipend, cashing the check and squirreling a few dollars away into my paltry savings.

Things were pretty calm when we moved in. Leah seemed to thrive in the atmosphere. I hadn't gone to church in a long time, and wished I could connect with God again. Each time I tried to make a neighborhood friend, Jim would immediately find fault and forbid me from seeing them again. I kept busy taking care of Leah, cleaning the house and reading my romance books, transforming my life and my marriage into the fiction I read every day. It was the only way to survive.

CHAPTER 23
THE MUSTANG

Things seemed to be going fairly well for Jim at work and I thought he may be keeping this job until one day when the Mustang screeched into our driveway, skidding tires burning rubber. He slammed into the house and announced we were moving. Leah ran over to me and sat down next to me on the couch, pushing hard against my side, shaking with fear.

"That no-good fool! He doesn't know how to run himself out of a paper bag, let alone run a jobsite. I told him a few things today." Jim was pacing as he cursed and ranted. I immediately began to pray to God for protection. "We don't need this place, or any of his other pieces of crap rentals! I told him we'd be out this weekend! He can have this tenement and his job! Telling me I seem irrational and making mistakes on the job. I know how to run a project. So I've been late and have missed a few deadlines, big deal! It's not brain surgery; it's a commercial building!" Jim began taking a few jackets out of the front hall closet and throwing them onto a pile.

Leah and I watched silently as he continued the tirade. In an instant, Jim looked at Leah and me and began to scream at us.

"What, are you deaf or something? I told you that we're moving. Now get your lazy butts off the couch and start packing!" Jim was hovering over us and we were afraid to move. He leaned in closely and screamed at the top of his lungs. "Now I said! Can you hear me? I said, now!" With that Leah and I quickly and carefully maneuvered by, hunching as we passed Jim to avoid a hard slap on the back of the head.

We took refuge in Leah's room and began throwing things into boxes. I had long ago kept every box when we moved from place to place. The boxes never unpacked and slid into the closets and on shelves. I gave up unpacking completely; it was useless. With this system, our few possessions could be ready for a truck at anytime and moving could be extremely efficient. Leah and I worked side-by-side. Jim left with a slam a few minutes later and Leah and I worked into the night, bringing the boxes into the living room and stacking them neatly into rows.

With everything back into storage, we returned once again to life at the Cozy 8 Motel. Just like old times, we got our second floor room and paid rent by the week. Jim was always gone and with one car, Leah missed a lot of school. I had little money with my unemployment checks barely covering essentials. Desperate and frightened, I sought more intimate time with God. Jim could hurt my physical body, but he couldn't take away my prayers. I prayed repeatedly for a job, pleading with God to work a miracle.

Daily I walked to the front office, picked up the used newspaper, and scoured the help wanted ads. A few days into our arrival at the roach motel, I spied an ad for an outside sales representative for a local San Jose electronics company. God *was* listening, the answer to my prayers jumped off the page: "Salary, commissions, benefits, and a company car, experienced need only apply." I felt confident I could do an outside technical sales job; Motorola had given me such excellent training on professional sales and electronics. I had a glowing letter of reference from Lou and record-breaking sales results; I was certain this job was a perfect match and it offered *a company car*.

I approached Jim about the job and he acted nonchalant. I explained I might be able to make more money working this new job than I had at Motorola. His eyes lit up. A few days later, Jim willingly drove me to the local library to update my resume. It was hard using my phone number at the Cozy 8, but when I received the call a few days later, I quickly lied and told my prospective employer my husband and I were relocating to the area and looking for a permanent residence.

After a successful interview, I landed the job; my sales were record breaking and healthy commission checks began to roll in. Within two months, we moved into a contemporary townhouse in San Jose. Life seemed to be settling down. Since Jim wasn't working, I drove the Mustang to work each day. Although I never did see the car payments, Jim assured me that he was making them. There was no way I would ever challenge him, it wasn't worth the abuse. I cashed my checks and handed most of the money to Jim to pay the rent and the bills. I squirreled away a few bucks each week into my secret savings account and silently rejoiced when the account balance reached $2000.

A month after we moved into the townhouse, Jim came in with a huge bouquet of red roses and to-go plates from a local steak house.

He landed a great job with another local construction company and would be starting immediately. Jim, Leah, and I celebrated and ate steak, lobster, and baked potatoes. Jim acted loving towards me, holding my hand over our small dining room table, telling me he loved me more each day. Jim spoke of future dreams for our family telling Leah and me that things were going to change for the better. I sat there trying to enjoy the moment wishing I could change Jim into the nice, compassionate man sitting across from me. Unfortunately, I realized he would never change. Throughout the last seven years there were sporadic splashes of happiness living with Jim; however, the abusive nightmarish episodes stood out prominently, with the happy moments fading quickly.

One morning, Leah and I went out to get into the car for our daily commute only to find that someone had stolen our car. Frantically, I ran into the house to alert Jim who was nursing a very bad hangover. Jim began barking at me to shut up as soon as I wakened him with the news. Once awake, he began to laugh in a sick and drippy tone, red eyes glaring and hair askew. "What do you think, you idiot whore? You think the bank lets deadbeats keep new cars without making payments? It's repo'd!"

I swallowed hard. What? Not making the bills? I handed over my hard earned money for that car and what happened to it? It went to the dealer for drugs—that's what I yelled at Jim inside my head but said nothing for fear of another bad fight. Leah sat on the couch downstairs by the door not saying a word.

"Is there any way to get the car back? I need to work," I said as softly and timidly as possible. Jim yawned and rolled over.

"They want the $2500 we owe, and I'm not giving it to them. Be thankful you've had it this long without making payments. They

232

just couldn't keep track of where we kept moving." Jim laughed at the thought he'd cheated the bank and kept them wondering where the car actually was. "You can call your boss and get them to give you that company car they promised. That was part of the deal, right?" I nodded silently, panicking about my next move and grieving for the loss of my car.

I called my boss, telling her I had car trouble. I wanted to tell her the truth; I had car problems all right. I hated lying. She understood and told me in a few days she would have the leased car and after signing the agreement I would have a car to drive. She allowed me to work a few days from home making customer contacts.

Thankfully, a few days later, the leasing agent came by our townhouse and picked me up in my new company car. This was one of the best days of my life. I had wheels. My company owned the car and paid the insurance. My territory performed well; I worked tirelessly on my accounts; and was elevated to the top sales person in the company, breaking all sales records. At work, I was a hero—the president, CFO, the managers, and all of my colleagues seemed to genuinely like and respect me. At home, I was a piece of dog crap, a worthless used-up hole and less than half a woman; I couldn't have a baby. Jim never let me forget that fact.

THE MUSTANG

CHAPTER 24
KITTY

One night, Jim came home after midnight, very stoned. He began yelling about the house smelling like a cat. I panicked and jumped out of bed to see what the commotion was. A few weeks earlier, Jim brought home a little kitten and had given it to Leah. Leah kept the kitten hidden away in her room, using a small box filled with dirt for the litter box. Each day, she faithfully cleaned the box to keep the house from smelling. The cat must have gotten out and had an accident, I thought, as I raced down the stairs smelling the same odor. Jim was pacing downstairs back and forth, screaming and looking for the evidence.

"Here! Do you see this?" Jim pointed to a cat pile in the corner by the front windows. "Cat crap! You see!" he screamed at me. I stood there not saying anything, watching his wild eyes as he let out a string of obscenities. "Where is that cat?" Jim screamed and in two leaps was up the stairs and crashing through the door of Leah's room, wood splinters flying. I heard Leah screaming, pleading, crying for her daddy to please, please let go of the kitty, promising him it was just an accident.

The next thing I saw was the kitten flying through the air down the stairs and smashing hard into the front door. Leah was screaming inconsolably, while Jim pounded down the stairs and callously swept the mangled body of the kitten back towards the wall as he slammed out the door. I took one look at the kitten, knew it was too late, and frantically ran up the stairs to console Leah. I held her young body as she screamed and shook, stroking her hair, trying to calm and soothe her. We sobbed together, both of our hearts shattered into small pieces, rocking back and forth and praying that neither of us were living the nightmare that was our reality.

Days passed with no sight of Jim; Leah and I continued as if nothing had happened. I couldn't talk about it. I was in total denial and tried my best to keep working, driving Leah to school and pretending my life was picture perfect.

Jim finally came home one Friday night while Leah and I were just sitting down for dinner. Jim acted like he had just gone out for a pack of cigarettes, and as usual, had on all new clothes and smelled like alcohol and perfume. Leah looked over at me and said nothing, neither of us acknowledging Jim. He grabbed a bottle of beer from the fridge and pulled up a chair, joining us at the table. I could tell something was different. It seemed Jim was somber and wasn't his normal self. It was probably the drugs, I mused.

Jim looked at me and grabbed my hands, holding them in his, forcing me to look at him face-to-face. Leah stared at us not speaking. Jim had tears coming down his face and was holding the gaze intensely. He must feel really sorry for what he'd done.

He *was* crying, I thought. I felt a familiar stirring of compassion flood my heart as I watched the tears come down Jim's cheeks. This was a man whom I had loved at one time and now when I looked at him, I felt sorry; I justified his behaviors and realized he was a very broken man due to the disturbing and abusive childhood he'd experienced. Immediately, my heart began to soften, although I tried not to feel anything at all. My heart was young and still hoped for a healthy relationship. I was desperately lonely and wanted a man to love and cherish me. I was a young woman who had so much love to give, so much life to live. I wanted to have a happy and normal life. Jim could sense my softening as he kept staring into my eyes.

"Jeanette," he said his voice raspy and breaking. "I. . . I. . . I can't live without you. Please, please. . . ." Tears rolled down his cheeks. I felt my heart twisting in two—the anger, the resentment, the brokenness being washed away. "Please, can we please try to make this thing work?" Jim leaned towards Leah and took her hand. Leah didn't move, but I knew she loved her daddy. Most kids love their parents no matter how abusive they are. Leah was no different; she wanted her daddy to love her, treasure her and keep her safe.

"Leah, my baby, daddy wants us to have a happy family. . . to have a love gang again." Leah watched her daddy continue to cry while waiting for my cue that everything was back to "normal" again. Jim turned his gaze on me again.

"Jeanette, you don't want Leah to have a broken family, do you? She deserves a mother and a father. Since she's not yours, if anything ever happened to us, she wouldn't have a mother," Jim said sincerely.

237

I heard this loud and clear. Professing his love and threatening me at the same time. Leah looked at me; I was unmoving. Jim reached into his pocket and took out a black velvet box. Opening the box, he put it on the table in front of my plate. It was the diamond he had given me a few years ago, back from the pawnshop and presented as a gift. He was buying me back with a piece of jewelry. It was beautiful. I smiled a slight crack, and Jim saw my face move. He took the ring, flashed me a huge white smile and put the ring onto my finger.

"Come on, little wifer, let's have a love gang. I've missed you guys." Leah was smiling and hoping her life was back together again. I entered into the "love gang" by sitting on one of Jim's knees, Leah on the other. We all embraced and kissed as a love gang; my heart softened a little and immediately pulled right back again. This was a ploy, he was at it again. When was I going to figure this out? My heart was now 100 percent encased by a thick cover of hurt, deceit, and abuse and unable to be vulnerable and love anymore. My mind raced through visions of escaping and of a new life as a different person. To keep the peace, we had a love gang moment and Jim began telling us excitedly about his new job building hotels for a large company based out of Los Gatos. Jim had a suite at the Toll House Hotel, and we could come over tonight to see the place.

We went outside to see a brand new 1986 company truck sitting in front of the townhouse. It had electric everything, all the bells and whistles, sporting custom plates and door logos from Jim's new company. Leah and I jumped into the truck, and we drove to the Toll House Hotel in Los Gatos. The staff treated Jim like royalty as we walked through the grand lobby.

Jim's suite was impressive! Leah ran from the bedroom to the dining room, to the workout room, to the bathroom, excitedly jumping into the dry oval Jacuzzi. Jim smiled and winked as he saw my shock at everything. He sure knew how to end up on top, I thought feeling angry. He kills Leah's kitten in a drug rage; leaves home without clothes, a car or a job; and comes back with a new truck and a suite at one of the most exclusive resorts in the area. Jim was a master con artist, we all fell for it. I was primed and ready for a miracle, ready for some help. Jim could tell he'd "fixed" the relationship again; his manipulation was working.

Leah lay back on the bed and flipped on the television, thrilled when her dad told her to order room service. Jim and I went to the Toll House Restaurant and enjoyed a seven-course gourmet meal. I felt like I was nineteen again and back in Newport Beach. Jim was attentive and loving, pulling my chair out and holding my hand. Jim ordered us expensive champagne, lobster, prime rib, Caesar salad, and chocolate mousse for dessert. Waiters came at frequent intervals to make sure their special guests were enjoying the night. I pushed back the thoughts of how bizarre my life was. I had a home and a job, but my husband, who had been missing for several weeks, was now living in a hotel treated like a king. I pretended Jim was not a monster but a doting, attentive and loving husband. For the moment I lied to myself and felt happy wishing it was true.

On Sunday afternoon, Jim took Leah and I back to the townhouse. He made sure to let me know he paid the rent in full as he handed me the receipt showing we were not past due anymore. This made me feel secure. . . at least for now. Leah bragged to me about how her daddy was going to buy her a new kitty and how he was building a new hotel. Being down this road for almost eight years with Jim, I wanted to see more than a few months of the "new man" before I would buy any of it. I craved a normal and healthy marriage and didn't want to embarrass my family with a divorce. If only Jim didn't melt down and change all of the time things might have been different. But for now, we were living the high life. Two new cars, both of us working, and all of the bills paid. Life seemed to be picking up.

CHAPTER 25
CASA CLARA

A few months passed and Jim's new hotel project was progressing well. To my relief, Jim only came back to the townhouse one or two days a week. He lived at the hotel the rest of the time. I was sure he was cavorting with women, but I didn't really care. He left me alone. Life was calm during those days; Leah and I carried on our daily routine in San Jose, and on weekends we stayed at the Toll House Hotel. Jim didn't dare yell there – even though we were in a large suite, you could hear muffled voices down the halls. This fact kept Leah and me safe. It was like having a vacation every weekend. We signed up for spa treatments, drinks, and food— charging everything to the hotel.

This went on for a several months. It seemed Jim was working hard every day. I prayed that maybe this time he had put the drugs away for good, would stay employed and wouldn't explode in anger. I carefully brought up the fact we had two households and maybe we shouldn't be paying rent while having a free suite to live in. Jim didn't respond but must have been thinking about it. As Leah and I were getting ready to leave on Sunday afternoon, Jim agreed that maybe we *should* store our things and live at the hotel for a few months. I was fine with it. We could save more than a thousand dollars a month, live in luxury, and I wouldn't get hurt.

When I drove back to the townhouse with Leah, I couldn't get my key to work. I walked to the property manager and asked if he could help with the lock. The manager stuck out his chest and announced they had changed the locks; we were out! He gave Leah and me fifteen minutes to go into the house to get as many things as we could and blurted out that they had a moving truck coming in the morning to take our things to a storage facility. He was evicting us because we had not paid rent in six months. I began telling the manager about the receipt. The manager laughed letting me know he thought we were "white trash" and hadn't seen a penny from Jim in more than six months. The only thing Jim had given him was a few joints to smoke and a lot of excuses.

Leah and I made as many trips as we could into the townhouse, filling the trunk and inside of my car with our clothes, toiletries, and anything else we could grab quickly. Leah was crying because she couldn't take her fish, and her prized collectibles and personalized clock would have to stay. I empathized with her promising she would eventually get her things back. We drove in silence to the Toll House quietly walking up the back stairs to the suite carrying a few boxes and paper grocery sacks. I knocked with my foot and Jim answered the door wearing a brand new navy-blue satin robe, smoking a joint. I didn't complain to avoid a fight and softly told him we had been evicted.

"I told you guys to move in here today, didn't I?" he chuckled. I didn't think it was funny. "Don't get mad, come on. It could be worse. It could be the Cozy 8." Jim was pretty stoned and laughed at his joke, while Leah and I started to put our things into the drawers.

"Come on, I'll help you bring in the rest of your stuff." Jim was right. It wasn't a bad place to be evicted to; after all, it wasn't the second floor of the Cozy 8. It was a fabulous suite. We moved in quickly, Leah went to bed, and Jim and I went down to the bar for a drink. Life was crazy. I was confused and angry and at the same time happy. Jim couldn't hurt me at the hotel. I lived in a dream, pretending I was a happily married woman, pushing down the pain that I felt deep inside.

Six glorious weeks passed with us living like celebrities at the Toll House. Although I was fairly certain Jim was still using drugs and having affairs, I kept working hard and eventually paid all past due bills, depositing a few dollars into my secret savings account. The lack of chaos stirred internal anxiety and was unsettling. I kept waiting for the other shoe to drop, but it didn't. The time allowed me to reflect on my life goals and evaluate my life. I still wanted to go back to school some day to finish my degree and I craved having a family. I so desperately wanted to raise a baby of my own. Each time I thought about my predicament, I became bitter and depressed. Maybe someday there would be a surgery I could afford, and who knows, maybe I would adopt a baby. Immediately I argued with myself. It was crazy enough having Leah involved in the life I lived with her father, I should never consider bringing another innocent child into our mess. I continued to pray for God to hear my prayers and frequently thought of my family and missed them terribly. I hadn't spoken to any of them in the longest time.

A few weeks later, God answered my prayer. Out of the blue my brother Tom called me at work and told me our folks were coming back from Denmark in a few months. That fact excited and terrified me. How could I face my parents without them knowing something was up? When they realized how horrible my marriage was they would be disappointed. If I said anything to my parents about Jim and his drug use and Jim found out, he would threaten them and could hurt or kill them. I shuddered as I pictured an out-of-control Jim and my much smaller retired father facing off.

Jim came home late one Friday after work, smelling like booze again. Leah and I were eating a four-star meal from hotel room service and watching television in bed, when Jim swung the door open too hard, startling us. We knew the drill and moved closer together under the sheets as Jim paced back and forth through the suite. I didn't say a word. Jim stopped pacing and stood at the foot of the bed, face bright red, eyes glazed.

"They're between projects. Think we should relocate temporarily, and our expenses ran a few grand extra last month." Jim fumed. He looked at me and ripped back the covers spilling the dinner tray all over the bedspread. "These. . . these red toenails," Jim pointed at my shiny fresh polish. "They showed me the bill. Twenty dollars, plus a tip!" Jim barked forgetting that *he* had urged me to get a spa treatment and had told me to leave a nice tip on the hotel charge. I didn't want a fight and sat unmoving.

"Now, we need to move out for a while until the next phase starts. I can move back in when that time comes. . . solo." Jim spun around, opened the drawers of the large mahogany bureau and pulled out a handful of my clothes, throwing them onto the floor. "Well, guess what that means my *gold-digger wife*? It means we are out on the street. I don't have a job, and we don't have any money until the next project starts again in a few months."

I was a gold-digger wife? Where did that come from, I wondered? Oh yeah, I was a real gold digger—living on pennies, being evicted, and working hard to support his free-basing cocaine habit. Leah and I were frozen in place and didn't say a word for fear of a huge eruption.

"What do you think about that?" Jim screamed with his face inches from my ears. I nodded, tears starting to run down my cheeks. "Get up and start packing, you brainless slut!"

Jim yanked me hard off the bed. I landed bottom first, bumping the back of my head on the nightstand. Rubbing my head to make sure I wasn't bleeding, I dutifully got up and carefully, watching every move Jim made, inched my way to the dresser and quickly threw on a t-shirt and jeans. Leah followed suit. She was almost ten now and knew that we needed to move slowly without any grumbling or we'd have to pay for our attitude. I could tell by the level of Jim's anger that even though he may have a job waiting for him, he wasn't afraid to let them know he was furious about moving out unexpectedly. Leah and I began to pack up our things as quickly as possible, making a long line of grocery sacks leaning against the wall from the front door through the entry hall.

I wondered where our things were stored as we were shuffling back and forth through the suite—Leah and I not saying a thing but giving each other loving and reassuring looks as we passed; Jim grumbling and cussing under his breath, many of the accusations about wild spending aimed at me. We left the palatial palace the same way we moved in—late at night and down five flights of stairs, stuffing everything we had into my company car. Jim drove us into an older section of Santa Clara and pulled up in front of the only place we found with a vacancy sign, the Casa Clara.

When we first pulled up to the place, I gasped. I had seen this motel in the daylight. It was a low-end, kitchenette motel with faded pink stucco and a huge, cracked blacktop parking lot. It looked better at night and that wasn't saying much. I handed over most of the cash I had in my purse for our first week's stay. We had to pay in advance.

Jim pulled the car in front of Unit 7 and opened the door letting us in. I took one look around and was immediately disgusted. The carpet was almost worn through, the bedspreads looked extremely old, and when I walked into the kitchen, I saw bugs scatter from the cook top of the small stove. We waited while the manager brought in a rollaway cot for Leah to sleep on. I didn't want to put my things into the drawers without cleaning them first, but Jim shoved whatever we had into the small brown chest of drawers and lined up the rest of our bags against the faded brown paneled walls.

I checked the sheets making sure they were clean and free of bugs and went into the bathroom to get some toilet paper and soap so I could wipe down the kitchen and bathroom counters. Leah's cot would only fit along the side of the wall next to the small kitchenette and I watched as she lined up her little ponies and began playing with them and telling them they were moving today and would have a new home in no time at all. My heart broke. She was such an angel and deserved to have a decent life. Jim looked outside the window, noticed there was a liquor store close to the motel and took off in search of beer and cigarettes. I finished putting our things away and turned on the small TV to watch some mindless show. This certainly wasn't the Toll House of Los Gatos.

We were now living in the Casa Clara, a pay-by-the-week, one-room-kitchenette motel with a few extra critters as guests.

Monday morning Leah and I left Jim at the motel and began our commute to school and work. I called Tommy to get more information about my parents coming back. He told me they wanted to come up to the Bay Area to see me. Great, now what would I do? Meet them at a coffee shop? I asked Tommy to give my work number to them, and when they got home have them give me a call. I hadn't seen my parents in more than seven years. Now they were finally coming home, and I was afraid to face them.

A few weeks later, I received the call at work that I had been fretting about. The familiar voice flooded the phone and tears immediately filled my eyes.

"J for Jeanette! Is that really you?" my father said exuberantly. I turned my back so none of my colleagues would see me cry. All of a sudden I wanted to burst. I wanted to tell my father everything, I wanted to let him know I was afraid, that Jim was violent, and he had hurt and threatened me. I sniffed hard.

"Daddy. . . Daddy, it's really you! You're home!" I cried now, tears of happiness mixed with relief ran down my face. "I've missed you so terribly." My throat closed and I swallowed hard, taking a deep breath.

"Little girl, your mother and I want to come up to see you and see how you are doing. When is a good time for us to visit?" My father asked with urgent concern.

I should have told him to come now, bring Mother, and rescue me, but then my thoughts clouded; what about Leah? She wasn't mine. I couldn't leave her there. . . and if I did leave. . . what would happen to her and what would happen to me once Jim tracked me down? I knew he had murdered before and wouldn't think twice about putting a bullet into my head. I quickly fumbled and tried to explain things to my father.

"Well, you see Daddy, we. . . uh, don't really have a house right now. We're looking for a place. . . and, uh. . ." My father could hear what I was saying between my words; he recognized I was in trouble.

"Listen Jeannie, Mom can stay at home. I can come up, and we can look for places to buy. Tom told me Jim was building a hotel and you have a steady job making good money now. Well, you shouldn't rent a place anymore. You're what, twenty-six now? You and Jim should settle down and quit moving around. If you owned a place of your own, you could put down roots."

I agreed with Daddy, but who would rent to us, let alone sell to us? Our credit was awful. A bankruptcy, a repossessed automobile, late bills, evictions. . . I couldn't even consider telling my dad about what transpired during the past seven years since he had gone to Europe with Mom.

"Daddy, I don't think we could qualify for a house. Our credit is not the best." "Bad credit" was almost a dirty word for my father. He was the son of immigrant Italian parents, who scraped an existence, pinched pennies, and built a life in America. My father joined the Navy, put himself through college, married, bought a home, saved his money, and invested wisely.

"Little girl," my father said with such love that I began to cry again. "You don't need to worry about a thing. I'm coming up. We can start to look for a place to buy. Your mother and I have excellent credit. We can be creative, as long as you and Jim are willing to work hard for it." I smiled; maybe my daddy could be my hero and save me from this mess I'd gotten myself into.

Jim went along grudgingly the day my father came up to help locate houses to purchase. Dad pulled his new white Mercedes Benz up to Unit 7 at the Casa Clara and I pretended to look cheerful, hiding my apparent disgust for our living arrangement, certain my father could see right through it. I ran to him and hugged him hard, tears of happiness flowing down my cheeks. Jim gave my father a half-hearted handshake, still holding his beer in one hand, cigarette between his fingers. Leah didn't know my father and approached timidly. He opened welcoming arms and gave Leah a warm grandfatherly hug.

We spent the next few weekends performing the same drills: Daddy drove up and Jim, Leah, and I piled into his Mercedes combing city after city for a house that would be our next place of residence. Every house we could afford was in a questionable area. After scouring every city within a fifty-mile radius of my office, we decided to look at property outside the Bay Area. We drove about seventy miles to a city named Tracy where the houses were about $150,000—still way too expensive. My father explained to us he was looking at the total cost and a fixed loan amount—a payment we could afford allowing us to establish credit and not default on the payments. Jim scoffed and told my father we should be looking at more expensive neighborhoods. He thought the range should be closer to $200,000. Daddy listened and nodded, driving further from San Jose.

Once we got to a city named Manteca, the houses were about $120,000. Daddy looked at me and said these were still too high, completely ignoring Jim's childish snorts and eye rolling. The next stop was a very small town named Ripon where the homes were $100,000—still too high. The sales rep showing the model homes in Ripon handed us a flyer for homes in Modesto selling for $74,000. Daddy looked at me and winked. The last stop that day was a little housing development south of the main city of Modesto. There was one house left for sale that day, it had just fallen out of escrow. The home was a brand new, darling grey house with white shutters. It had three bedrooms, two baths, a brick fireplace, two-car garage, on a corner lot, and included front yard landscaping. The house was selling for $74,950.

I was on cloud nine. This house was a dream come true. Wall-to-wall carpet, central air, a laundry room, and the payment was only $675 to own! Daddy spoke with the agent and after a few price negotiations, worked up the paperwork. With my parents' excellent credit, we could finance the house with only 3 percent down plus closing costs – the total out of pocket would be $3,150. The agent took a few Polaroid pictures after Daddy signed off on the loan and gave them a deposit check of $500.

On the ninety-mile drive back to Santa Clara, I sat in the back seat of the Mercedes staring at the pictures of my new home. I couldn't believe it. We were going to live in a new home—not a rental, but as owners! Although I was excited about the house and the stability this allowed, my life was clouded by the prison I lived in.

During our long car ride back to the Casa Clara, Daddy discussed with Jim and me how we'd finance the house. Daddy would buy the house and prior to the closing of escrow, Jim and I would pay $2000 for our share of the down. Daddy would finance the $1150, and we'd pay him back at $50 a month until his personal loan was paid back in about two years. We would make the $675 payment each month, depositing the house payment into a secure checking account. After a few years, if our credit was established, Daddy would sign the house over to us. I knew I would not let my father down and would be responsible for not missing a payment. I was so thrilled to be moving out of the Casa Clara in about six weeks! Leah would have a back yard and her own room. We would have a chance again to start a normal life. I childishly dreamed of the three of us in the house, one happy love gang. It was a dream I wished were true, but realized was not reality.

CHAPTER 26
THE DREAM HOUSE

Struggling each week to save for our down payment was extremely difficult. Jim received a few paychecks from the Toll House handing me a couple dollars toward the deposit. I received a few paychecks but with weekly rent at the Casa Clara, it was almost impossible to save more than a few hundred dollars. Daddy was extremely generous, but he was a businessman and I was certain he would not sign the final papers unless we contributed our share as agreed. I gently pleaded with Jim each week as I counted the days until escrow closed and fretted about the amount we needed to deposit. Jim brushed me off, telling me more than a few times what he thought of my father and that "Daddy would save his little girl."

Daddy called me at work each week sending his love and also asking for updates on our portion needed for the down payment. I reassured him we'd have the money once it was time for escrow to close. I panicked and worked harder during the next few weeks than I had in the last two years, calling every customer I could think of and closing a record number of sales. That month I broke my own sales record and earned enough for the down payment and a few extra hundred for our living expenses. I had to hide the house money and kept it locked in my desk drawer, telling Jim I mailed it to my father each week. Many nights during drug binges, Jim would get frantic looking around the motel for drug money; he would go through all of our clothing and pockets, and he cleaned out all of my purses looking for spare cash, trying to uncover a secret stash of money. I kept my small passbook account tucked away in my desk at work. Whenever I needed to access it, I would keep it hidden inside my shoes for fear of getting caught. My balance was more than $2,100 now, and I knew if Jim ever found my account and saw all the dates I had deposited a few dollars, I would pay severely for the deception.

On a sunny Saturday afternoon in May of 1986 Leah and I happily packed our paper bags and cleared out our things from the Casa Clara. Jim even seemed like he was in a good mood as we drove the ninety miles to our new home in Modesto. We were going to meet my folks at the title company to sign final papers and receive our house and mailbox keys. Our car stuffed to the brim with all our worldly possessions, we drove to meet my parents. We would be sleeping in our new home that night!

When we finally reached the title company, I ran to greet my mother. She smiled enthusiastically and walked toward me looking almost the same as she had the last time I'd seen her—her petite frame, soft, curly chestnut hair glistening now with a touch of gray, arms open wide, eyes moist with tears. I knew I had put her through a lot of turmoil during the past few years by not keeping in contact like I should have. But now embracing my mother in a tight and loving grip, we were together. My parents were home! I was overcome with a flood of emotion and confusion and began to cry. My parents were here; however, my life still seemed all wrong. I kept pushing down the thoughts of my explosive and abusive relationship with Jim and painted a rosy picture to my parents of a happy little family.

We walked through the new home in Modesto, and Mother was very happy, remarking about how lovely it looked and the two of us buying fabric to sew some curtains and make quilts for the beds.

Daddy wanted to get on the road and I surreptitiously handed him the down-payment envelope with a cashier's check for $2000. Daddy winked and then he ushered us into the kitchen, placing a document onto the counter for us to review. It was a contract detailing all legalities of the house agreement. At first I was unprepared and felt worried signing a contract but understood my father was a savvy businessman. Jim balked as he read the typewritten agreement and began pacing around the empty house venting his disapproval. It clearly outlined a few rules about owning the house. Daddy made it a necessity that we take care of the property, make each payment plus the extra $50 on time, establish good credit, and he added a clearly defined line item that stated: "If anything transpires between the relationship of Jeanette Miani-Miller and Jim Miller, causing them to break up prior to the transfer of said property, Jim Miller must vacate the property and Jeanette Miani-Miller shall have sole use of the property."

Jim fumed and let out a string of obscenities when he read the protection clause telling us he didn't want to sign the agreement because it was ludicrous. Daddy told him it was up to him; however, he would never have a chance to buy the place if he didn't agree.

255

Reluctantly and with outward disrespect for my parents, Jim signed the house agreement. My folks hugged Leah and me, said goodbye to a sulking Jim, and left for Orange County.

Life in the new house was peaceful during the first few weeks. We didn't have any furniture except for a used mattress and box spring I bought at a local garage sale, but I didn't care. I felt this house could be the new start we desperately needed, and after a month or so Jim somehow managed to get our things out of storage. Jim still wasn't working back at the Toll House yet, but promised he would be starting soon and was out all hours of the night. Jim seemed to be taking drugs very heavily, and in the depth of his drug abuse, his personality seemed to be non-existent. He barely spoke and would mumble things about needing to meet someone and out the door he went on foot.

There was a run-down sleazy bar a mile or so from our new house. While driving to the store with Leah one Sunday afternoon, I saw Jim standing in front of the local biker hangout with his arms around a young petite blonde. I tried not to react because Leah was sitting next to me in the front seat, but I could see the small frame leaning back against Jim. The girl looked very young, probably just out of high school, wearing tight jeans and a black leather vest. Jim didn't see me drive by. My stomach tightened as we passed and I realized when Jim had another love interest, he left me alone; however, when he had casual flings, he would force himself on me after his dalliances. This was how I kept getting those horrible female diseases—from his lust relationships. I swallowed hard and thanked God Jim had a love interest because it prevented him from raping me.

My company allowed me to shift territories handling the area from Milpitas to Reno, requiring me drive into the San Jose office only once a week for sales meetings. A new slew of customers kept me very busy. Leah was registered at the local elementary school. Jim stayed home during the days, sleeping in and staying out most nights. After a few weeks, Jim announced that his job at the Toll House was starting again and he was supposed to pick up his new work truck at the local dealership a few miles into town. I dropped Jim off to pick up his truck on a Sunday afternoon and feigning the adoring little wife, kissed Jim goodbye and wished him luck, immediately praying he would never return.

The summer of 1986 unfolded hot and dry in the Central Valley. Leah and I made a great team working on backyard projects and traveling around my sales routes together. We decorated our quaint house and enjoyed our two-person family. Jim was in the Bay Area and he rarely called. I made the house payments each month, depositing the payment plus the extra $50 into the house account. Enjoying peace and working full-time gave me an opportunity to meditate about my future. Leah and I could stay together, but the longer I put off completing my education, the fewer opportunities for advancement I would receive. Few top corporations would hire a technical sales rep with only a high school diploma.

I researched the class offerings at Modesto College and decided to consult with a counselor. I completed several units of general education back in Orange County and after attending part-time, could get my Associate of Science Degree. My counselor explained the units I needed while developing a part-time class schedule that would allow me to complete my AA in about two or three years. I desperately sought an education, but if Jim found out I was going to school without asking, it would be a very bad scene.

Jim came home the following weekend in an excellent mood. As was normal for his pendulum behaviors, he brought a large bag of "goodies": food, gifts, cards, toys, and flowers for me. Leah was almost eleven, and she longed for her father to love, protect, and take care of her. I, on the other hand, had been burned for seven years and to keep the peace, played along with the "love gang." I wasn't waiting for my prince to sweep me onto his white horse, steal my heart, and ride away with me into the sunset. I resigned myself to the fact that my life was over, never to encounter true happiness or love again. During our dinner and over a glass of wine, I carefully brought up the subject of school to Jim. He immediately frowned.

"What a brainless thing to do, why do you want to go to school? I make great money. You make enough money, and didn't I just buy you this brand new house?" I stiffened. If I acted like I was too excited about starting school, it would tip Jim off and he would put his foot down. I tried a different method.

"Uh, I guess I don't really want to go back to school. I would have hours of homework and the additional raise at work wouldn't be that much." Jim's eyes brightened.

"They're offering you a raise for going to school? Well, how much more?" Jim asked, putting a forkful of broccoli salad into his mouth. I pretended not to be that interested and left a long pause before answering.

"Oh, I doubt that much. When I'm done, they told me the AA degree would give me only $500 more a month," I emphasized, "before taxes!" I snorted and took a drink of my wine.

"That's a lot of money! Why don't you consider the classes? You don't need that many units, do you? And it's 6K a year. We could use the money!" Jim drained his wine and as expected, said goodbye to Leah and me to take off for his evening out.

As soon as the door shut and I heard the sound of the motor fading into the distance, I jumped around the house for joy with Leah following. Turning on my small radio to a local rock station, Leah and I danced and cleaned the dishes, having a personal celebration of a huge victory. I was going back to school.

CHAPTER 27
NOTHING BUT TRASH

I registered for two classes and started a few weeks later, attending one early morning and one late night class. Although I wasn't that much older than the other students, I felt decades older. These young people had their whole lives in front of them. I was trapped, unable to escape my situation. I did well and tried to keep my books hidden in the house so Jim wouldn't be able to find them. If all went well, I would be able to graduate in the spring of 1989—fourteen years after graduating from high school.

One rainy Friday afternoon Jim came home early. Leah wasn't home from school yet, and I was studying at the kitchen table, books spread out in a huge circle around my chair. I heard the garage door open and jumped up to see Jim looming down the hallway toward me, face red with anger.

"What are you doing. . . work? What's this mess on the table?" Jim barked, looking at my papers littering the table. I backed up to the wall not moving as Jim began flipping my things around and looking at the content. "So, you are a student, huh?" Jim began to get angrier and came over to me pressing both of his hands around my throat, cutting off my air supply. "Why would you be so brainless that you didn't tell me?" He began to spew a long string of obscenities. "Are you screwing the students now, or the professors? You brainless stupid idiot! You think your puny brain is smart enough to go to college?" Jim let go of my throat, throwing me aside and grabbed a handful of my papers and began shredding them. "If you're that smart, then I guess you won't need these!"

Jim laughed while I stumbled to my feet, rubbing my throat, anger rising in my chest. I did need these papers he was shredding. My research paper was due in a week. I'd spent hours of work on it. Jim watched my face turn red and then saw tears run down my cheeks. He continued to laugh manically knowing he was hurting me with every destructive move he made. The final stab to my heart was his methodical ripping of my used textbook. I cried quietly while Jim did his best to render the text unusable. He was successful. Jim ran out of the house carrying my pile of papers and two altered books, laughing the whole way. I stood in the kitchen looking out the windows as Jim threw my research paper and what was left of my books into the trash.

I stood unmoving as Jim came back into the house, looking like he'd just conquered the world. He sneered at me again.

"You should have told me you were back at school, you sneaky little thing. You got what you deserve!" Jim spun around and slammed out the door, screeching the tires of his truck as he sped down the quiet residential street. I waited until I was certain Jim was gone and went out to the garbage, filling a clean paper sack with my stained, torn, and filthy books and papers. I must have been a sight—out in the street, crying and stuffing grocery bags with old garbage.

I argued with myself that my life just wasn't fair. How could Jim treat me like he did? I thought of my passbook and the money in my account; I desperately wanted to flee, but fear for Leah and my safety kept me there. It just wasn't fair! I stormed into the house and began a secret project of lightly washing each piece of paper and drying them in the back of Leah's closet. Those papers that weren't in bad shape, I put into numerical order, figuring I could tape the books back together.

Leah came home, and we ate a quiet dinner together, thankful Jim was out bar-hopping and would come home late. The next morning when I awoke, I found him asleep on the living room couch with a new gold pinkie ring adorning his finger. ·

Leah and I quietly left for the store Saturday afternoon. When we came home, Jim was awake and watching television. We came in and put the groceries away, not saying a word. Jim acted like there was nothing wrong. He didn't choke me, scream obscenities at me, and throw my books in the trash, did he?

"Hey, look who is home: Leah and my little wifer. Come here!" Jim motioned for us to come over. Leah bounded onto the couch and hugged Jim. I started to move in his direction, but couldn't get close because I was so angry. Jim looked up at me, his eyes looking sincere. "Hey, you know I love you so much. Don't get mad. I just want you to tell me the truth, to talk to me about school, that's all." I nodded, inwardly wanting to tear his head off. I looked down at the new carpet.

"Jim, you told me to register, remember? I was getting a raise." I said quietly. Jim remembered because he let out a belly laugh, so loud that Leah yelped.

"Oh yeah, you did tell me. I forgot, I guess. Did you get your stuff out of the trash?" Jim asked, laughing hard at the scene he created. I nodded. "Well, I'm starved, how about a nice sandwich?"

Leah jumped off her daddy's lap and we knew the cue. I went into the kitchen and made Jim a sandwich and a nice glass of ice-cold pink lemonade with a little spit stirred into the foaming bubbles on top. Leah and I smiled triumphantly at each other in the kitchen. Leah understood the abuse and constant pain her father put me through. We were partners in crime as we served Jim his lunch. Yeah, I thought, you throw my books in the garbage – you are nothing but trash! Feeling some sense of relief at my spit and my defiant thoughts, I was comforted through the knowledge Jim confirmed I was going to school. I was certain as long as I lay really low with my studies, I might have half a chance of graduating from college someday.

CHAPTER 28
FORTUNE 5

In the fall of 1987, Jim was still working intermittently on the Toll House project, and life erupted about every month with obscene screaming, yelling, broken dishes, and holes in the walls. Jim knew I didn't leave any valuables or dangerous things out any more; I had no sharp knives in the house and what few tools we owned I kept in the trunk of my company car. The only way he could hurt me now was by breaking the house and punching out the windshields of my company car, which he did a few times. When he became angry now, Jim would pull out my flowerbeds and punch his fists through the walls of my prized home. These antics always made me cry frustrated angry tears of helplessness.

I was putting more than 200 miles a day on my company car, and although my sales results were excellent, I longed to have a local job, local customers, less windshield time, and began to scour the Modesto Bee in search of a sales career advancement opportunity. Finding good job opportunities wasn't the problem

– having proper qualifications was. I found an excellent listing for an account executive with a Fortune 500 communications company—"Modesto office, salary, commission, expenses, car allowance, benefits. Proven sales results, college degree preferred. Mail resume to. . ."

My eyes lit up. The ad didn't say, "college degree required," but preferred! I had the proven sales. I quickly updated my resume on the college library typewriter and mailed it out a few days later. I would be graduating in a year or so and figured with my sales results at Motorola and my current job, I may have a chance.

I began to get disheartened as Thanksgiving approached and there was still no update on the dream job. I bristled thinking they should at least send me a thank you for your resume note, but nothing arrived in the mail. Just as I put the job out of my mind, I received an official looking envelope with a familiar blue sphere-shaped logo on the front.

As if carrying a newborn babe, I took the envelope inside, my heart pounding. I sat down at the table and opened the letter slowly to avoid tearing the paper.

The letter thanked me for my resume and instructed me to call an HR manager at the corporate location in Los Angeles during business hours to schedule an employment test. I quickly called and spoke with the HR manager who explained that AT&T selected my resume and was in the process of reviewing my qualifications for a potential account executive position. In order to proceed to the next phase in the AT&T hiring schedule, I needed to travel to downtown Oakland and take an SAT-standard hiring examination. If I passed the examination, I would be granted a first interview.

My heart pounded enthusiastically and I tried not to sound overly excited as I calmly agreed to attend the next available testing date.

I shared very little with Jim for obvious reasons. I didn't want him to do anything to jeopardize my chances for career advancement. The testing day arrived and I drove to Oakland giving myself ample time for parking and finding the location. I was ushered into a room full of eager young candidates and nervously took my seat. I eyed my competition and prayed silently as the instructor told the class there would be four sections to the test. Each section was carefully timed and after the test, if we did well, AT&T would conduct our first interview.

Taking the test, I thanked God I was in school. The information was fresh in my mind and I felt confident as I turned in my test and answer sheet to the facilitator. I sat and watched as the training facilitator called person after person out of the testing room until only one young man and I remained. They called the young man and then shortly after, called me. I was bewildered and overwhelmingly depressed. I thought I tested well and felt deflated at failing my lifetime opportunity for career advancement.

The female facilitator led me down a long hallway and into a small office where I met an older, balding man in a navy blue suit and tie. He stood up, offering his hand and smiling congenially.

"Congratulations, Ms. Miller, you passed the test with flying colors." I listened in total shock and disbelief as the hiring manager for Northern California relayed the AT&T standard hiring information and disclaimers. There was no job or salary guarantee and no guarantee of start date. I passed the test successfully and AT&T would contact me within a few weeks to schedule a second interview if there was a local position. I answered a list of standard questions and was quickly ushered out of the building, leaving with more questions than answers.

A few short days later, I received a surprise call from an AT&T sales manager. He introduced himself, congratulated me on passing my test and asked me to schedule a second interview. The next week I made the long three-hour drive to Bakersfield, arriving at the Central California branch. I completed a grueling personnel interview conducted by AT&T executives and branch managers. The opportunity was outstanding and added to the nervousness I felt. During the interview I never relaxed and was certain the executives could tell I was shaking. They concluded the interview and asked if I had any questions. I told them I had only one.

"When will I start my new position?" I smiled, making direct eye contact, wearing my confident and bold work persona, leaving my whipped–dog, abused wife personality at home. The room erupted with laughter.

My confidence worked. They told me I would receive a hiring package via mail within the week. If all my references and personal driving record checked, I could plan on training the first part of 1988. I drove back to Modesto bursting with excitement. I landed a job that would change my life.

Working for AT&T was a dream. I began my technical training, loved the challenge, and thankfully, stayed in Bakersfield for weeks at a time. Jim was unemployed again, and although he grumbled about me being gone, Leah just turned eleven and could cook and clean for him. As long as he had a girlfriend, he was fine. I did worry about Leah and Jim abusing her, but pushed those thoughts out of my mind. As long as I paid the bills and left money from my paycheck, Jim didn't complain.

On weekends, I would come home and a majority of the time Jim was gone. He enjoyed partying and found a home at the Double Eagle, the skuzzy bar he discovered when we first moved into Modesto. I tried to avoid Jim getting close to me – the last thing I needed was another venereal disease. Jim barked at me each week when I arrived home warning me he'd kill me if I had a boyfriend. He hurled profanities and threatened if he ever found me with someone else, he'd throw acid in my face so no one would ever look at me again. Jim also bragged with a broad smirking smile that he'd have me killed for a packet of coke. I left my training manuals in plain site, shook my head and remained quiet.

In February of 1988, I completed my AT&T technical training in Cincinnati, Ohio, at the University of Sales Excellence. It was two marvelous weeks without threat of Jim yelling or hurting me; two carefree weeks of room service and catered lunches, dinners out, and music with new friends—two wonderful weeks of bliss. Students in my eight-person class politely asked about my family. I smiled and lied, telling them I had a wonderful eleven-year-old daughter and a happy marriage. I was so good at spinning the lie I even believed it myself. Dreading my flight home and walking back into an abusive and loveless house, I packed and hugged new friends, telling them goodbye, promising to call once we were back at our new offices.

FORTUNE 5

CHAPTER 29
NEW ROOMMATES

Nothing could have prepared me for the scene I found as I walked through the front door of my home. There were white lines of drugs on small mirrors with razor blades scattered about most of the flat surfaces, empty beer bottles, half-consumed large tequila bottles, and cut limes and salt shakers everywhere. It was only four in the afternoon on a Sunday, and it appeared the party had gone on for quite some time, probably all weekend. I didn't see Jim or Leah or anyone inside the home, but heard a lot of music and voices outside as I dragged my luggage into the hall.

I walked from the hallway to the main living room, grabbed a handful of beer bottles and began cleaning up the mess. Dumping out a few bottles I turned around to make another trip when I ran hard and fast into the hairy chest of a toothless, gnarly, and scary-looking old biker. He wore greasy leathers, a red bandana, and sported chains hanging from his belt. He laughed a drunken and drug-induced guffaw as he looked at my surprise and eyed my blue

271

business suit and matching heels. I backed up creating distance between us.

"What are ya doing here, little lady? Shouldn't you be in church?" he said slurring his words. He reached to the counter and grabbed a bottle of tequila, pouring some into an unmanned cup and reaching for a lime. "See," he said, demonstrating how to drink a large shot of tequila with lime.

"You do it just like this." The man took a large gulp and made a disgusting noise as the liquor burnt his throat. "Aahhh, just like this." He poured another shot. "Here, this one's for you. . ."

I backed up shaking my head, and upon seeing my fear he let out another loud laugh. "You must be Jim's whore, eh? He told me all about you. It's nice of you to work to take care of his drug habit and the bastard kid and all. You're a real Mother Teresa, you are." The biker slung back the other shot, spun, and warbled out the back slider, slamming the door so hard it almost came off the track. I could hear the man yelling for Jim out in back, announcing my homecoming.

As I walked carefully into the back yard, it was like entering another planet. The yard was full of bikes and people. Biker girls and guys sat together on lawn chairs, hanging on each other, drinking and smoking pot in broad daylight. There was a group of men drinking from vodka and tequila bottles and laughing loudly, examining several guns and shooting them excitedly into the dirt. I located Jim on the side yard. He was absorbed in a knife throwing game and didn't see me as I walked up, his young thing clinging to his side. Someone nailed up a board as the target; however, there were still about a dozen large knives sticking out of the fence destroying the new wooden gate. As soon as he saw me, Jim quickly pushed the young girl away and walked up to me, a large grin on his face. My heart began pounding with fear.

"You're home!" he gushed, drunk with drug-glazed eyes. I panicked and didn't want to make a scene. It probably would have been the last second of my life; these bikers would have killed me in a flash, if Jim, their honored host commanded them to. I smiled weakly and walked up to Jim, allowing him to plant a gushy wet kiss on the side of my face. I could see the young girlfriend stomping her foot and scowling from behind Jim's back.

"Yes, my flight came in early," I said. "I am really tired and need to study and get some rest." I smiled at Jim again and felt like I was going to throw up or pass out.

"Why don't you loosen up for a change, party with me and my friends, do a line of coke and have a beer?" Jim commanded. He walked over and grabbed a beer from the cooler and handed it towards me. I shook my head and could tell Jim was immediately irritated. I didn't give him the answer he was looking for. I wasn't any fun. I was a stuck-up prude and not a partier.

"No thanks, babe; I'm just really tired," I said as sincerely and soothingly as I could. "You and your friends have fun; I'm going to study and will be in the house if you need anything." I turned and started to walk toward the house, my high heels sinking deep into the soft moist grass.

Making my way slowly toward the back door I could feel all eyes burning a hole into the back of my head. Jim reached me as I neared the patio, grabbed my arm hard whirling me around, and with a red face and eyes squinting, spat into my face.

"You better watch it, whore – you do one thing to screw with my party, or my friends, or you think for a second about calling

273

the cops…"Jim paused and looked around at his friends. I was the recreational event and they stopped all activity to watch my reaction to Jim's tirade. "And this will be your last day. They'll never find the pieces!"

Jim let go of my arm and launched me hard onto the cement. I hit with a thud, my legs spread apart, my skirt hiked up. Jim laughed cruelly, his friends joining in as I quickly got up and scurried into the house, my face flushing with hurt, fear, and anger. Leah came home a short time later, knocking on the guest bedroom door and wondering what happened to the place. Apparently she had gone to a friend's house to spend the night and went on a shopping trip with their family. With Leah and me gone, Jim had a great place to throw a biker party, inviting all of his new friends and girlfriend. I opened the door and let Leah in, asking her if she had been safe while I was gone. She assured me she was fine; her dad was gone most of the time. She told me her dad had brought a few friends around. . . one was a girl. Leah took me into the master bedroom and showed me where the new girlfriend had moved some of her hanging clothes right next to mine in the closet.

I was full of confusion and fear. This was a great thing for me! With Jim having a girlfriend, I would be safe; however, I *was* paying the house payment, and he had his girlfriend living in *my* bedroom. My mind began to spin and talking about my afternoon would have catapulted me into a complete nervous breakdown. To feign some normalcy, Leah and I made peanut butter sandwiches and sat on the guest room bed with the door closed, eating and chatting like two young sisters. Leah told me about her sleepover, the shopping trip and school, showing me her papers and writing assignments. It all appeared pretty normal from the outside. I was Leah's mother, sitting on the bed talking about school as any mother and daughter would. The reality of the situation was more than bizarre—four of us now living in the same house. Jim – the handsome, rich Newport Beach doctor; me - the abused wife, struggling to cope and get ahead in life; Leah – a child he'd fathered with a girlfriend he never saw; and now adding to this family, a slightly emaciated, young, drug-addicted girlfriend, who didn't know I was Jim's wife!

Leah went to bed a few hours later, setting out her clothes for school as she normally did. I took the ironing board into the guest room and began to ready my clothes for work the next day. My stomach clutched tightly as I heard laughing coming from outside and heard the front door fumble. I stood still holding my breath as Jim and his girlfriend came into the house talking and laughing, while they made their way down the hallway towards the master bedroom. The door slammed shut and giggling continued. I heard a few low voices, silence, and then the door of my bedroom banged open sending the ironing board and iron spilling onto the floor. Jim poked his head into the room as far as he could crane. Looking at my face he uttered a threat.

"If I so much as hear you breathe tonight, you won't wake up. Is that clear?" I gulped and nodded not moving, not changing my gaze. With the master bedroom door shut, muffled laughing and low voices became blurred by the addition of the country music playing harmonically from the stereo. That night I prayed and cried and cried and prayed. I prayed for God to hear me, to answer my prayers, I prayed for a miracle. I prayed for God to save me from my situation or to take my life. I fell into a fitful sleep.

Early the next morning, exhausted, I readied for work and took Leah to school. The only sound coming from the master bedroom was the twang of the music on the stereo. I didn't know what I was going to do after what happened. I couldn't stay in my house, but how could I leave? I was making the payments and promised my parents I would be responsible. I went to work and pretended I was the "golden girl."

Once at work, Dave Boyd, a technical branch manager, called me into his office gesturing me to sit down. He looked serious, and I was immediately afraid I had done something wrong. Dave looked at me from his desk; a genuine smile crossed his face.

"Jeanette, I sure am hearing good things about you from the techs. They like the detail you are putting into the sales packages, and our local results are higher than they have ever been." I smiled and nodded my head. "We need to keep our crews employed. With a new, energetic sales gal, they feel encouraged this will be a good year for hours and overtime." Dave smiled again and shuffled some papers into neat piles on his desk. He began again:

"I'm going to Fresno today to look at a project and wanted you to come along so you could quote the equipment portion of the job. Are you available to quote the job?" Dave asked. This was an excellent opportunity for me, being ushered into a project I would probably close with little effort. I nodded my head.

"Dave, this sounds like a great opportunity. When are you planning on leaving?" I asked.

"Well," Dave looked at the clock on his wall, "after the crew gets out to their jobs, I have a call with my area foreman and then we'll leave." I stood up and agreed.

We drove the few hours to Fresno and performed the site survey. As we drove back to Modesto, Dave began telling me about his children and wife and about his happy marriage. He laughed when he mentioned he had to stop at the grocery store to pick up some chicken. I was surprised as Dave told me he usually cooked for Pat and the kids since he got home first. I received a rare glimpse into a normal marriage and a loving relationship. Unexpectedly I felt a lump form in my throat and tears well in my eyes as I realized there was no way I would ever be happily married or have the joy of conceiving and giving birth to a baby.

Dave looked over, noticing my tears and pulled the car off the road. "Hey. . . hey, what's wrong? It can't be all that bad, can it?"

I laughed in embarrassment as I realized the awkwardness of the situation. Dave put a fatherly hand on my shoulder, and I began to cry softly into my hands. Dave began questioning me.

"Are you in trouble?" I didn't answer, but kept crying, unable to stop. "Is your husband mean? Is he hurting you?" I nodded my head up and down, the tears continuing to roll down my cheeks. Dave sat there for a while, not moving the car and began his speech. I never said anything, but listened, trying to gain composure.

"Listen Jeanette, I don't know you very well. You seem like a swell gal and all. I want to tell you that no man should ever hurt a gal, no matter what! A guy should love and cherish his wife. Sure, it isn't the easiest thing in the world to get married and stay married; add a couple of kids and some bills and things can get pretty stressful. But I know this: If any man ever lifted a hand to a woman, well, he's not really a man at all." I sniffed and nodded, feeling like my daddy and God were talking directly to me. I knew this. I knew things were bad and had progressed beyond believable. I lied to everyone around me, spinning the tale of my perfect fairy-tale life. Something in me changed that day; I finally allowed myself to admit to another person I was a domestic prisoner.

277

"Jeanette, no woman should stay with a man who hurts her. Now, my wife and I are churchgoers and don't believe in divorce and all, but that is one situation where I would tell a gal to leave. Most church counselors would say the same." I nodded and felt vindicated. My secret was out. Dave knew that I was in a bad marriage. Although I didn't feel I could share the graphic details, he knew I had been hurt and was scared of the one person who was supposed to protect, cherish, and love me.

CHAPTER 30
THE CONFRONTATION

After pulling my car into the garage, I walked into the house slowly, not hearing anything at all, thankful no one was home. Leah's backpack and books were in her room. I put my briefcase and purse down in the guest room, closing the door behind me. I lived quietly in the bedroom, eating, sleeping, readying for work in the small basic quarters. I had moved a few more of my clothes into the room, trying to be sly about getting my things. I had no idea how drugged up Jim may be and knew he had a few new guns around the house.

The rest of the week was uneventful. I made my sales appointments without running into Jim or his girlfriend. He brought her home each night, the laughter and drunken chatter continuing until wee hours each night. I made sure to leave early to avoid getting hurt.

Thursday night, I heard Jim come home, but didn't hear the laughter as I had all week long. I heard Jim enter Leah's room and ask her a few questions. I held my breath and waited until I heard the doorknob turn. Jim crashed into the room standing over the bed as I lay motionless.

"So, I guess this is it with us, is it?" Jim asked, almost sounding like he needed a new girlfriend. I wasn't quite sure how to answer, not wanting to say the wrong thing.

"I guess so," I said softly. As soon as I saw the look on Jim's face I knew I had said the wrong thing. I clutched onto the sides of the bed as Jim grabbed the mattress with super-human strength and turned the bed upside down throwing me under the mattress squished between the box springs and the bedding. Jim pulled the mattress off of me and raped me, screaming at me with each thrust.

"Why are you doing this to us? You know I have always loved you! Now look at what we have. Nothing! You and I are nothing. You can't give me the one thing that I really want from you – a baby. I want a son! You can't give me a son. You're nothing but a used-up broken hole!" I heard Jim fumble around and grab something as he slammed out of the room. I lay there hurting with each humiliating motion, feeling destroyed and useless. He was right. I was sterile and would never be able to give him or anyone else a baby.

Jim left me sobbing under the mattress, bleeding from both arms where he'd clawed my skin, bruises on both thighs from the pressure of his knees, bumps on my head where my head had hit the box springs. I cried out to God for Him to please take the pain away. I didn't want to live. I couldn't go home for fear Jim would kill my parents. I couldn't leave because he promised to kill me and anyone I ever got involved with. My life was over, and I was ready for it to end. I prayed harder than I'd ever prayed in my life.

Lord, if you're up there, please, please hear my prayers. I am hurting, Lord. I am ready to go home, Lord. I just can't take another day here. Please Lord, please help me. Protect Leah, Lord; keep her safe. I just can't take another day on this earth, Lord. Please help me. I'm crying out to you, now. Lord, if you don't take Jim's life tonight, take mine. I just can't take it anymore.

I woke up early, thankful the night was over so I could get out of the house and go to work. As I readied to walk out the door I realized what Jim had grabbed before storming out of the bedroom—he'd taken my purse.

Three, four, five soft steps and I reached my purse. The handle was a long strap that hung down along the side of the sink. Looking over, the coast was still clear; he was asleep. Quickly I grasped the square body of the purse and began to lift. . . a little too quickly. The strap lifted and wrapped around the knob of the vanity cabinet. As I pulled the purse towards my body the cabinet door opened and then swooshed closed with a loud slam! A loud stream of profanity began to spew from his mouth.

"Where do you think you are going?" he slurred. I could smell the alcohol and cigarettes projecting from across the room. I should have shut up and cowered, but was seething with anger. He raped me the night before, I was very angry at being a prisoner in my own home and felt my life was hopeless with no way out. I felt my cheeks get hot.

"To work. . . one of us has to earn a living," I said sarcastically. As soon as it came off my tongue, I panicked. Glancing at the dresser, I noticed a hammer. He must have been working with his tools and forgot to put the hammer away. As soon as I spied the hammer, I noticed his eyes on it at the same time. Enraged, he flew out of bed, crossing the room, grabbing the hammer in one motion. I dared not run. If I ran, he would claw me in the back of the head. I might have a chance if I didn't try to fight back. I crumpled down by the vanity, crouching on both feet, my hands up in a defensive position and watched in the wall-sized mirror as he filled the room, looming larger than life. I looked up at him and then I saw it as clear as day. He stood above me with the hammer poised to come down, crushing into my skull. His face was contorted and looked like a person possessed by the devil. His eyes were bloodshot and in the darkened room looked like red slits of blood. This was it. This was my last moment of life. The hammer started to come down. I saw the scene unfold as if the seconds were all in slow motion.

I prayed a silent prayer for God to be with me now and suddenly felt laughter rise up from inside of my belly. I let out a loud laugh, and it startled Jim and me.

"Go ahead!" I yelled, a new miraculous strength conquering my fear. "Go ahead and do it!" I screamed looking at Jim frozen in the mirror, hammer poised over his head, me not cowering at all, but challenging him to kill me. "Kill me, Jim! Go ahead; kill me now because today I know something. . ." I smiled up at him, facing his eyes and not glancing away. "I know I'm not afraid of you anymore. You have no power over me because I'd rather be dead than live another day with you!" I faced Jim off and for the first time wasn't afraid of him. I felt a spirit of boldness flooding through my body and watched as Jim backed off like a confused child, dropping the hammer to the floor, walking around in circles mumbling indistinguishable phrases.

I was dumbfounded at Jim's response and felt the boldness of God empowering me. I gathered my purse and without any fear in my body, left the house without turning back. I knew this would be the last day Jim would ever have the chance to hurt or abuse me again.

CHAPTER 31
THE ESCAPE

My boldness vacillated to timidity as I played the hammer scene over in my mind. During work, I went through the motions, my mind spinning with fear, my stomach sick immediately, unable to eat or keep anything down, my mouth dry – what had I done? What was I going to do? I had to go back to the house to rescue Leah. I needed to pack my things, but how? In the early afternoon, I drove by the house a few times, passing without stopping in case Jim may be home. From what I could tell, no one was home. I eased my car around the corner, parked it and quietly slid through the back gate. I couldn't get in through the back door, so I made my way to the front, unlocked the door and went inside.

To keep the house safe from "undesirables," Jim installed motion sensors, an alarm, and keypad to use for a security system. As I quickly punched in the digits, the beeping would not stop. I reentered the code several times and realized frantically that Jim had changed the code! I knew in less than thirty seconds, the alarm would blast out and the police would arrive. No doubt Jim had already called local law enforcement, letting them know they should expect a break-in.

Running through the house, I quickly grabbed armfuls of my clothes, make-up and anything else I could carry and threw it onto a pile in the back yard. The alarm blasted and I made a few more quick trips, my arms scratched by the metal hangers. I threw three loads of clothes and shoes into my car and I screeched out of the quiet neighborhood, homeless once again.

I wanted Leah to be home so I could take her with me. Why wasn't she at home? I lamented as I drove from the house, wishing I had her in my car. My heart was breaking in two. I loved Leah; she was my daughter, but I knew if I took her, I wouldn't stand a chance legally and would certainly lose my life in the process. Jim knew Leah was the joy of my life and to make sure he hurt me, he would never let me see her again. The thought of losing my daughter made me sob uncontrollably as I drove blindly around the streets of Modesto for hours trying to calm myself and figure out what to do. I did have some savings, but that had dwindled with the closing costs of the house and a few extra furnishings. I barely had $500 saved.

With no extra cash on me, no credit cards, no family or friends in the area and no place to sleep, I pulled up to the house of a colleague—Kevin Flowers. Kevin was a senior sales executive and had helped to mentor me and give me a few tips for success on the job. He was very gregarious and had invited me over to his house for lunch, right after I started working at the branch. I met his lovely wife Rita and their two young children.

After sitting in my car for a long time, I finally had the composure to walk up to the door and ring the bell to ask if I could please sleep on their couch for a few nights until payday. I would no doubt have to explain my whole embarrassing story hoping they wouldn't judge me, try to call Jim, or try to convince me to go back. Things would never change. I finally realized that.

I hesitantly rang the doorbell. Rita answered the door. She took one look at my tear-stained face and without saying anything opened her arms wide. I fell into her embrace, sobbing into her shoulder, my body shuddering in spasms. Kevin and the children stood behind in silence. Rita took me by the hand and sat me down on the couch. Kevin ushered the kids to bed and came back, making small talk, while Rita fixed a kettle of tea.

For the first time in my life, I told the truth. I had nodded to Dave Boyd about my secret, but couldn't bring myself to vocalize it. That night, over a few cups of tea, Rita and Kevin sat and listened to my tale of living as a domestic prisoner for almost a decade, trying not to let the shock show on their faces. They saved my life that night, becoming an answer to my prayer. Jim didn't know them, didn't know where they lived, and there was no way for him to find me. I was safe.

Rita put together a makeshift bed on the couch, while Kevin and I carried my worldly possessions into their small home, hanging up as many of my things as we could. Kevin brought in a few cardboard boxes from the garage and soon enough I had all of my things in order, giving me a sense of peace. I went to sleep that night feeling dreadfully unsure of my future, worrying about Leah and also feeling indescribable freedom and relief from a huge boulder lifted off my chest. My secret was out. I left Jim and was going to meet with a lawyer to get a divorce. I would never allow myself to get into an abusive relationship again.

I met with a divorce lawyer later in the week, sharing the details of my abusive relationship with Jim. She questioned me about Leah, asking if I ever legally adopted her. With a lump in my throat, I admitted I hadn't and had no legal right to her. She said the process without property and without children would be fairly easy. California was a no-fault divorce state; you didn't need grounds to file, she explained. We would evict Jim from my parents' house and split the possessions 50/50. I would file for divorce, serve Jim the papers, and he would be forced to show up at court. It would take six months, and then the divorce would be final. She kept saying the "d" word, and I had fearful visions telling my parents I was getting a divorce. I handed her an envelope containing all of my savings for her retainer and told her I'd pay for the rest of the divorce in payments. I left her office looking over my shoulder, feeling fearful Jim was watching me.

Kevin and Rita were very gracious hosts; however, I really longed to have a little privacy. I remembered an older woman named Lori, who shared one of my night classes, mention she had a small room with a private entrance for rent. I saw Lori the following night at school. I was relieved when she informed me the room was vacant, very affordable, and I could move in immediately. My quarters had a mattress on the floor, a small bathroom and a wire rack to hang up a few clothes. It was wonderful, anonymous, and best of all, Jim didn't know where I was. I was able to drive to and from work, and was safe. I cried each night as I thought of Leah, and the fact I had escaped without her.

My parents were unaware of the situation, mainly because I was afraid to face them. I felt a dread in divulging the truth, feeling it was my fault; they had warned me! I hadn't listened! Guilt flooded my body. I felt filing for divorce was a sin, a huge failure and an embarrassment to the family. I was fearful once Jim received divorce papers he would retaliate, most likely by killing me and maybe my parents as well. I called them from work a few weeks later not mentioning what was going on. Mother sounded happy to hear my voice, talking to me about the family trip up to Lake Tahoe in a few weeks. They asked if Jim, Leah, and I could come up for a few days. I told my mother that I could take the time off, and would be coming up alone. I could tell by the way my mother said goodbye she was very worried about me.

THE ESCAPE

CHAPTER 32
LAKE TAHOE

Lake Tahoe has incredible natural beauty, huge pine trees, wildlife, and the serene deep blue of the lake. I always loved the lake as a girl but now felt nothing as I gazed upon the handiwork of God. At the cabin I crossed paths with my brothers and their families, hugging quickly and exchanging greetings as I came and they left. My sister Debbie was going to stay. It would be just us two girls and our parents at the Incline Village lake-view cabin.

I was a complete zombie. We hiked and went for picnics; I went through the motions of the days performing without feeling. I had a huge lump in my throat that just wouldn't leave. When Debbie finally left, my parents and I had one day alone at the cabin. This would be my chance to tell my parents the truth.

We sat on the deck overlooking the vast mountains, the look of worry crossing my parents' faces. With coffee cups in hands, they sat without speaking as I unfolded the decade-long story of my true life with Jim Miller. I cried as I began confessing my horrid and secretive journey, leaving out the graphic details of the rapes, the diseases and the drugs. They listened intently to my story. When I finally reached the current events and shared that I had already filed for divorce and nothing they thought or wanted would change my mind, they hugged me and cried and apologized that they hadn't seen the signs. They both reassured me I was making the right decision and would stand behind my reasons for divorcing Jim. They were thankful I had survived and escaped my prison and would be my support whenever I needed them. The feeling of complete and unconditional love poured out from my parents. There were no "I told you so's." They only loved me and wanted to help. I was extremely relieved wishing I would have confessed the truth years earlier.

The divorce proceedings were scary. I only made it through with my father standing by my side. Jim would direct dagger eyes and threatening stares to me every time he saw me, smirking any chance he had. He would whisper death threats under his breath, trying to scare and intimidate me. I still didn't care if he killed me during those days; I was free and would never let myself become an abuse victim again. His threats scared me, but I knew, day-by-day, I would get stronger and would be building a new life without Jim.

I felt comforted in the knowledge that God had taken me out of a horrible situation. I trusted He had a plan for the rest of my life. Daddy vowed to help me through the divorce proceedings, promising to be there next to me for every court appearance. He also told me he would keep me safe and that Jim would never lay a hand on me again as long as he was alive. True to his word, when we finally regained possession of the little house, Daddy moved in with me—cleaning, mowing, fixing walls, and getting the house back into shape. After several months passed, I had a fellow student move into the house and convinced I was safe, Daddy went home to live with Mother.

CHAPTER 33
THE NEW LIFE

Work was amazing. I poured my energy into my accounts and made more money than I had ever made in my life. Locally, AT&T made a sweeping organizational decision: the Modesto branch where I worked was realigned and became managed by the Sacramento regional office. Our direct line of support now came from Sacramento. At the transition I was assigned a new manager and went back to using my maiden name. No one in the new branch knew me or knew I had been married, except Kevin Flowers, Dave Boyd and a few techs. I was thankful my life wasn't a focus of gossip or questioning looks. It all worked out perfectly.

I was left financially devastated by Jim. Each trip to the mailbox would reveal an ever-mounting pile of bills to pay off, including things he had charged to my name. I was in debt several thousand dollars and to pay my overdue bills, I decided to take another job. I worked for AT&T full-time during the week and as a waitress on the weekends. It worked, and slowly the pile of bills began getting paid off. I started putting a few dollars back into my savings account and getting my life in order.

School was plugging away and in the spring of 1989, my parents proudly came up to watch me walk across the stage and pick up my diploma from Modesto College. I smiled sheepishly as they urged me to stand in front of the large sign for the college, adorned with cap and gown and diploma in my hand for a picture. They loved me and were proud of my accomplishment; they had the opportunity to witness me reach one of my greatest milestones. My parents shared the exhilaration I felt in reaching one of my life goals, made more dramatic because of the adversity I endured.

CHAPTER 34
MODERN DAY MIRACLES

I felt a stirring in my heart and a deep emptiness I knew only God could fill. As a Catholic I knew unless I had my marriage annulled, I couldn't receive communion and would not be a "true" Catholic as a divorcee. Each Sunday I tried to enter into the service; however, I fell into a deep depression and pushed down the envious feelings as I watched the happy young families with their children worshipping God. I desperately wanted to connect with God and prayed for Him to help me heal from my horrific ordeal.

Time was my friend and allowed me to try to make sense of my past and to grieve for the innocent young girl, abused by a man who was suppose to be her protector. I was aware many women repeat patterns when pairing off and I was rightfully afraid of getting into another relationship with a man who was an abuser. I knew the signs and shared a date with a man who used colorful profanity when talking about his ex-wife; that was the last time I saw him. I was done with men and certain I would never marry again.

One evening while hosting an AT&T Technical Booth at a local business fair I met Sam, a very handsome young business owner. We chatted easily and began a friendship that grew with each conversation and date we shared. Any man I dated at this time of my life was highly scrutinized. I was not going to get involved with anyone who would not respect me like my father respected my mother. I found Sam to be a lot like my dad. Sam shared his deep convictions and faith with me and I grasped onto the freedom gained by believing in Christ and of the plan God had for my life. Sparing the gruesome details, Sam listened empathetically as I unfolded the story of my life before meeting him. I was completely honest as I explained I would probably never be able to carry a child. Sam was never married before and had no children; I knew in my Italian family, a man would rarely marry a woman knowing she was infertile.

Our relationship grew deeper and I began devouring one of the first gifts Sam gave me: a Bible with my name printed on the cover in shiny gold script. Each day of my newfound Christian walk felt liberating and free. I could feel my heart heal and during unabashed times of worshipping Him in a fervent and innocent way, tears flowed freely down my face as I bathed in complete love and restoration. God was working a real-life modern day miracle in my life. I was thankful for the truth I was shown, and forever indebted with my life for His saving grace. I vowed to serve Him for all of my days as partial payment for the saving of my life and the answering of my prayers.

As I recounted the hard, cold nights and angry, frustrated times, I never held the long years I suffered against God. I didn't blame God for my situation. I reflected as I looked back and clearly felt

God was with me all of those years, crying with me as I cried, holding me as I sobbed, and comforting me as I reached out to Him. He showed me a love that would never leave me nor forsake me, a love that would be pure and never hurt, and a love that was always on my side, unconditionally for every day of my life.

Receiving counsel and hearing the wisdom of my pastors, I immersed myself in good Christian counseling and allowed my church friends to pray for continued emotional healing. I knew it would take years to completely heal from my traumatic past, but clinging to God my Father allowed me to feel safe and secure once again.

My relationship with Sam blossomed into a tender and trusting love and late in 1990, we had a fairy tale white wedding on the lawn of his parents' riverfront estate—I was the princess, my heart given to my prince. We walked down the aisle as family and friends smiled at the young couple with a bright future. I smiled up at my handsome new husband with that familiar lump in my throat, hiding an underlying fear I would never be able to give him a child.

My marriage to Sam was a dream come true—true love made in heaven and blessed by God. I felt cherished and for the first time in my life, I wasn't afraid to open my heart to love. Sam loved me tenderly and showed me his patient ways, honest dealings and love for Christ. He wasn't a Bible-thumping, "repent or you'll burn in hell" Christian. He showed the true life of Christ by how he lived. Was he perfect? Is any person? No, but he was so genuine and funny and hard working; he was made of the same moral and honest fiber as my father.

We sought out the services of a San Francisco fertility specialist and after several months of unbearable pain and emotional disappointment were overjoyed with the news of a positive blood test. Our final treatment was successful and I was carrying Sam's baby inside of my womb. We immediately called our parents relaying our good news, and embraced each other thanking God for the miracle growing within me. Sam boasted to anyone who would listen about me carrying twins, a boy and a girl. I didn't say anything because he was so proud – I loved watching his happiness and wouldn't dare dash his enthusiasm.

Our first ultrasound revealed a very successful fertility treatment indeed. I had conceived, and clearly detailed on the monitor we gazed in awe over, were two tiny babies: a boy and a girl. I wept tears of joy and knew God had revealed our children to their father. We were overjoyed, immersed in our love for each other, and witnessing the miracle of life, thankful to our God for protecting my body. I loved being pregnant and Sam made me feel like a precious gift, carrying his two wonderful children. At thirty-one weeks gestation, I went into pre-term labor and had an emergency C-section, delivering the twins nine weeks prematurely. Although our babies were only two and three pounds, they suffered no health issues and day-by-day continued to thrive. After growing and gaining weight, we rejoiced and finally brought our twins home with us near Easter of 1992. I would look down at my twin babies, asleep together in their bassinette and cry and pray and thank God for His miracle delivery of two tiny precious gifts of life.

CHAPTER 35
BUILDING AN EMPIRE

My life divided into twenty-minute increments around the clock, full of midnight feedings and diaper changes. Although my maternity leave was almost three months, I spent most of that time caring for my infant twins in the hospital preemie ward. A friend at church recommended I interview a nanny she once hired for her young son. Angelica was a caring and capable young lady who out of necessity immediately came to live in our home to mother our two tiny infants. I wept the morning I left for work having only four short weeks to spend at home with my babies and felt an overwhelming pang of guilt for leaving.

I poured myself into work; instead of satisfaction as I once felt, I began feeling angered by the constant travel and account presentations. Bombarded by the constant guilt of raising kids and keeping the momentum in my career, I stressed nearing my breaking point. If I could have, I'd quit and become a stay-at-home mom, but our finances just wouldn't allow it. Late in 1994,

I consulted with the women at church, lamenting my situation and sharing my feelings of inadequacy as a mother who was never there. One wise woman asked me what my heart was telling me. I told her I wanted to quit my job because my heart craved staying home with my children. She nodded and matter of factly told me to trust God and quit my job! She looked me square on and said we serve a big God. What? What was she saying? Trust God and quit my job? What would I do? How would I make enough money for us to make ends meet?

The thought of quitting my job played over and over in my mind and after discussing my desperate feelings with Sam, we both agreed I needed to spend more time with the babies. Sam suggested I speak with my direct manager at AT&T and inquire about a permanent part-time position—one that would allow me to work less hours and help with the family finances. The branch manager called me at my office and explained he understood my situation; however, they simply didn't have the flexibility for an employee to job-share or work my account executive position part-time. That was not the answer I was looking for.

Not understanding what God was doing, but certain I was making a solid decision, I decided to trust Him and quit my job. With the support of Sam and my friends at church, I typed out the resignation letter and turned it in to Charles Silver, regional vice president for AT&T. Charles and I had a very good relationship and when he received the letter, immediately called me to discuss my reasons for leaving. I explained I had given birth to twins who were born very premature. I told Charles I spent my entire maternity leave alone at home while my babies were in the hospital. When they finally did come home, I continually left them with my nanny.

I expressed I just couldn't do the eight to five and overnight travel anymore, relaying I felt this was my only option. Charles understood, confiding he was a husband whose wife was a stay-at-home mom. He told me he would be in touch and wished me well.

When the call came from Charles a month later I was surprised. He explained: "Jeanette, our area results have dropped significantly since you left the territory. I was hoping there was something you and I could come up with to help." I listened to Charles, having loved the month at home with my children, and resolving *even if* he offered me a huge raise to come back to work, I wasn't going to take it. I murmured my acknowledgement to his situation.

"Remember last month when you asked me about job-share or part time? Well, we didn't have the headcount for an employee with a part-time expense, but we would be able to bring you on as an AT&T contractor."

My mind was abuzz. Contractor? Charles rushed on, trying to explain, "Well Jeanette, AT&T has sanctioned a firm to become a national sales agency and branches like mine are hiring these 'agents' to fulfill territory sales positions. You would be the first 'independent California-based sales agency' for AT&T and could get a business license, cards, and we'd provide everything else you needed. . ." Charles paused sensing my hesitation. "*And* you could work as a consultant as many or as few hours a week as you wanted. You'd be your own boss. You wouldn't have to travel; we'd loan you a phone system and computer system for your house. You'd be connected to the branch, *and you can work at home.*" I started considering what Charles was saying, feeling bitter that I had walked away from my retirement and benefits a month earlier and now presto-magic, have the job I was looking for.

I began hesitantly. "Okay, Charles, you have my attention. I get my business license and become a contractor for you, doing what I did before, except working from home, and being my own boss. How do I get paid?" I asked.

Charles explained, "I'll have Betty Abraham call you in a few days. She'll work with you on all the details. Pretty much, you manage accounts like you did as an employee; use our paperwork to submit orders and when the month is over, we'll present you with a commission statement overview. You approve it and send us an invoice to pay. I think you would be really good at bringing on new agents, training, and supporting them as they worked for you. You make the overall commission and pay your agents a percentage. This could be a little empire for you, Jeanette."

I couldn't believe my ears. My mind was spinning, working from home with my children and earning income. This was an answer to my prayers. . . and little did I know, the opportunity of a lifetime.

CHAPTER 36
LEAH'S RESCUE

Although I settled into a life of satisfying motherhood and a fulfilling career, I often mourned deeply for the loss of my first daughter, Leah. On many occasions I placed anonymous calls to Child Protective Services hoping they would send someone to investigate a home where I knew drugs and abuse would reign. I prayed for Leah asking God to protect her and keep her safe until she grew up, hoping I would see her again. I could only imagine the lies Leah's father told her when I escaped and I prayed she would one day forgive and understand my actions.

To complete his domination and abuse, when the court evicted Jim from the house we lived in, he moved a few doors down in the same neighborhood. Several years later when Sam and I married and I became pregnant with the twins, I was not comfortable living in the little house my parents helped me to buy, so we rented out our house and purchased a wonderful home a few miles away. I left my work number with Mrs. Torres, an elderly neighbor, asking her to keep an eye on our renters and never to share my number or whereabouts with Jim. Mrs. Torres had heard screams coming from the little house and figured out that Jim was not a nice man. She promised she would keep my number private and watch the place for us.

One day when the twins were almost a year old, I received a frantic call from Mrs. Torres. Mrs. Torres witnessed Jim beating Leah outside of their house and intervened, yelling at Jim. Jim finally relented and Mrs. Torres pulled Leah out of the clutches of her abusive father. Leah was sobbing, battered and bleeding. Mrs. Torres took her in knowing she could not keep Leah safely in her home and worked to reunite her with her natural mother. As I heard Mrs. Torres describe Leah's horrid beating I was confused, afraid and desperately wanting to save my little girl. My mind was a mix of emotions as I questioned Mrs. Torres.

"How is Leah doing now?" I asked pensively, the thoughts of my sweet twins asleep in their cribs flooding my brain. Mrs. Torres began.

"Well, we've been calling her mother in Orange County unsuccessfully all day, and I called her father and told him I'm bringing her to the train station and putting her on the 4 o'clock to L. A. I can't keep her here and I knew you had a good life now with the babies and all. I really didn't want to bring you into all of this, but I just don't know where to turn. I can't put her into foster care. Do you think you could take her until we can find her mom?" She sounded like my grandmother, full of concern, but knowing she was intervening into a potentially lethal situation.

"Mrs. Torres, Jim doesn't know where I live and you know I'm happily married and have the twins. I haven't seen Leah in over

304

five years. I don't know if I can help you or not; I will have to call Sam at work and tell him what's going on. Let me call you back." We hung up and I called Sam, explaining the dire situation.

Sam told me to choose a safe place to rendezvous with Mrs. Torres, pick up Leah to keep her safe and we would worry about finding her mother later. Tears streamed down my face as I drove to the church where Mrs. Torres brought Leah. I thanked God for protecting her and for blessing me with a husband who had His heart.

I pulled up to the empty church and began walking through the classrooms following the sound of a young woman's frantic voice. As I entered the classroom, my heart stopped, the familiar lump in my throat. I couldn't see Leah's face, but her voice was familiar. She sat with her back to the door of the room, her long dark hair cascading down her back, talking on the phone. She was pleading.

"But Mom, Mom, I know it's the middle of semesters at school... I know I've gone to three high schools, you just don't understand what happened." Leah took short breaths, sobbing and choking filled with emotion. "No, I can't stay with my dad, you don't understand – he's hurting me, Mom, he's beating me up. Last month he called the police on me! On me! I spent my sixteenth birthday in juvenile hall surrounded by scary gang members because my dad told the police I was a problem!" I stood still with my heart breaking, tears streaming down my face, listening to my now-grown daughter pleading with her birth mom to take her away from the horrible prison that I had already escaped from. The phone hung up and a desperate Leah leaned over and cupped her face into her lap, sobbing uncontrollably. I had to go to her, but I was afraid.

I didn't know if she would reject my heart, my love, my shelter. I started out softly.

"Leah, are you ok?" I asked, knowing she wasn't. Leah stopped crying for a moment as she recognized my voice and turned around. When she faced me, I almost fainted. Here in front of me in the matter of a second, Leah grew up from the eleven-year-old young girl I had left, into the beautiful sixteen-year-old young woman standing in front of me. I couldn't control my heart. I opened my arms and invited her to hug me, hoping she would run to me, afraid her rejection would crush me in two.

"Mommy!" Leah said as we both knew in that instant we were meant to be together, mother and child. We were united with an outpouring of years of pent up emotion. We hugged and cried for a long time, silently sharing each other. We did not have to talk about the drama that pushed us together, thankful that we could hold one another and comfort and understand without a word spoken. After a long while, I looked up at her, holding her grown face in my hands and I cried all over again, this time tears of happiness as I gazed upon her face and sorrow as I realized I lost over five precious years of her life.

While Leah and I drove back to her new temporary home, I explained how Mrs. Torres called me trying to help, fearful she would be hurt if she mentioned my intervention. We talked briskly, trying to catch up on each other's lives. Leah settled into our home very quickly. I knew the shocking difference in the home I lived in with Sam compared to the sentence Leah left behind. There were no broken dishes or profane threats. There were no holes in the walls or broken door jams. Our home was filled with the love of God, an imperfect couple, loving and respecting each other and joyfully raising our children. Leah seemed so at peace in our home. When we finally connected her with her mother several months later, it was a sad day; however, we both knew nothing would keep us apart again.

Sam and I remained a part of Leah's life from that day forward. Every chance we had we spent time with her in Orange County. The children got to know her and grew to love their "big sister." We saw each other often and would share the emotional stories we survived. We tried to help one another make sense of our captivity and work towards healing. I loved Leah; however, I always felt a pang of guilt when introducing her in any social situation. I called her "my God-daughter" or "adopted daughter," none of these validating the child I kept close to my heart, a child I sacrificed my own life to protect. Leah in my life was a constant reminder of the horrific past I endured, and sharing our relationship with new acquaintances was a secret I would not reveal to anyone.

CHAPTER 37
PRESIDENT

The local AT&T agency began to bloom, and I worked diligently at each function, keeping processes I felt made sense and ditching those that never did. At the end of the first year, I hired my first employee, a young lady who hit the ground running. Together our sales results were on the top of the charts and getting local attention. Charles Silver called me with the news and enthusiastically encouraged me to replicate what I was doing in different territories. He told me to go out and recruit new sales agents. With twins in tow and my parents helping to baby-sit, I covered the state filling in sales territories with new agents for AT&T. By the end of our second year, the company had eight employees and our sales results were exceeding a half-million dollars.

My personal reputation earned during the eight years as a direct AT&T account executive opened doors; managers throughout the state contacted me and asked me to train and mentor their new agents. During one meeting AT&T offered my company over 350 territory sales positions. I did mull it over and thankfully declined, reminding myself I trusted God and walked away from my career to be a mother and if that meant my company wouldn't be a mega corporation that was fine with me. I was working long hard hours, but scheduled my time around toddler naps and play schedules. It was perfect. I pushed down the past and covered the unbelievable story of my abuse. It was behind me and I wasn't going to look back. The whipped dog and doormat, abused wife persona was almost dead. In her place was the educated, accomplished, hard-working, street-smart, business owner. I was blessed. I took time off to take my kids to the zoo and be a working-mom, confident my sales reps were trained and working in their territories. My business continued to thrive.

CHAPTER 38
HEALING A HEART

Suffering the loss of a few pregnancies, one which almost took my life, leaving me unable to carry any more children, Sam and I prayed about growing our family. During one hormonal Sunday, I read the Parade section of the newspaper. There was a feature article written by the late Dave Thomas, founder of Wendy's, explaining his life as an adopted child. The article shed light on the national plight of the foster child. My heart went out to the children without homes, the staggering numbers totaling over 150,000 in the North America Welfare System awaiting permanent homes.

I immediately began praying Sam would feel the same way about adopting a baby as I did. When we first married, he always told me not to worry about getting pregnant. He said he'd be very happy to have our own or to adopt. Well, now he could have both. Hesitantly I mentioned my heart, feeling God had another life for us to bring into our home. Sam looked at me smiling his agreement; we were on the same page.

We received the call after nearly two years of waiting as trained foster/adopt parents; there was a baby, she was bi-racial, four and a half months old and ready for permanent placement, *and* she had a two-year-old sister. My heart dropped. I had stressed with the twins, feeding one then the next, changing one while the other cried, always feeling frantic and out of control. I had a vision of me sitting in a rocking chair feeding and cuddling a little baby. I didn't envision growing our family again, two-by-two.

Sam and I made our first trip to social services, our five-year-old twins along, to meet the foster children. They were so different. The baby was tiny with pink cheeks, soft brown hair, brown eyes and caramel colored skin. Her sister in contrast was blond, blue-eyed, with glow-in-the-dark white skin. They were desperately needy, absolutely adorable, and we all immediately fell in love with our two new additions. I made a mental inventory, thanking God we were ready for two more children; we had two cribs, two high-chairs, two car seats and a double stroller. We had two of everything and welcomed our precious kids into our lives. Life in our home was rambunctious and overflowing with four young children, and thankfully never the same.

I managed the business as the mother of four, with the business incorporating, naming me as president and CEO. Our staff was comprised of some of the industry's top technical associates, many whom I worked with at AT&T. We provided technical applications, hardware, software, wire, and service to businesses all over the United States. Our sales topped five million with more than thirty employees. In 1999, the National Association of Women Business Owners, (NAWBO) honored my accomplishments at an awards ceremony. I earned the recognition as a woman working in a nontraditional field of technology. I stood at the podium receiving my award: 1999 Woman Innovator of the Year, Jeanette Towne, President and CEO. The lump was back in my throat as I thanked God, who allowed me to escape my prison and blessed me with a family and a part-time job that turned into a thriving enterprise.

Amazingly the business landed MetLife in 2001 allowing our California-based corporation to sell product and support technical communication installations nationally, for a global giant. The MetLife engineering staff soon trusted our technical and sales staff and enjoyed the attention we devoted to supporting their account. Supporting MetLife brought me to travel to New York City a few times a year. Throughout my tenure with AT&T I had traveled alone and with my obvious knowledge of how awful some people were, I was very careful. Sam would stay home with the children while I left to do short bursts of travel. We rarely took our children to babysitters and flexed hours to make sure we took care of our growing family.

In 2007, during a long drive home from our church's family Mexico mission trip I found the courage and finally shared my story with a single gal I had grown close to through the week. She openly shared her story of abuse at the hand of an ex-husband, a situation similar to mine. I listened and felt God tugging hard at my heart. Over the period of several hours in the car, I unfolded the story of me, the girl who made one really poor decision in her life, and the catastrophe that ensued. I rejoiced with her in the miraculous rescue and restoration I received from God my Father. My friend urged me to write this story, to tell the truth in hopes of helping to save another. In that moment of the long car ride, I realized my heart had finally healed, for it was now thirty years since I met Jim Miller and almost twenty years since I had seen his face. For the first time ever, I was talking about my story. It was time to connect my past with my present and to uncover the journey, no matter how nightmarish it was. By keeping my life a secret, I not only invalidated what God had done in my life, but I invalidated my relationship with Leah, leaving her confused and feeling insignificant. Two weeks later, I received a hand-written two page letter from my church friend. She continued to tell me how inspiring she thought my story was and encouraged me to use my story for the good of another.

I started the journey a young and innocent girl, losing the end of my teens and most of my twenties. I had been trapped in the convoluted and intricate web that entangled me, kept me frightened, unable to feel I could escape. There was one thread constant through the time of captivity: I never lost faith that God could hear me. When I cried out to Him I did feel Him comfort and carry me through many very difficult days.

God worked a miracle in my life, giving me a man with His character, a fairy-tale wedding, miracle twins, and a successful corporation. I was a victim, trapped, and He allowed me to escape and brought me to a place of solace and healing. Am I completely healed? Absolutely, not. We have open wounds that if deep enough will heal over time, but the scars will remain, maybe tender for a long time and then finally as a reminder of the pain that once was.

I had a prayer session in my closet with God one day shortly after the car ride with my friend. Sounds funny, I know, as I write this I still think it sounds this way, but I heard God speaking to my heart that evening. I felt God telling me I needed to share my story to help another and honor the miracle He performed in my life. I pray the words penned here will be passed to another and find their way into the hands of those who need to hear.

EPILOGUE

Leah called me after 9/11 crying out for a family to belong to. Sam and I encouraged her to move up to Northern California permanently to settle, which she did. Leah met the man of her dreams and when they married a few years later, Sam proudly walked her down the aisle as our friends and family looked on. Leah has grown up to be an incredible young woman and is in my life today, enjoying a happy marriage, an excellent career, and raising an active toddler.

I have never run into Jim since the court appearances, but in the first few years after escaping, I dreamed of being abused and frightened, and in later years of actually praying for and forgiving him. One day on a whim, I Googled Jim Miller and found a frightening public record about a violent domestic abuse case he was mentioned in. The police report said there was so much blood spatter in the residence that it looked like a homicide scene. They found his current girlfriend naked, battered, and laying unconscious in the street. Jail time ensued.

EPILOGUE

I continued to work hard in my business and eventually went back to school to receive a business and marketing degree. I am proud of finally finishing an advanced degree years after I left high-school, completing a goal I set as a young woman. Today I am residing president and CEO of my multi-million dollar corporation and will embrace the past as part of who I am today. Although I have experienced more tribulations than most people have in their lives, I am living proof that God works true miracles in the lives of ordinary people today, allowing them to break free, to escape chains, to overcome, to thrive, and to not remain a prisoner of their circumstances.

FROM PRISONER TO PRESIDENT READERS' GUIDE

QUESTIONS FOR DISCUSSION

1. Chapter 1: The beginning of the manuscript details a horrific scene of abuse. Jeanette went back into the bedroom to collect a personal item. What was the item? What were Jeanette's feelings as she entered the bedroom?

2. Chapter 2: Where is the college Jeanette attended located? What course of study does Jeanette choose? Do you think there is anything about an innocent student that makes them a perfect "target" for the perpetrator? Why?

3. Chapter 2: What was the nature of the first speech Jeanette gave to Jim? Where did this speech take place? Why do you think Jeanette felt compelled to make this speech?

4. Chapter 3: Who was Iris? What are her two major employment titles? Do you think there are a lot of Irises out there in the world? How do you think innocent young women get coerced into becoming "working" girls? Do you think there was real danger of being killed by Savage or Iris that night?

5. Chapter 4: What did Jeanette's mother think of Jim? What did Jeanette's mother say to her as she was readying to leave? Do you think Jeanette's mother had God-given intuition about Jim? Have you ever felt an internal "alarm" when meeting another person?

6. Chapter 7: Who was Ken Tuttle? What was his relationship with Jim Miller? Was Jeanette rightfully concerned? Do you think people often use children as pawns in relationships? Why?

7. Chapter 8: What was the incident that resulted in the scene of "First Abuse"? How did Jeanette react to this? What did she do? Did she reconcile with Jim? How did this make you feel?

8. Chapter 10: Donny's Beach House is the scene of a violent episode. Who was the victim and how did he become the abused? Did the abuse end at the restaurant? What was the scene at the trailer? How did Mrs. Phillips help Jeanette? Do you think Jeanette should have said something to Mrs. Phillips?

9. Chapter 12: Why did Jeanette see a lawyer? How did this make her feel? Do you think many people get into marriage relationships without knowing the financial situations of their spouses? Do you think pre-marital counseling should include a

financial aspect?

10. Chapter 13: What law did Jim and Jeanette break in court? What did Jim do to perjure himself? How did Jeanette become involved with this? How did Jim feel about the law? Why do you think when Jeanette is hurt and angry she then allows Jim to work his way back into her heart?

11. Chapter 13: Where did Jeanette get a job? How did she get to work? Where was Leah during the day? What does a typical victimizer do to a victim to keep them in the relationship? Did Jim do this to Jeanette? What one thing did Jeanette do financially to make her feel a sense of accomplishment?

12. Chapter 16: Where did Jeanette uncover the information about a teaching opportunity? What was the job? How did she learn the information? What product and manufacturer did she mention? What was her thought about this product and how it would be received in future markets?

13. Chapter 17: What shocking realization did Jeanette make about Anne? What were Jeanette's thoughts about her mother-in-law and abuse? What explosive incident did Anne endure? What thoughts do you as the reader have about the generational inheritance of abuse?

14. Chapter 18: What did Jeanette realize about Jim's addictions? Who is Frank and what does he ask Jeanette for? Who is Rick? Why does Jeanette feel she needs to call him? Do you think she

QUESTIONS FOR DISCUSSION

made a mistake by calling Rick? Did you feel Jeanette "asked for
the abuse"?

15. Chapter 19: What was the Cozy 8? Were other families living
there? Do you think motels of this kind house other homeless
families? Do you think drug and alcohol addictions contribute to
families' homelessness? What steps do you feel would be helpful
for families with addictions? Would identifying the addictions and
working to control them help situations like Jeanette's?

16. Chapter 20: Where did Jeanette land a job? How did her
computer skills enable her to get consideration? Who did Jim go
to Hawaii with? What was the confession Jim gave to Jeanette?
Who called Jeanette on the phone looking for Jim? What did
Jeanette do with the note?

17. Chapter 21: What revelation did Jeanette have about the
"Shameful Disease"? Why do you think she should or shouldn't
have realized Jim was the source? Do you think she was naïve or
trying to ignore the truth? What was the name of the family the
Millers lived with?

18. Chapter 22: How did Jeanette feel as she walked back into
the Hutsill's house after being missing for a night? What did
Karen accuse her of? What did Jim do to the wedding rings? Why
do you think the Hutsills ignored the clear evidence of spousal
abuse? What was the contrast between Jeanette's work persona
and that of her home?

322

19. Chapter 25: What horrific drug-raged episode do you read about in this chapter? Why do you think Jim unleashed his abuse on an animal? Why do you think abusers use the innocent to gain control? What was the name of the hotel where Jim lived? How did Jeanette feel about the living accommodations?

20. Chapter 26: What was the Casa Clara? How did this location contrast to the Toll House? Who called Jeanette to tell her important family information? How did Jeanette feel when speaking with her father? What goal did Jeanette's father have? How did he agree to help Jeanette? Where was the new house?

21. Chapter 28: What one life goal did Jeanette have since her early 20's? What happened when Jim found out she was going back to school? What did Jeanette do to "spike" Jim's lemonade? Why do you think a small defiant act made Jeanette feel triumphant?

22. Chapter 29: What Fortune 500 did Jeanette interview with? How did the college classes help Jeanette with the employment testing? Where did Jeanette drive to conduct a second interview? In what city was the two-week training Jeanette attended held?

23. Chapter 32/33: What gamut of feelings did Jeanette experience after her escape? Where did Jeanette find refuge? Where did Jeanette confess the abuse to her parents? What was their reaction?

24. Chapter 34/35: What step in Jeanette's life goal did her parents witness? Who did Jeanette meet in Chapter 35? Who did she liken Sam to? What did Jeanette do to try to begin the healing process? What two major life events did Jeanette write about in this chapter? What miracle did God reveal at an ultrasound appointment? How did God protect Jeanette?

25. Chapter 36: What did Jim do to make a final threat and gain control over Jeanette? Who was the neighbor and what did she do to help Leah? Where did Jeanette find Leah? What fear did Jeanette have as she encountered Leah for the first time in years? What was the positive outcome for Leah and Jeanette?

25. Chapter 37/38: What business opportunity did Jeanette consider? How was the business opportunity an answer to prayer and faithfulness? Whose story in Sunday's *Parade Magazine* caught Jeanette's eye? What did Sam and Jeanette do to grow their family? When did Jeanette finally share her past with a friend? What realization did Jeanette come to about her healing heart? When Jeanette covered the secret of her past, how did that impact Leah? What did God impress upon Jeanette encouraging her to share the journey?

ABOUT THE AUTHOR

Jeanette Towne jokingly tells friends she slices her days into twenty-minute increments, busy running her company, supporting her family and keeping pace with extracurricular activities. She enjoys the challenge of work; however, spending time with her husband Sam, and their four children is extremely rewarding. With a fairly young family, after work hours, she can be found serving nachos in the school cafeteria as a volunteer parent, or sitting in the stands cheering at basketball games.

In addition to family and work responsibilities, Jeanette donates her time and energy investing into a real-life ministry in Mexico. Many summers her family of six uses their vacation time to build basic homes for hard-working needy families. Jeanette enjoys anything active and outdoors, hiking, swimming, biking and skiing activities with her family. One of her favorite activities is investing in her local church and teaching Sunday school to 3rd and 4th grade classes.

ABOUT THE AUTHOR

Jeanette loves to share her incredible and miraculous story and is available for inspirational speaking engagements geared towards women's groups. Please fill out a contact form on her website or call directly.

www.prisonertopresident.com

Toll Free @ (877) 521-8821 x 2121

AUTHOR'S NOTE

For any person who may read this book, please know you are not alone. There are hundreds of people who feel trapped; some appear to be the "perfect families" who suffer, silently entangled in domestic violence. Know the abuse is not your fault! Abuse knows no race, sex, age, religion, educational or economic strata. Abuse is an ugly trait passed down from one generation to the next, whereas the helpless abused and victimized child turns and becomes the victimizer and abuser.

The American Medical Association reported that as many as 1 in 3 women will be assaulted by a domestic partner in her lifetime – 4 million in any given year. ("When Violence Hits Home." *Time*. June 4, 1994).

Where to find help
The National Domestic Violence Hotline
(800) 799-SAFE
Or (800) 787-3229 TTY
Anonymous and confidential help
www.ndvh.org
24 hour access all 50 states – translators available

Intermedia
Publishing Group

Publishing That Works For You

Do you need a speaker?

Do you want Jeanette Towne to speak to your group or event?
Then contact Larry Davis at: **(623) 337-8710** or email:
ldavis@intermediapr.com or use the contact form at:
www.intermediapr.com.

Whether you want to purchase bulk copies of *From Prisoner
to President* or buy another book for a friend, get it now at:
www.imprbooks.com.

If you have a book that you would like to publish,
contact Terry Whalin, Publisher, at Intermedia Publishing
Group, (623) 337-8710 or email: twhalin@intermediapub.
com or use the contact form at: www.intermediapub.com.